DAILY DEVOTIONS FOR DEACONS

260 INSTRUCTIONAL AND INSPIRATIONAL DEVOTIONS

RUSSELL R. COOK

CROSSBOOKS

CrossBooks™
A Division of LifeWay
1663 Liberty Drive
Bloomington, IN 47403
www.crossbooks.com
Phone: 1-866-879-0502

© 2012 Russell R. Cook. All rights reserved.

No part of this book may be reproduced, stored in a retrieval system, or transmitted by any means without the written permission of the author.

First published by CrossBooks 2/10/2012

ISBN: 978-1-4627-1328-8 (hc)
ISBN: 978-1-4627-1330-1 (sc)
ISBN: 978-1-4627-1329-5 (e)

Library of Congress Control Number: 2011963557

Printed in the United States of America

This book is printed on acid-free paper.

Certain stock imagery © Thinkstock.
Any people depicted in stock imagery provided by Thinkstock are models, and such images are being used for illustrative purposes only.

Because of the dynamic nature of the Internet, any web addresses or links contained in this book may have changed since publication and may no longer be valid. The views expressed in this work are solely those of the author and do not necessarily reflect the views of the publisher, and the publisher hereby disclaims any responsibility for them.

Dedication

To my Savior,

the Lord Jesus Christ, the greatest Servant of all.

To my family,

my wife, Marsha Cook, who lovingly encouraged me to write and assisted me with much of the editing and typing to complete this book; our children, Bryan and Lisa Cook, Phillip and Angela Cook, and Aaron and Joy Swensen; and our precious grandchildren. Thank you for your love and support.

To my Ministry Assistant,

Janice Maynard, who compiled, formatted, and typed several early drafts of this book. I am very thankful for your arduous labor of love. You are a true servant.

To my fellow servants:
the Deacons of Western Park Baptist Church
Dallas, Texas, 1976-1982.

the Deacons of First Baptist Church
Vinita, Oklahoma, 1982-1987.

the Deacons of Clearview Baptist Church
Broken Arrow, Oklahoma, 1987-1996.

the Deacons of the churches of Pottawatomie-Lincoln Baptist Association,
Shawnee, Oklahoma.

the Deacons of the churches of the
Baptist General Convention of Oklahoma.

the Deacons of the churches of the
Southern Baptist Convention since 1845.

Thank you for your historical service to the body of Christ.

Endorsements

As a Pastor, I truly appreciate resources that encourage and equip Deacons for ministry in the local church. I firmly believe that this work, *Daily Devotions for Deacons,* is a rare find and will be incredibly helpful for any Deacon body. Russell Cook incorporates his many years of experience in working with and teaching Deacons in these biblical and relevant devotions. I encourage you to give a copy of this book to each of your Deacons to strengthen them in their walk with the Lord and service to the body of Christ.

Todd Fisher, Senior Pastor
Immanuel Baptist Church
Shawnee, Oklahoma

Russell Cook has written a resource that will last for decades. Now, more than ever before, the North American church needs servants. Deacons need to be spiritually healthy so they can minister to the needs of the body of Christ. Any Deacon can be assisted by these *Daily Devotions for Deacons*, no matter what his spiritual maturity, to become all Christ means for him to be. I wholeheartedly recommend this book for new and seasoned Deacons.

Monty Hale, Pastoral Ministries Specialist
South Carolina Baptist Convention
Columbia, South Carolina

Russell Cook has done an outstanding piece of work on these *Daily Devotions for Deacons.* They are informative, instructional, and inspirational. These will help Deacons in their walk with our Lord, their families, their churches, and their ministry. When a Deacon is maturing as a disciple of Jesus, everyone wins. This is an excellent assist in that journey. Every Deacon in every church should have this book on his night stand or in his prayer closet.

Jim Henry, Pastor Emeritus
First Baptist Church
Orlando, Florida
Author: *Deacons, Partners in Ministry and Growth*
Deacons, Growing in Character and Commitment

As you are looking for a devotional for Deacons, let me commend, with no reservations whatsoever, this wonderful book by Russell Cook. Deacons are an untapped reservoir of useful energy for God's Kingdom. When they are inspired, trained, and loosed to do ministry, they become a mighty force for the church. These devotions will encourage your Deacons to be the best they can be for the Kingdom. I highly recommend it to you.

> Johnny Hunt, Senior Pastor
> First Baptist Church
> Woodstock, Georgia
> Author: *The Deacon I Want to Be*

Russell Cook has invested more in equipping Deacons for effective service than anyone I know of in the Southern Baptist Convention. With this book, *Daily Devotions for Deacons*, he provides a new tool to inspire and instruct men who have been set aside to serve as Deacons in Christ's church. Every devotion is anchored in Scripture and uniquely illustrated. Any Deacon who will walk day by day through these devotions will mature spiritually and grow in ministry effectiveness.

> Anthony Jordan, Executive Director-Treasurer
> Baptist General Convention of Oklahoma
> Oklahoma City, Oklahoma

It is nothing less than embarrassing to realize how little has been written about the role of the Baptist Deacon. Russell Cook distills decades of careful thinking and pastoral experience in this new book, *Daily Devotions for Deacons*. We are all in his debt for the work.

> R. Albert Mohler, President
> Southern Baptist Theological Seminary
> Louisville, Kentucky

For those of us who have served and led local churches, the importance of a healthy and vibrant deacon ministry cannot be overstated. These *Daily Devotions for Deacons* reflect decades of wisdom, measured out in daily doses, for instructing and inspiring those called to serve as Deacons. Russell Cook's passion for mature, able Deacons who contribute to mature, healthy churches is stamped on every page. Without hesitation, I am delighted to recommend *Daily Devotions for Deacons* to every Deacon in every church in America.

> Thom S. Rainer, President and CEO
> LifeWay Christian Resources
> Nashville, Tennessee

I am pleased that Russell Cook has been led by God to take on the task of training Deacons through a year-long devotional format. Exceptional insight is packed into each day's valuable devotion. The author has helped the Deacon by grouping these scriptural teachings into a variety of series. *Daily Devotions for Deacons* would be an excellent gift from a church to each of its Deacons, whether active or reserved.

> Henry Webb, Retired
> Deacon Ministry Consultant
> Hermitage, Tennessee
> *Author: Deacons: Servant Models in the Church*

So often, Deacons are ordained by their church and placed in the important role of serving, only to be overwhelmed by the enormity of the task. These wonderfully written *Daily Devotions for Deacons* by Russell Cook will serve as an encouragement to Deacons and their families, that they may not grow weary in their responsibilities.

> David Whitlock, President
> Oklahoma Baptist University
> Shawnee, Oklahoma

Contents

Foreword xiii

Introduction xv

The Deacon's Qualifications 1
Week 1, Day 1 through Week 4, Day 1

The Deacon's Spiritual Fruit 19
Week 4, Day 2 through Week 5, Day 5

The Deacon's Personal Life 31
Week 6 Day 1 through Week 9, Day 1

The Deacon's Commandments 49
Week 9, Day 2 through Week 11, Day 1

The Deacon's Common Ministry 61
Week 11, Day 2 through Week 23, Day 5

The Deacon's Relational Characteristics 127
Week 24, Day 1 through Week 29, Day 1

The Deacon's Giftedness 155
Week 29, Day 2 through Week 30, Day 3

The Deacon's Caregiving Ministries 165
Week 30, Day 4 through Week 35, Day 5

The Deacon's Doctrine 195
Week 36, Day 1 through Week 38, Day 5

The Deacon's Greatest Challenges 213
Week 39, Day 1 through Week 52, Day 5

Foreword

It is refreshing to find a pastor/teacher, who now serves as a Director of Missions, who has such a passionate heart for the Deacon ministry. This devotional book by Russell Cook is a timely, powerful, and much-needed tool to encourage and strengthen the biblical Deacon's ministry of servanthood. What the author has written comes from years of study, teaching, and training Deacons to be followers and servants of the Lord Jesus Christ. He genuinely loves Deacons, and his only desire is to see them fulfill the ministry of serving the body of Christ and glorifying our Lord.

If you will read, study, receive the truth written in these devotions, and implement it into your daily life, you will grow in grace, becoming an example of Christ. Jesus said, after washing the feet of His disciples, "For I have given you an example that you should do just as I have done for you" (Jn. 13:15).

This is much needed in an era when some are saying the office of Deacon is unnecessary and no longer beneficial to the modern and contemporary church. The Deacon ministry will never be outdated or unneeded. It is vital to the church.

This book fills a void in respect to the ministry and service of the Deacon. There is no other devotional book that directs itself specifically to the heart, life, and soul of the Deacon. It is masterfully formatted, accurate to the text, and insightfully applied.

As you read through *Daily Devotions for Deacons*, you will find nuggets of biblical truth, practical illustrations, and principles that will enrich you spiritually. You will be challenged to become more and more like the Master/Servant!

These devotions come from a heart that yearns to see the church empowered with the dynamic presence of the Lord Jesus. As a Deacon, you can make a difference. You can be used of God to bring renewal, revival, and reconciliation to your church family. Permit the Holy Spirit to fill you and open your heart to the joy of being a Deacon. These devotionals will give you a freshness in serving the Servant of all, the Lord Jesus Christ.

Ed J. Ethridge, Director of Missions
North Texas Baptist Area,
Lewisville, Texas

INTRODUCTION
A Personal Introduction by the Author

In *Deacons: Servant Models in the Church*, the highly respected author, Henry Webb, identifies four characteristics that describe the qualities of a servant-leader in the church. He says, "Deacons will demonstrate growth toward a mature faith, Christian family life, personal and public morality, and a life accepted by God and the church."[1] Webb then explains in some detail what those qualities should look like when observed by others.

It is my belief that many Pastors and Deacons in the church today know generally what their service should look like, but so few have a close, devotional relationship with God that allows them to actually live out those qualities. This book of devotions is an attempt to give Deacons another tool to help them not merely adopt the principles of servanthood but to also apply the qualities of servanthood in their everyday lives.

Though it is grammatically questionable, I have chosen to capitalize both Pastor and Deacon throughout this book. I believe these to be the only legitimate New Testament offices in the church today. Each office is emphasized and identified as imperative to the effectiveness of the church.

Perhaps by daily reading what God has said and how God has worked in the lives of other great servants, today's Deacon could be motivated to even greater maturity. No book of devotions or even books of academic and theological instruction will, in and of themselves, produce a mature servant. Only God Himself can do that. I hope this work will bring the reader closer to Him—to His presence as you pray, to His truth as you obey, and to His church as you give yourself away.

Considerations for Using the Top Twelve Applicable Devotions Record Sheet

The following page is provided for the reader to use in recording at least twelve of his most meaningful and applicable devotions. They may be used in any of a variety of ways:

1. You may enter one devotion from each month, choosing from approximately twenty you'll read.
2. You may simply enter devotions spontaneously as you read without regard to monthly entries.
3. You may read through the twelve months of devotions with other Deacons in your church and at each monthly Deacon's meeting, share and compare your entries.
4. You may use the applicable devotions as a guide to help you prepare and deliver a devotional presentation to others (Deacons, Sunday school, discipleship group, etc.).
5. You may choose to enter one applicable devotion from each of the sections identified in the table of contents.

Surely, out of 260 daily devotions, God will speak to you specifically and directly in at least twelve. Each time through the book, you may be given twelve new applicable devotions.

Personal Entries of Your Top Twelve Applicable Devotions

The following devotions were especially meaningful to me:

1. Week # _____ Day # _____ Page # _____
   Title: _____

2. Week # _____ Day # _____ Page # _____
   Title: _____

3. Week # _____ Day # _____ Page # _____
   Title: _____

4. Week # _____ Day # _____ Page # _____
   Title: _____

5. Week # _____ Day # _____ Page # _____
   Title: _____

6. Week # _____ Day # _____ Page # _____
   Title: _____

7. Week # _____ Day # _____ Page # _____
   Title: _____

8. Week # _____ Day # _____ Page # _____
   Title: _____

9. Week # _____ Day # _____ Page # _____
   Title: _____

10. Week # _____ Day # _____ Page # _____
    Title: _____

11. Week # _____ Day # _____ Page # _____
    Title: _____

12. Week # _____ Day # _____ Page # _____
    Title: _____

The Deacon's Qualifications

Week 1 **Day 1**

DEACONS: SERVANTS OF GOD
Exodus 23:25

"You shall serve the Lord your God and He will bless your bread and your water; and I will remove sickness from your midst."

Webster's defines *servant*, "one that serves others or performs duties about the person or home of a master or personal employer."[1] A servant is one who performs tasks at the direction of and for the benefit of another. One of the Old Testament titles of the Messiah is "Servant of the Lord" (cf. Isa. 52-53). The New Testament uses two primary words for servant. *Doulos* refers to a slave or bondservant who completely subjects his will to another. *Diakonos* (from which we get our English word Deacon) defines a helper or minister who is ready and willing to meet the needs of others.[2]

> May the prayer of my heart always be: "make me a servant today."

Christians are considered by God to be bondservants completely subject to the lordship of Jesus Christ. As servants in the church, we are uniquely focused on caring for and meeting the practical and spiritual needs of other believers. Jesus said, "The son of Man did not come to be served, but to serve, and to give His life . . ." (Mk. 10:45).

As a servant in the church, you will focus on the person you ultimately serve (the Lord your God), the provision made by the one you serve (bread and water), and the protection given to you by your Master (to remove sickness from you). Though we serve other people in the church, we do so in obedience and reverence to God. Perhaps you could make a song by Kelly Willard your prayer:

> Make me a servant, humble and meek;
> Lord, let me lift up those who are weak.
> And may the prayer of my heart always be:
> Make me a servant, make me a servant, make me a servant today.[3]

God will answer that prayer from your heart. It may take the rest of your life, but He will make you a servant. What could bring more satisfaction and completion to your life than to invest it in service to Him and His people?

Lord, make me a servant, starting today.

A DEACON WITH A GOOD REPUTATION
Acts 6:3a

"Select from among you seven men of good reputation."

Reputation may be defined as "over-all quality or character as seen or judged by people in general; recognition by other people of some characteristic or ability."[4] The word used in Acts 6:3 carries the idea of a "supposed opinion assumed by one person in regard to another."[5] All of us have a reputation in the eyes of others. In fact, other people's opinions of us matter a lot to God. The apostle Paul described the character of servants in the early church: "he must have a good reputation among outsiders" (1 Tim. 3:7). In other words, unbelievers should have no reason to hold a servant of God in ill repute. They may not always agree with us, but they should have an honest respect for us if we are maintaining a godly reputation. Ideally, our reputation should reflect the character of Christ.

> **Unbelievers should have no reason to hold a servant of God in ill repute.**

B. B. McKinney captured this thought well in his great hymn:

> While passing through this world of sin
> and others your life shall view,
> Be clean and pure without, within, let others see Jesus in you.
> Your life's a book before their eyes,
> they're reading it through and through.
> Say, does it point them to the skies, do others see Jesus in you?
> Then live for Christ both day and night, be faithful, be brave and true,
> And lead the lost to life and light, let others see Jesus in you.[6]

As a servant of Christ, are you maintaining a good reputation in the eyes of God, in the eyes of other believers, and in the eyes of the world? Do others really see Jesus in you?

Lord, please control my mind, emotions, and will in such a way that Your very character will be demonstrated in my life today.

A Deacon Controlled by the Holy Spirit

Acts 6:3b

"Select men full of the Spirit . . ."

Perhaps the classic New Testament passage describing the "Spirit-filled" life is Ephesians 5:18ff: "do not get drunk with wine, which leads to reckless actions, but be filled with the Spirit: . . . making music to the Lord in your heart, giving thanks for everything . . . submitting to one another in the fear of Christ." To be full of the Spirit is not just a matter of Him indwelling you but literally controlling you. It is essential that the servant of God be under the complete control of His Holy Spirit. That means we will think like He thinks, talk like He talks and act like He acts. It means we will be daily and consistently "conformed to the image or likeness of His Son" (Rom. 8:29).

> "The Holy Spirit is God's imperative of life."

A. W. Tozer correctly asserted, "The Holy Spirit is God's imperative of life."[7] The Holy Spirit gives us life, guides our lives, guards our lives, and lives His life in and through His servants. Apart from the fullness of the Holy Spirit, a person is simply wasting time trying to be of service to God. The would-be servant who is controlled by the flesh (i.e., the whims of human inclination) sets his mind only on what man can do, which is natural and futile. The Spirit-led servant who is controlled by God's Spirit (i.e., the clear directives of His Word) sets his mind only on what God can do, which is supernatural and profitable.

Are you living your daily life under the full control of God's Holy Spirit? If not, perhaps you might pray:

> Heavenly Father, as Your child and Your servant, I humbly ask that You cleanse me from all sin and fill my life today with Your powerful Holy Spirit. Control my life in every respect today.

God will honor your prayer and empower you to do things you never dreamed you could. Daily confession leads to daily forgiveness and cleansing, which leads to daily infilling.

Lord, please take complete control of my life, that I might serve in Your power and strength.

A DEACON WHO IS WISE
Acts 6:3c

"Select men full of wisdom . . ."

The effectiveness of the servant of God is measured, to a great degree, by the wisdom he possesses. Wisdom is not identical to knowledge, but they are closely related. Wisdom, according to *Nelson's Bible Dictionary* is "the ability to judge correctly and to follow the best course of action, based on knowledge and understanding."[8] This wisdom is God given and not human produced. Thus, we are encouraged to pray for wisdom (James 1:5) and seek to exhibit the characteristics of wisdom that is "*from above*" (James 3:17). James 3:17 lists these characteristics: (1) pure, (2) peace-loving, (3) gentle, (4) compliant, (5) full of mercy and good fruits, (6) without favoritism, and (7) without hypocrisy.

> To know and apply the wisdom of God, I must saturate my mind with Scripture.

D. Martyn Lloyd-Jones wrote, "Surely the essence of wisdom is that before we begin to act at all, or attempt to please God, we should discover what it is that God has to say about the matter."[9] Our service for Christ and His church is to be ordered and directed by God Himself through His Word, the Bible. Someone has well said, "The Bible is God's wisdom written down." If I want to know and apply the wisdom of God, I must saturate my mind with Scripture. Hear it, read it, study it, meditate on it, memorize it, and live it out, and you will thus become a wise servant of Christ.

Pray this prayer:

> Lord Jesus, I admit to You that my mere human understanding is inadequate and fails to produce a servant's heart. I ask that You supply the wisdom You alone possess so I can serve You, Your church, and other people, even as You did.

As you study God's Word, you will gain God's wisdom. As you apply God's wisdom, you walk in His ways. You will, in fact, fulfill
God's will for your life.

**Lord, I ask for Your wisdom to serve
You faithfully according to Your Word.**

A Deacon With Dignity
1 Timothy 3:8a

"Deacons likewise, should be worthy of respect . . ."

The term used for *worthy of respect* refers to that which is honorable, venerable, and grave. Being a servant is a serious matter. A Deacon in the church should be as diligent in his sacred work as he is in his secular employment. John Phillips, in his commentary on this text, states, "It is astonishing how some deacons put their hearts and souls into their careers and then turn around and render indifferent service to the church."[10]

A servant of God and His people—the Church—must take his responsibility seriously. One of the biggest problems in the twenty-first-century church is that we are not taken seriously. The world does not take us seriously because we do not take God and His Word seriously. We are not *worthy of respect*. Often this is because of a poor understanding of who we are in Christ and what is expected of us as His servants. We must have a seriousness of purpose and self-respect in conduct.

The servant of Christ in the church is not inherently worthy of respect. God actively regenerates (Titus 3:5), redeems (Titus 2:14), reconciles (2 Cor. 5:18), and re-creates (2 Cor. 5:17) the believer and makes him to become a worthy servant. Clearly, our worthiness is not a matter of upbringing, education, career, family, friendships, or worldly success. Our worth and worthiness are exclusively discovered in relationship to Christ alone.

> **Being a servant is a serious matter.**

Consider the apostle's prayer for the servants in the Colossian church:

> We are asking that you may be filled with the knowledge of His will in all wisdom and spiritual understanding, so that you may walk worthy of the Lord, fully pleasing to Him, bearing fruit in every good work and growing in the knowledge of God (Col. 1:9-10).

Are you a servant of God who is worthy of the respect of God and the church?

**Lord, make me a worthy servant
from this day forward**

A Deacon of His Word
1 Timothy 3:8b

"Deacons must not be double-tongued . . ."

This is the only use of this word in the entire New Testament. It literally means saying the same thing twice or given to repetition. According to John Phillips, a *double-tongued* person says something to one person and then, when talking to another person, puts an altogether different slant on the subject.[11] Today we might refer to this person as "talking out of both sides of his mouth."

God intends for His servants to be men of their word—men who know what they are saying, mean what they say, and say the same thing with the same meaning even to different people or in different contexts. The tongue of the Deacon can be used for good or evil. "With it we bless our Lord and Father, and with it we curse men, who have been made in the likeness of God; from the same mouth come both blessing and cursing. My brethren, these things ought not to be this way" (Jas. 3:9-10).

> **God intends for His servants to be men of their word!**

Clearly, it is the duty of the servant of God to guard his tongue. We must join the psalmist and pray, "Set a guard, O Lord, over my mouth; keep watch over the door of my lips" (Ps. 141:3). The Scriptures are filled with verse after verse instructing us on the use and misuse of the tongue. What we say, how and when we say it, and to whom we say it matters a great deal to God. Jesus makes this extremely clear in His words to religious leaders (would-be servants) of His day:

> But I tell you that every careless word that people speak, they shall give an accounting for it on the day of judgment. For by your words you will be justified, and by your words you will be condemned (Matt. 12:36-37).

Whenever you are tempted to lie, especially in your service to other believers in the church, know that God is listening. He listens to your words and weighs your motives (Prov. 16:2). Determine from this day forward not to be double-tongued.

Lord, remind me when I misspeak and take control of my tongue!

A Deacon Who Is Temperate

1 Timothy 3:8c

"Not drinking a lot of wine . . ."

The matter of temperance or, as the text literally reads, "given to much wine," has been the subject of debate among believers for centuries. It has certainly been debated among Baptists, and the discussions continue. Though a fully agreed-upon position has not been endorsed by all, most Baptists have held to total abstinence with regard to alcohol as a beverage. This has become especially important in relation to servant-leaders in the church. When servants in general and Deacons in particular are looked to by the church for a good, godly example of Christian living, then temperance and discipline become more crucial than ever.

The word for "wine" is the same word used in Ephesians 5:18, where intoxication is evidently in view. In 1 Timothy 5:23, Paul advises his young colleague to use a little wine moderately for medicinal purposes. But as important as anything for God's servants is the example they set. The New Testament warns against indulging in anything that might cause a brother to stumble. This practically rules out the use of wine altogether (Rom. 14:21). Any use of any amount of fermented alcohol has a stimulating effect on the human brain, the blood stream, and all the body's systems. And since the servants of God are admonished not to "get drunk with wine, which leads to reckless actions, but be filled with the Spirit" (Eph. 5:18), it makes sense that only total abstinence can guarantee a temperate Christian life. After all, what could be worse than a drunken Deacon?

> **Only total abstinence can guarantee a temperate Christian life.**

Ask the Lord in prayer:

> Lord, please help me to lead a disciplined and temperate life, abstaining from the use of any substance that would alter my mind. Let my mind be constantly renewed and protected by the purifying power of Your Holy Spirit. And from this day forward, help me to live with the mind of Christ (cf. 1 Cor. 2:16).

Lord, please help me live a disciplined and temperate life.

A Deacon Who Is Not Greedy
1 Timothy 3:8d

"Not greedy for money . . ."

The servant in New Testament times was much more interested in how he could please his master than how much money he could accumulate. Proverbs 15:16 states it well: "Better a little with the fear of the Lord than great treasure with turmoil." Times, cultures, and people change over the years. Now, in twenty-first-century America, we have employees who care very little about pleasing their employers. Their primary focus is upon their own salary and benefits. It has become an obsession with many to want to "get all you can, can all you get, and sit on the can." Greed has done us no favors in our homes, our churches, our businesses, or our government.

A rather wealthy rancher and land owner in West Texas was once asked, "How much land do you want to have, anyway?" To which the rancher replied, "Not a lot, really . . . just that which joins mine!" Greed can be a deceptive thing. It is much easier to compare our resources with those who have more and thus develop a greed for more than it is to compare our resources with those who have less and thus develop a spirit of generosity.

> "If someone wants to be well paid for his service, he is probably disqualified."

The man of God who would serve the people of God must know in his heart that "the love of money is a root of all kinds of evil, and by craving it, some have wandered away from the faith and pierced themselves with many pains" (1 Tim. 6:10). As one preacher put it, "No person should be in the ministry merely to make money. If someone wants to be well paid for his service, he is probably disqualified."

> Dear Lord, please instill in me a heartfelt attitude of generosity. Help me to use money to serve people rather than use people to make money. Show me how to rightly view material possessions, never exploiting others for my own gain. Help me give what I cannot keep in order to gain what I cannot lose.

Lord, help me to develop a spirit of generosity in my service for You.

A DEACON WITH A CLEAR CONSCIENCE
1 Timothy 3:9

"Holding the mystery of the faith with a clear conscience."

In the New Testament, *mystery* refers to a secret that is revealed by God to His servants through His Spirit. One text that exemplifies this is 1 Timothy 3:16, "The mystery of godliness is great. He was manifested in the flesh, justified in the Spirit, seen by angels, preached among the Gentiles, believed on in the world, taken up in glory." These are *mysteries* to many, but they are great and precious truths to the servant of Christ. When held to with strong conviction and practiced with sincere devotion, these mysteries serve as the foundation for our faith.

It is essential that God's servant have a working knowledge of these truths and hold them with integrity or with "a clear conscience." The word *clear* actually means "cleansed, free from any mixture with impurity, unblemished." *Nelson's Dictionary* describes *conscience* as "a person's inner awareness of conforming to the will of God or departing from it, resulting in either a sense of approval or condemnation."[12] The apostle Paul said, "I thank God, whom I serve with a clear conscience" (2 Tim. 1:3).

> Do you have an inner awareness—in your conscience—that your service is met with the approval of Christ?

Do you have an inner awareness—in your conscience—that your service is met with the approval of Christ? Your inner awareness should grow out of your understanding and application of God's Word—the mysteries of God revealed in His Word, the Bible. We can serve God most faithfully when we serve Him with a clear and pure conscience.

> Heavenly Father, create in me, today, a clean and pure heart.
> Please clear my mind of any sinful thoughts. Remind me regularly of my need to confess my sins, repent of my sins, and live in the cleansing power of Your Spirit and the complete perfection of Your Word.

**Lord, clear my conscience today
of anything displeasing to You.**

A Deacon Who Is Tried and True
1 Timothy 3:10a

"And they must also be tested first . . ."

John Phillips says of this text and referring to these Deacons, "They are to be proved before they are promoted . . . deacons are to be put to the test before being put in trust."[13] It is a good thing for a church not to select and elect men so they may become Deacons but to select and elect those who are already servants at heart. Their lives and deeds have proven again and again that they are men who serve the church with a pure heart.

Most of us recall courses we have taken in school that required a test either during or at the end of a semester. The end test was usually referred to as "the final exam." We often feel a sense of apprehension or uncertainty about tests either because we did not apply ourselves or because we had little or no interest in the subject. The test is given nonetheless. In the final analysis, course credit is received and perhaps greater responsibility given to the one who passes the test.

> The Lord allows us to be tested, not to harm us but to help us.

Such is the work of the servant-leader in the church. His selection and election and perhaps even ordination hinge upon his having passed certain tests in his Christian life. It might be nice if, once elected as a Deacon, the tests were over, but actually they continue for the rest of our lives. The Lord allows us to be tested, not to harm us but to help us; not to hinder our service but to enhance it; not to bring us to failure but to elevate us to great success.

Dear Lord, I pray that you will build into my life the spirit of discipline I need to prepare for and pass the tests before me. I ask that You would so control my life that I would remember lessons learned and tests completed. May I be prepared for every good work.

**Lord, help me to be tried and true
as one of Your servants.**

A Deacon Who Is Blameless
1 Timothy 3:10b

"If they prove blameless, then they can serve as deacons."

The term *blameless* can also be translated *above reproach*. It does not suggest absolutely flawless character or perfection. It does refer to a servant whose character is reflective of Christ and against whom no charge of wrongdoing can be brought with success. A servant in the church is wise when he daily makes the prayer of the psalmist his own: "God, create a clean heart for me and renew a steadfast spirit within me" (Ps. 51:10).

> Circumstances never create character; they merely reveal it.

Over time—sometimes months, sometimes years—the church has ample opportunity to evaluate the calling, character, and competence of the servants who surround them. Such servants should be set aside as Deacons only when the church has observed their behavior and found them blameless or above reproach. Again, this does not mean perfect but clearly implies a good reputation.

Someone has well said, "Circumstances never create character; they merely reveal it." A man's true character is developed over years of obedience and discipline in God's Word. It comes through glorious encounters with God in worship and grows out of deep, deep valleys of trial and struggle. As James puts it, "Endurance must do its complete work, so you may be mature and complete, lacking nothing" (Jas. 1:4). It is this obedience, this discipline, and this endurance that proves to a congregation the blameless character of a Deacon.

Abraham Lincoln once said, "Character is like a tree and reputation its shadow. The shadow is what we think of it; the tree is the real thing."[14] Live your life in such a way that others may see your good works and know they follow a blameless character. May others, then, give glory to your Father who is in heaven.

Lord, please empower me in this and each day hereafter to conform to the likeness of Jesus and consistently exhibit His character.

A DEACON AND HIS WIFE
1 Timothy 3:11

"Wives, too, must be worthy of respect, not slanderers, self-controlled, faithful in everything."

Those who enter the ministry vocationally are almost always reminded, "Your wife can either make you or break you!" No less can be said of a Deacon in the church. A Deacon's effectiveness in ministry hinges greatly upon the character and attitude of his wife. The four qualities of a wife listed by the apostle Paul are clearly intended to complement the character traits of her husband. She is respectable, kind, self-controlled, and trustworthy. When these qualities are evident in the wife of God's servant, it challenges the Deacon himself to exhibit godly character.

The idea of a ministering couple is not new. However, it is an idea that has been lost in too many servants in today's church. When service happens at all, it is usually rendered by a man or by his wife but seldom together. How refreshing it is to witness the work of a ministering couple in the church. Such couples often attribute their successes to each other. They are usually well disciplined, like-minded, and full of love for God and others.

> **It only makes sense for a servant of Christ to double his ministry through his wife.**

It only makes sense for a servant of Christ to double his ministry through his wife. Can you imagine a ministry couple correcting the likes of the "scholar-Pastor" Apollos? That is exactly what Priscilla and her husband Aquila did in Acts 18:26. Like Priscilla and Aquila, you and your spouse can have a great impact on the lives of others. The advance or retreat of your church may depend upon your faithfulness as a ministering couple.

*Dear God, I thank You for my spouse.
I pray You will enable us by Your Spirit to become
worthy servants—together—in Your church.*

A Deacon and His Family
1 Timothy 3:12

"Deacons must be husbands of one wife, managing their children and their own households competently."

John Phillips, in his commentary on this passage, refers to Philip, one of the seven servants identified in Acts 6, as a good example of a godly Deacon and family man. He states, "Philip was not only hospitable but also had a houseful of daughters who were pure in character and able to articulate the Word of God." Phillips suggests, "Paul must have been delighted to see his idea of the model Deacon personified in Philip."[15]

The question often arises from the reading of this verse (3:12), "Should a divorced man be ordained as a Deacon?" Though some Pastors and churches make exceptions, the vast majority of Bible-believing scholars (and churches) hold this passage to mean the Deacon should have only one living wife, if he is married at all. This is certainly taking the high ground on the subject but is more likely to reduce criticism and enhance effectiveness in the long run.

> **The first service a Deacon must render is to his own wife and children.**

One might also ask, from this text, "What constitutes a good manager?" One thing is sure: the success or failure of an adult child does not necessarily mean that the parent was a bad manager. However, until such time as children grow up and are on their own, it is imperative that fathers not "stir up anger in their children, but bring them up in the training and instruction of the Lord" (Eph. 6:4). The first service a Deacon must render is to his own wife and children. Only then can he be effective in serving the church.

The hymn writer B. B. McKinney captured this truth when he wrote:

> God, give us Christian homes: Homes where the father is true and strong, homes that are free from the blight of wrong, homes that are joyous with love and song; God give us Christian homes.[16]

Lord, guide me to serve You by serving my wife and children. Grant me Your love and wisdom to manage my household well.

A Deacon Who Is Faithful

1 Timothy 3:13a

"Those who have served well as deacons . . ."

Every deacon at one time or another has asked himself, "How can I know if I'm doing a good job?" In other words, "Am I serving well?" The best judge of our service is usually someone besides ourselves. But even the notice or compliments of others don't necessarily prove that we are doing well. In the final analysis, our faithfulness in service is measured by God Himself. Fortunately, He has given us His written Word, the Bible, to show us how well we are serving Him.

Numerous examples are given in the Bible of the faithfulness of God's servants. Men like Abraham, Isaac, Jacob, Joseph, Moses, and David were all men who served well . . . not perfectly, but well. There are others like Matthew, Mark, Luke, John, James, Peter, and certainly Paul. These were all faithful servants of God and His people. Of course, the greatest example we have of one who served well is Jesus. He said of Himself, "Even the Son of Man did not come to be served, but to serve, and to give His life—a ransom for many" (Mk. 10:45). He gave His life in service to us. The least we can do is give our lives in service to Him.

> **Faithfulness to God is our first obligation.**

We know we have served well when we have obeyed the clear teachings of Scripture and have followed the clear example of the Savior. There is no greater calling. There is nothing that will bring greater reward—maybe not here, but certainly in eternity.

Iain H. Murray said, "Faithfulness to God is our first obligation in all that we are called to do in the service of the gospel."[17] Serve Him faithfully; serve Him well.

Lord, may all who come behind me find me faithful.
Let it be said of me now and especially
when I'm gone, "He served well!"

WEEK 3 **DAY 5**

A DEACON IN GOOD STANDING
1 Timothy 3:13b

"Deacons acquire a good standing for themselves . . ."

It can be seen from this text, those who diligently discharge their duties as Deacons make a great investment in their own future. We do not serve as we do in order to gain greater responsibility in the future, but that is often what happens. Jesus said, "Much will be required of everyone who has been given much" (Lk.12:48). Clearly, there are degrees of responsibility in service and therefore degrees of reward for our service.

Serving well is rewarded with greater opportunity to serve. At least two of the seven servants selected in Acts 6 served well and thus were given even greater responsibility. Stephen became the great defender of the faith (Acts 7), and Philip became a great evangelist (Acts 8). The "standing" of these men in the early church was very high. They were held in high regard, not because they were better at what they did but because they were extraordinarily faithful in their service. If you want greater service, then exercise great faithfulness in the service you now have.

> **There are degrees of responsibility in service.**

> The credit belongs to those who are actually in the arena, who strive valiantly; who know the great enthusiasm, the great devotions, and spend themselves in a worthy cause; who at the best, know the triumph of high achievement; and who, at the worst, if they fail, fail while daring greatly, so that their place shall never be with those cold and timid souls who know neither victory nor defeat.[18]
> — Theodore Roosevelt

Lord, I pray that You will order my steps of service, not that I should receive glory or that my standing may be above others. Reward my service with right standing before You.

WEEK 4 — DAY 1

A Deacon With Great Boldness
1 Timothy 3:13c

"Deacons acquire . . . great boldness in the faith that is in Christ Jesus."

Great boldness in the faith is no better modeled than in the life and death of Stephen, one of the seven servants selected in Acts 6. He was a model servant by virtue of his defense of the Christ, but he was especially bold in his faith when he faced his death by stoning, as we read in Acts 7:54-60.

> "Courage is fear that has said its prayers."

Boldness seems to be a rather inconspicuous virtue in the church today. We speak of it in our sermons, we sing of it in our hymns, but we seem to dismiss it in our evangelism and in our daily lives.

When Peter and John were put in jail for proclaiming the gospel and threatened with their lives if they resumed the practice, they immediately went back to the church and prayed (Acts 4:24-30). They did not pray, however, for deliverance from their enemies or their godless government. They simply prayed, "Lord, take note of their threats, and grant that Your bond-servants may speak Your word with all confidence." More than anything, they wanted great boldness in the faith.

As servants of Christ in the church today, we need great boldness in the faith. We need boldness to stand for what is right regardless of the consequences. We need boldness to proclaim the gospel to anyone who will listen and even to those who won't.

Someone once said, "Courage is fear that has said its prayers." May the Lord grant us the courage and boldness we need to serve Him faithfully in this life.

Dear Lord, grant that I may speak Your Word with all confidence and serve You with great boldness of faith.

The Deacon's Spiritual Fruit

WEEK 4 **DAY 2**

A Deacon Who Loves

1 Corinthians 13:13

"The greatest of these is love."

Of all the virtues that could be attributed to the servant of God, none ranks any higher than *love*. God's love for us and God's love through us is the greatest motivation we have to serve. The Bible says, "The love of Christ compels us" (2 Cor. 5:14). Some versions render this word "motivate." A servant of God is motivated to minister to God's people because of the great love of God. It is out of God's great love that He sent His Son to the cross. It is out of His love that we have been saved. Out of His love He places us into service. With His great power, He instills within us His own love (Gal. 5:22), the love that compels us to expend our lives for the sake of others.

W. H. Griffeth Thomas said, "Love is the outgoing of the entire nature in sacrificial service."[1] The greatest love calls for the greatest surrender, makes the greatest sacrifice, and renders the greatest service. The greatest love ever expressed took the absolute surrender of the Son of God to the will of His Father. It called for the greatest sacrifice ever made. And it provides eternal salvation for everyone who believes.

> **The greatest love calls for the greatest surrender, makes the greatest sacrifice, and renders the greatest service.**

As you fulfill your service in the church, perhaps it would be wise to pray that what you do will be done out of a sincere love for God and others. Allow God, by His Holy Spirit, to produce His own love in you and demonstrate His own love through you. This will certainly call upon you to give more than you receive and put the needs of others above your own. Remember the words of Richard Braunstein, "It is possible to give without love, but it is impossible to love without giving."[2] For God so loved the world that He gave His only Son—the greatest, sacrificial Servant of all.

**Dear Lord, may Your love motivate me to
sacrificially love others and serve them.**

A Deacon With Joy

Philippians 4:4

"Rejoice in the Lord always. I will say it again: Rejoice!"

In the Christian life, happiness depends on happenings, while joy depends on Jesus. Most of us have heard the acrostic J=Jesus, O=Others, and Y=You. The acrostic has an intended order to it. In a life of service, we put Jesus first, others second, and ourselves last. This is service that is "inexpressible and full of glory" (1 Pet. 1:8). Serving God and others out of a heart of love brings great joy.

Joy is usually experienced after service not before. For the joy set before Him, Jesus endured the cross (Hebrews 12:2). So many believers today expect to have joy in their hearts without giving anything of themselves to others. It is not others who bring us joy. It is our service to others, motivated by love that brings us joy. The joy of Jesus can never fill the heart that is filled with self-indulgence, self-love, and self-service.

> We remain weak in our service when we lack the joy of the Lord.

We remain weak in our service when we lack the joy of the Lord. After all, it is the joy of the Lord that is our strength (Neh. 8:10). Isn't it amazing that service brings joy and joy brings strength? As a faithful servant of Christ, you have the great capacity for joy. His joy, in you, will give you greater strength for more service.

When God sent His Son into the world to be our Savior, the angel said to the shepherds, "Do not be afraid; for behold, I bring you good news of great joy which will be for all the people" (Luke 2:10). The good news of great joy is still at the heart of our service. Nothing and no one will bring greater joy to your life than the good news of Jesus known personally and shared regularly.

Dear Lord, please empty me of me enough that I might give more of myself away to others—leaving plenty of room for You to fill me with Your joy.

A Deacon With Peace
John 14:27

"Peace I leave with you; My peace I give to you . . ."

Jesus was not only the sacrificial Servant of the Father. He was also the Prince of Peace (Isa. 9:6). Even when He was faced with the darkest hour and the most destitute of circumstances, He maintained a steady peace with the Father (Jn. 17).

As a Deacon in the church, it is important for you to live a life of tranquility. The apostle Paul assured Timothy that through prayer "we may lead a tranquil and quiet life in all godliness and dignity" (1 Tim. 2:2). A life in turmoil can provide little service to another life in turmoil. The servant in the church must have made peace with God and know the peace of God before he can ever administer peace to others. This means regardless of the circumstances surrounding you—in your family, in your church, on your job, or in your government—you can still have a lasting and abiding peace in your heart.

> The effective servant of God will keep his mind stayed upon the Lord.

The prophet Isaiah, in his acknowledgment of God's peace, said, "You will keep in perfect peace the mind that is dependent on You, for it is trusting in You" (Isa. 26:3). The effective servant of God will keep his mind stayed upon the Lord.

Frances Havergal stated this beautifully in the classic hymn, "Like a River Glorious":

> Stayed upon Jehovah hearts are fully blessed,
> Finding, as He promised perfect peace and rest.[3]

This may be a day in your life when your anxiety outweighs your peace. You may have been bombarded with hurts, fears, discouragement, and stress. Would this not be a good time to pray? "Don't worry about anything . . . let your requests be made know to God. And the peace of God will guard your hearts and your minds in Christ Jesus" (Phil. 4:6-7).

**Dear Lord, grant to me Your peace,
that I might serve You with a spirit of tranquility.**

A Deacon With Patience
James 5:11

"You have heard of the patience of Job . . ."

The word for *patience* in most of the book of James can also be translated "endurance." For example, James 1:3 says, "Knowing that the testing of your faith produces endurance (patience)." Webster defines *patience* as "the bearing of suffering, provocation, delay, tediousness, etc. with calmness and self-control."⁴ It is not merely an ability to wait. It means we wait in confidence that the Lord is sovereignly in control.

> The man of God who would serve the people of God must so allow God's Spirit to control his life that he endures whatever he must.

Most scholars believe that Job may be the oldest and earliest book in the Bible. If that is so, God must have seen man's need for patience very early in history. Remember what God said to Satan in Job 1:8: "Have you considered My servant Job?" Yes, Job was a servant of God, much like you, who listened to God, followed God, faced great opposition, and yet served Him patiently through it all. Hopefully, God will not say to Satan, "Have you considered My servant _____ (put your name in there)?" But if He did and you were tempted and tried in every imaginable way, would you be able to say along with Job, "Though He slay me, I will hope in Him" (13:15)?

Patience is a great virtue. It is not something discovered quickly in the Christian life, though we are given many opportunities to do so. The man of God who would serve the people of God must so allow God's Spirit to control his life that he patiently endures whatever he must.

Life is a symphony, and we lose a third of it by cutting out the slow movement. You may feel as though you are accomplishing so little in your service for Christ. Remember the patience of Job. Sooner or later—and it may be later—God will reward your patience. "Job died, an old man and full of days" (42:17).

Lord, grant to me Your power to endure hardship and to be patient even when my service for You seems meaningless.

WEEK 5   **DAY 1**

A Deacon Who Is Kind

Ephesians 4:32

"Be kind and compassionate to one another . . ."

A servant of God is intended to express both by his words and his actions a disposition of gentleness, graciousness, and consideration. The word used in this text for *kind* is a common expression of goodness of heart. This is a virtue that is unique to God but one that is manifested in and demonstrated through His servants. Most of us are not naturally kind or compassionate or tender-hearted—especially we men. Somehow we have assumed that this is a virtue for women and children but not men. Nothing could be further from the truth.

In fact, no greater kindness or compassion has ever been shown than that shown by Jesus Himself. Whether it was toward a widow who had lost her son (Lk. 7:13), a blind man who had lost his sight (Matt. 20:34), or a multitude who had lost their way (Matt. 9:36), Jesus was moved with compassion. It is this sort of kindness that today's Deacon in the church should exhibit. Someone has well said, "Kindness is a language that the deaf can hear and the blind can see." It may be conveyed in a gentle touch of someone's hand or shoulder. It may be expressed with a tender hug.

> "Kindness is a language that the deaf can hear and the blind can see."

Whether by word, touch, or attitude, this beautiful disposition of kindness is one of the most valuable expressions of God's love. Since this virtue is uniquely found in Christ, every servant of God must maintain a deep, abiding, consistent love relationship with Him. To discover and live in the kindness of the Lord is great motivation to share it with others.

Remember, every moment is the right one to be kind. Determine, in this day and every successive day of your life, that you will be kind to others.

> **Lord, I desire to express Your love and kindness toward others. Please empower me by Your Holy Spirit to be kind and show compassion to someone today.**

A Deacon Who Is Good
Acts 11:24

"For he was a good man, full of the Holy Spirit and of faith . . ."

This verse applies to one Barnabas, a traveling companion of the apostle Paul. We are told his name literally means "son of encouragement" (Acts 4:36). What a model for the Deacon in the New Testament church! What a great need for any Pastor of a church. Barnabas was a friend to the Pastor, just as every Deacon should be. He was a servant of the early church. He did all of this not for the recognition of his peers or some award he might have received from a congregation but because he was a good man.

Goodness is variously defined. Often we think of the goodness in ourselves as compared to others. Since we can always identify someone else who is worse than we are, then we are fairly good or much better in comparison. The one thing that makes this goodness unique is that it flows out of the fullness of God's Spirit and is conveyed in faith. It is actually God's goodness in us.

> A good man will love God, his family, his church, his Pastor, and life.

This goodness compels us to befriend the unfriendly, love the unlovely, care for the careless, help the helpless, and give hope to the hopeless. A good man will love God, love his family, love his church, love his Pastor, and love life. Again, this goodness is not man-produced, for clearly "there is none who does good, there is not even one" (Rom. 3:12). But it is God-produced. It is God who, by His own Spirit, produces His own goodness in us and through us to others. Wouldn't it be an amazing thing if, after you were dead and in heaven, someone would have engraved on your tombstone, "He was a good man, full of the Holy Spirit and of faith?

Dear Lord, today and from this day forward would You produce Your own goodness in me? I acknowledge that apart from Your Holy Spirit infilling me, I can never know or express this goodness. Please fill me today with Your goodness!

A Deacon Who Is Faithful
Revelation 2:10

"Be faithful until death, and I will give you the crown of life."

The term *faith* is used in Galatians 5:22 in reference to a fruit of the Spirit. This identifies an important elemental and essential characteristic of the Christian life. Often translated *faithfulness*, it implies the way of life for the Deacon in the church. The faithfulness of a man of God who serves a local church is as important as any virtue found in Scripture, with perhaps the exception of love. The word speaks of loyalty, devotion, steadfastness, reliability, and trustworthiness. These are always to characterize the servant of God.

Years ago, the recording artist Steve Green popularized a song that conveys this idea of faithfulness quite well:

> May all who come behind us find us faithful,
> May the fire of our devotion light their way.
> May the footprints that we leave, lead them to believe,
> And the lives we live inspire them to obey.[5]

Only eternity will tell the impact of your personal faithfulness to Christ and His church. In the final analysis, we will not be accountable for the numbers of people we have witnessed to nor the amount of money we have invested in the church nor the number of services we have attended nor the number of years we have served, though all of these are important. On Judgment Day, we will be judged as to how faithful, trustworthy, and dependable we were with the time, talents, truth, and treasure given us by God.

> **Only eternity will tell the impact of your personal faithfulness to Christ and His church.**

Iain H. Murray said, "Faithfulness to God is our first obligation in all that we are called to do in the service of the gospel."[6] When Jesus returns or when you are on your deathbed, will He find you faithful? Be faithful until death and He will give you the crown of life.

**Heavenly Father, empower me by Your Spirit
on a daily basis, that I might serve You
and Your church faithfully.**

A Deacon Who Is Meek

1 Thessalonians 2:7

"We proved to be gentle among you . . ."

The word for *meek* or *gentle* in this verse, and many others, is a word not easily translated into English. In English the word *meekness* is commonly equated with *weakness*. But in the Bible it is a term used to describe Moses (Num. 12:3), Jesus (Matt. 11:29), Paul (here), and a submissive wife (1 Pet. 3:4). Obviously, it does not mean weakness for the servant of God. It has been suggested that meekness, at least in its biblical use, refers to *power under control*. It was meekness that prevented Moses from calling down judgment upon God's people (Exod. 32:12). It was meekness that kept Jesus on the road to Calvary (Matt. 21:5).

> Meekness is not weakness, but it certainly involves submission on our part.

As a servant of God in the church, you will do well to develop this virtue in your life. You have been given the power of the Holy Spirit of God to fulfill your role. He is the Master at controlling us and guarding us from our own self-service.

Meekness certainly involves submission on our part. "Submit therefore to God" (James 4:7). Give yourself over to His Lordship. His Holy Spirit's power in you can produce great service to the body of Christ. Serving the Lord with meekness will not come naturally, nor will it ever be something you do out of sheer determination. Live and serve in the fullness of God's Spirit, and He will develop meekness in you.

Geoffrey B. Wilson said, "Meekness is the mark of a man who has been mastered by God."[7] Allow God to master your life and you will be a blessed servant in the church. You will prove to be gentle among them.

Dear Lord, show me the ways in which I am
not submissive to You so that I may begin—or
begin again—to submit my will to Yours.
May Your meekness and gentleness characterize
my life and service.

A Deacon Who Is Under Control
Titus 2:2

"Older men are to be self-controlled (temperate) . . ."

Actually, whether you are old, middle-aged, or young, as a servant of God in the church you will want to exercise *temperance* or self-control. The word used here and in the list of the fruit of the Spirit (Gal. 5:23) is a word meaning more than mere self-control, for even unbelievers can show a good measure of self-control. Some unbelieving men believe temperance is the ability to "hold your liquor." Biblical temperance is much different than that.

Nelson's Bible Dictionary gives a sound description of temperance:

> It indicates a self-control that masters all kinds of sensual desires, such as sexual desire or the desire for material comfort. Through temperance Christians can discipline body and spirit, so that they are more capable of striving for their spiritual reward.[8]

Clearly, this virtue is needed among all men in the church but especially among those who serve as Pastors or Deacons. These servants of God are tempted by sensual desires regularly. You may be one of these. If so, be encouraged because God has indwelled you by His Holy Spirit and His Spirit is *holy*. When you surrender yourself—body and spirit—to the Lord, you then have the power to resist temptation. You have His power to maintain control over your desires and appetites.

> **Victory over sinful desires begins with your own honest assessment of your life.**

Your victory over sinful desires begins with your own honest assessment of your life. It is not easy to do this, but it is essential if you would be a servant with integrity. The man who resists self-examination can easily conclude that he needs it. Perhaps you would like to pray the prayer of the psalmist in Psalm 139:23-24.

> "Search me, O God . . . and see if there be any wicked way in me, and lead me in the way everlasting." Control my mind, my emotions, and my will so that I can live a temperate life before those whom You've given me to serve.

The Deacon's Personal Life

The Deacon and His Master

Jude 1:4

"Certain persons . . . deny our only Master and Lord, Jesus Christ."

The term *Master,* used here of Christ, refers specifically to one who has absolute ownership and controlled power over another. The term references slaves and masters (1 Pet. 2:18) but is uniquely applied to Christians and Christ. Quite literally, the biblical term means superintendent, overseer, or one who stands over. As applied to the servant of Christ, it means that Jesus Christ is to be in absolute control or mastery over your life. The Bible refers to false teachers "even denying the Master who bought them . . ." (2 Pet. 2:1). As servants of Christ, we know that we "have been bought with a price . . ." (1 Cor. 6:20).

Knowing this, we are compelled to listen to the commands of our Master; understand what He expects of us; and obey Him without reservation or hesitancy. As a Deacon in the church, you exemplify what it means to be a servant of your Master and Lord, Jesus Christ. You are not the only servant, but you are to be a model of service to others who have the same Master as you have (Acts 20:28).

> Jesus Christ is to be in absolute control or mastery over your life.

To experience the Lordship of Christ and His mastery over us, there must be a deliberate and genuine surrender of ourselves to Him. We give our minds to Him so we can think like He thinks. We give our feelings to Him so we'll feel as He does. We give our wills to Him so we will decide as He does. We are to "set apart the Messiah as Lord in our hearts" (1 Pet. 3:15).

Scripture makes it clear we cannot receive Christ as our Savior and refuse to obey Him as our Lord. We may serve any number of persons or things as our master, but we can never serve Jesus Christ or His church unless and until He is the Master and Lord of our lives.

Lord, I am sincerely surrendering my life to You as my only Lord and Master. I desire to hear You, understand You, and obey You from this day forward.

The Deacon and His Maturity
Hebrews 6:1

"Leaving the elementary teaching about the Christ, let us press on to maturity . . ."

Just as babies require a transition from liquid to soft food to solid food, so we must mature in our spiritual growth. The Bible gives a clear method for making this transition. It is called discipleship. Actually the preceding verse to today's text says, "Solid food is for the mature, who because of practice have their senses trained to discern good and evil" (Heb. 5:14). It is this practice of the Christian life that, over time, results in our spiritual maturity.

> It is imperative that spiritually maturing men be identified and placed into service in the church.

To think about training our senses raises a life challenge. We sometimes teach our preschoolers, "Be careful little eyes what you see, be careful little ears what you hear or be careful little hands what you touch." Unfortunately, we stop teaching it too soon and "post-schoolers" get into all sorts of trouble. The challenge in Christian maturity is continual training and consistent practice. That, of course, requires discipline, which is the essence of discipleship.

On a scale of one to ten (one being infantile and ten being fully mature) where are you in your spiritual maturity? A servant of God in the church may not be a ten or even a nine on such a scale, but he should certainly be striving in that direction. It is imperative that spiritually maturing men be identified and placed into service in the church. We have too many spiritual "infants" who, because of popularity, good business savvy, honorable family, or exuberant personality, have been elected as Deacons or other church leaders. The church continues to falter and fail at her assignment with "babies trying to raise babies.

Give yourself to spiritual maturity. Hear, read, study, meditate, and memorize Scripture. Consistently attend all the regular services of your church. Give faithfully of your time, talents, and treasure to the Lord's work. If you do, you will mature sooner than you think.

> **Lord, enable me by Your Spirit to train my senses and practice the principles of Your Word. Lead me steadily to a higher level of spiritual maturity.**

A Deacon and His Mind

Colossians 3:2

"Set your minds on what is above, not on what is on the earth."

Webster's Dictionary defines *mind* as "the element or complex of elements in an individual that feels, perceives, thinks, wills and especially reasons."[1] In the Bible, the word *heart* or *soul* is often used to describe the mind. In the New Testament, the mind was clearly thought of as either good or evil. *Nelson's Bible Dictionary* explains:

> Negatively, the mind may be "hardened" (2 Cor. 3:14), blinded" (2 Cor. 4:4), "corrupt" (2 Tim. 3:8) and "debased" (Rom. 1:28). On the positive side, humans may have minds that are renewed (Rom. 12:2) and pure (2 Pet. 3:1). They may love God with all their minds (Matt. 22:37; Mk. 12:30; Lk. 10:27) and have God's laws implanted in their minds (Heb. 8:10).[2]

The man who would serve the church in any leadership role should be developing his mind. How we think and reason has everything to do with how we serve. If we think that others should take care of themselves, no matter their circumstances, then we are not thinking *servanthood*. If we reason that "what's mine is mine" and others should never be given a handout—or a hand up—then we are far from being an effective servant.

> **The man who would serve the church in any leadership role should be developing his mind.**

There is a familiar Proverb (23:7) that says, "As he thinks within himself, so he is." Simply put, as you think, so you act. A servant thinks service. Give more of your time and attention to others. "With humility of mind regard one another as more important than yourselves" (Phil. 2:3). Then you will serve well as a Deacon.

Dear Lord, I acknowledge that my mind often strays from You, Your church, and Your people. Please build into me the mind of Your Son, that I might think and act as He did.

The Deacon and His Morality
1 Corinthians 15:33

"Do not be deceived: Bad company corrupts good morals."

The word translated *morals* in this verse is the word *ETHOS*. It is rare that we have a Greek word that is actually used as an English word, but this is one. *ETHOS*, in English, is defined by Webster as "the distinguishing character, sentiment, moral nature, or guiding beliefs of a person, group, or institution."[3] The King James Version translated this word "manners." It speaks of ethical conduct or principles of right and wrong in behavior.

Morality has many synonyms: ethical values, ethics, and right or wrong. In the New Testament, we are given numerous principles intended to help us discern right from wrong. In order to have a right and wrong, we must have a standard or a plumb line by which to measure our behavior. For the believer, and certainly for a servant of God in the church, that standard is the Bible. There are good morals, as indicated in our text, and there are bad morals. The Word of God shows us that clear distinction and admonishes us to practice what's good and right.

> The Bible, God's Holy Word, is your moral compass.

The now-deceased evangelist Vance Havner was known for saying, "Nothing is ever settled until it is settled right; and nothing is ever settled right until it is settled with God."[4] What is right for you to believe and do is settled. It is "firmly fixed in heaven" (Ps. 119:89). God's Holy Word, the Bible, is your moral compass. You serve as you do—or neglect to serve as you should—based upon your obedience to that moral compass. Don't be deceived: if you hang out exclusively with those who have a different moral compass, your own morals will be corrupted. Your service for Christ will be nullified.

> Dear Lord, I ask You to give me clear understanding from Your Word of the difference between right and wrong. And help me to adopt and practice good morals, especially as I serve Your people.

A Deacon and His Money
2 Timothy 6:10

"For the love of money is a root of all kinds of evil . . ."

For many years in many churches—especially Baptist churches—it was assumed that managing the money was the Deacons' main responsibility. However, in recent decades, that notion has changed. These men now devote more of their time and energy in servant-ministry to the church members. This still requires some management of funds but mainly as they relate to the benevolent ministry of the church.

How a Deacon earns, manages, and spends his money is of great concern to God. How much money we earn is not nearly as important as what we do with it. Most Christian financial counselors remind us that there are only a few things we can do with money: (1) we can earn it, (2) we can save it, (3) we can spend it, or (4) we can give it away. All of these uses are mentioned directly or indirectly in Scripture. A good passage to study on this subject is 2 Corinthians 8-9.

The man who is a Deacon should be one who gives serious attention to the money entrusted to him by God. You should set a good example in earning money. "If anyone isn't willing to work, he should not eat" (2 Thess. 3:10). You should set a good example in managing money. "You should have deposited my money with the bankers. And when I returned I would have received my money back with interest" (Matt. 25:27). You should set a good example in giving money. "They all out of their surplus put into the offering; but she [poor widow] out of her poverty put in all that she had to live on" (Lk. 21:4).

> Fall in love with Jesus, but never fall in love with the things He may supply.

Fall in love with Jesus, but never fall in love with the things He may supply for you (Lk. 12:15). Loving money or the things money can buy will cause you all sorts of trouble and render your intended service to the church void.

Dear Lord, please help me to grow in my love for You and not for the things You have provided for me. I acknowledge that my real blessing is You . . . not my money or things.

A Deacon and His Marriage

Ephesians 5:25

"Husbands, love your wives, just as Christ also loved the church . . ."

Thomas Adams stated, "As God by creation made two of one, so again by marriage He made one of two."[5] Jesus said, "For this reason a man will leave his father and mother and be joined to his wife, and the two will become one flesh" (Matt. 19:4). Since "Deacons must be husbands of only one wife" (1 Tim. 3:12), it makes sense that servants in the church should give attention to their marriage. Believers who are married are given a clear, functional role in the relationship. Husbands are to love and lead their wives (Eph. 5:23, 25) just as Christ loves and leads the church (His Bride). Wives are to submit to and respect their husbands (Eph. 5:22-33) just as Christ submitted to His Father and respected His role in the godhead.

It is true that a servant in the church is no stronger or weaker in his service than he is in his marriage. Most church leaders realize they definitely need their wives to help them in ministry. A healthy marriage, including mutual love and understanding, can only enhance the effectiveness of God's servants. You will picture the intended relationship between Christ and the Church; identify with the particular needs of families in the church; communicate by word and deed the plan of God for married couples; and leave a legacy of biblical family life for future generations.

> A healthy marriage ... can only enhance the effectiveness of God's servants.

The Pastor or Deacon who guards his marriage and trains his children to fear and follow the Lord will have made a great contribution to the Kingdom of God. Remember, your intended priorities should be to God, to your wife, to your children, to your church, to your employer, and then to the rest of the world.

**Lord, thank You for my wife and for our marriage.
Please help me to serve her and my family first so
I may serve the church better in the long run.**

The Deacon and His Management

1 Timothy 3:12

*"Deacons . . . managing their children and
their own households competently."*

The word for *managing* literally means "to stand before," hence "to lead, attend to" (indicating care and diligence), "to rule over."[6] The word is used in a list of seven motivational spiritual gifts describing general servant-leaders in the church (Rom. 12:8). It is used to describe one of the intended qualifications of Pastors in 1 Timothy 3:4-5 and again in 1 Timothy 5:17 to describe a principal function of the Pastor. It is used here to identify one of the qualifications and assumed functions of the Deacon.

The work of managing or ruling, for the servant of God in the church, extends beyond his family to his ministry to others. You will find yourself standing before others who are awaiting a word of direction or a gesture of care or maybe an admonition. You will often feel a compulsion to want to lead another person to Christ or back to Christ and help him or her better manage his or her spiritual growth.

> The more the Master manages you, the more effective your management of others will be.

How you develop this responsibility is a direct reflection upon your call and competence as a Deacon. Begin by managing your own household well and you will find managing your ministry much easier.

We can never truly call ourselves leaders unless we know where we are going and can identify others who are following us. As a servant-manager in the church, you must have the calling, the character, and the competence to take others where you are going. When your life and ministry are aligned with Scripture, you will serve as a "good manager" in your home, in the church, and in the community. Thus, you need not be surprised when others want to follow you or see you as a model of servanthood.

The more the Master manages you, the more effective your management of others will be. So let Him have His way with you today and each day hereafter.

**Lord, I desire to be a good manager of my home
and my ministry to others. By the powerful work of
Your Spirit, please be the Manager of my life.**

The Deacon and His Message
1 John 1:5

"This is the message we have heard from Him and declare to you . . ."

God has wonderful ways of bringing us under the proclamation and influence of the gospel message. Many are exposed to this message through servants in the church who are determined to tell the story. Anyone who has been the recipient of this message has an obligation—indeed a mandate—to share it with others. The message of the gospel in general (cf. 1 Cor. 15:3-11), once received and applied to your life, becomes a "life message" for you. The apostle Paul said, "My message was not in persuasive words of wisdom, but of demonstration of the Spirit and of power" (1 Cor. 2:4). Clearly, the message of the gospel had become Paul's message. Likewise, it should become our message.

> Anyone who has been the recipient of this message has an obligation—indeed a mandate—to share it with others.

In 1896 H. Ernest Nichol wrote a song that challenges the church to take this message to the world:

> We've a story to tell to the nations,
> that shall turn their hearts to the right,
> a story of truth and mercy, a story of peace and light.
> We've a message to give to the nations,
> that the Lord Who reigneth above
> Has sent us his Son to save us, and show us that God is love.[7]

This message of the gospel is yours. It is the message with which you have been saved. It is a message to which you have surrendered. It is a message you must be faithful to share. Tell your parents, your siblings, your wife, your children, and your grandchildren. Keep telling the old, old story of Jesus and His love. In so doing, you will be a faithful Deacon who "obtains for himself a high standing and great confidence in the faith" (1 Tim. 3:13).

Dear Lord, thank You for the great sacrifice You've made to bring the gospel message to my life. Empower me to believe, live, and tell the story as each day of my life unfolds.

The Deacon and His Methods

1 Corinthians 14:40

"But everything must be done decently and in order."

Most of us have heard or even made the statement ourselves, "There is a method to my madness." Webster defines a *method* as "a systematic procedure, technique, or mode of inquiry employed by or proper to a particular discipline or act."[8] The New American Standard Bible translates this verse, "But all things must be done properly and in an orderly manner." We definitely serve an orderly God. Just look at the Creation! He has intended for the church to function and fulfill its commission in an orderly fashion.

We who serve in the local church should never be passive, apathetic, or flippant about our service. We must not render service to the church without meaning and purpose. Methods may vary from church to church or servant to servant, but the principles of service remain the same—everything must be done decently and in order.

> **We must not render service to the church without meaning and purpose.**

The word for *decently* denotes "gracefully, becomingly, in a seemly manner." The way we maintain our buildings and grounds, the way we present ourselves to visitors, the way we teach our classes, the way we care for our children and our aged, the way we deliver our message, the way we give money, and the standards we uphold are all intended to be done decently and in order. As a Deacon in the church, you have a responsibility to order your private world and to bring order to the ministry of your church.

Fanny Crosby, though blind from childhood, captured the great need of the church:

> To the work! To the work! We are servants of God,
> Let us follow the path that our Master has trod;
> With the balm of His counsel our strength to renew,
> Let us do with our might what our hands find to do.[9]

Dear Lord, as Your servant I acknowledge my utter need for Your Holy Spirit's guidance, not only in what I do, but in the way or method by which I choose to do it.

The Deacon and His Mouth

James 3:5

"Though the tongue is a small part of the body, it boasts great things . . ."

Jesus made it very clear that "on the day of judgment people will have to account for every careless word they speak. For by your words you will be acquitted, and by your words you will be condemned" (Matt. 12:36-37). You will find much of James 3 is teaching on the tongue. It would do us all well to read that chapter at least monthly and be reminded how important it is to listen and think before we speak.

> Keep your tongue from evil and your lips from deceitful speech.

Many well-meaning servants in the church have a real challenge when it comes to "bridling their tongue" (Js. 3:2-3). A godly mother used to repeatedly tell her children, "You have one mouth and two ears. You should spend twice as much time listening as you do talking." Elected servants in the church will do well to heed this motherly advice. The more and the better we listen, the better we will understand how we should serve.

Proverbs 15:1 should be learned and regularly applied in Christian service, especially in godly counseling: "A gentle answer turns away anger, but a harsh word stirs up wrath." Not only is it extremely important what you say, but it is also just as important how you say it. With your mouth you may bless your Lord and Father, and with it you may curse men who are made in God's likeness. James says, "My brothers, these things should not be this way" (Js. 3:10).

Follow the admonition of the Psalmist (34:13): "Keep your tongue from evil and your lips from deceitful speech." Your service for Christ and His church will be much more effective when your speech is "gracious, seasoned with salt" (Col. 4:6).

> Be careful little mouth what you say,
> for the Father up above is listening every day.

Dear Lord, I pray You will guard my tongue. Enable me, by Your Holy Spirit, to be quick to hear and slow to speak but to speak clearly for You.

THE DEACON AND HIS MEMORY
Psalm 119:11

"I have treasured Your word in my heart so that I may not sin against You."

The idea of treasuring God's Word in our hearts is a somewhat foreign thought. It seems we are more conditioned at forgetting than at remembering. The child of God has the wonderful privilege of memorizing snippets of the mind of God. When we memorize a phrase, verse, paragraph, or chapter of the Bible, it is like gold stored in a secure safe. Of course, we will only benefit from what we have stored if we often unlock the safe. And far too many of us, because of idleness of mind, have forgotten the combination.

> When we memorize Scripture, it is like gold stored in a secure safe.

When the Bible admonishes us to "forget none of His benefits" we are challenged. We are challenged to remember "the Sabbath day" (Ex. 20:8), remember "your Creator in the days of your youth" (Eccles. 12:1), and remember the great sacrifice of Christ (Luke 22:19). "Do not forget the Lord" (Deut. 6:12). Individuals do it, and nations do it (Ps. 9:17). You will too, unless you "treasure His Word in your heart.

Scripture memory comes easier to some than others. But that is not an excuse to not do it. We all remember some things. You likely remember multiple addresses and phone numbers as well as certain facts related to your job and everyday life. Why not remember Scripture? It has something to do with what is really important or valuable to us. When knowing God and knowing what God has said becomes important enough, we will begin to remember Scripture.

A good little formula for Scripture memory is: read it, re-read it, repeat it, repeat it again, recite it, recite it again, review it, and review it again. Then repeat the whole formula. Repetition and review are essential to Scripture memory. Start with brief verses, and you will soon remember many. Before very long you will have begun to "treasure God's Word in your heart.

**Dear Lord, please develop a passion in me to know
You and to remember what You have said.**

The Deacon and His Magnitude
2 Timothy 4:7

"I have fought the good fight, I have finished the race, I have kept the faith."

Saul of Tarsus (i.e., Paul the apostle), in his younger adult life, had no idea that the Messiah he rejected would so transform his life and use him as He did. Like most servants of God, your present life is probably appreciably different than your past. You may have never dreamed that you would be a Christian and certainly not a Deacon in the church. The magnitude of Paul's life and ministry is immeasurable. Yours may be too!

None of the great patriarchs or prophets of the Old Testament even imagined the magnitude of their lives. The New Testament apostles, the authors of Scripture, the named, and unnamed servants in the early church never pre-planned the extent of their influence. They simply loved God with all their lives and loved others for whom God had provided salvation. They were faithful, obedient servants who were consistently unassuming. The magnitude of their lives has gone down in history and impacted multitudes for eternity.

> Stay focused. Be faithful, True, and consistent.

Perhaps you too, as an elected Deacon in the twenty-first-century church, should focus your attention on today's service and let the impact of your service be carried as near or as far as God would take it. A preacher once said, "If you will take care of the depth of your service, God will take care of the breadth of your service." Stay focused. Be faithful, true, and consistent. Don't try to do more than you can, but give yourself to do all that you should with God's Spirit enabling you. Then you, too, will have "finished the race and kept the faith.

Lord, enable me to focus on my present service and spend less time thinking about future opportunities. Help me to attend to the depth of my service while You tend to the breadth.

THE DEACON AND HIS MARGINS
Matthew 14:23

"After dismissing the crowds, He went up on the mountain by Himself to pray. When evening came, He was there alone."

Sometimes our free time or time we spend to ourselves is referred to as *marginal* time. The margin is the extra white space on a page that allows for the unexpected ideas that might come out of the body of the text. You probably have made notes to yourself in the margins of a book or magazine or your Bible.

The big question is, have you left any space in your life—any margins to your schedule, your finances, and your time? And if not, what is being neglected in your life that has no room to enter because the margins are all taken up? Servants in the church, especially Pastors and Deacons, tend to fill the margins of their lives so full that there is no room or space to "dismiss the crowds," much less "come away and pray.

The margins of your life are not intended for mere idle thinking. It is true, "An idle mind is the devil's workshop." Margins are intended for clear thinking—for meditation on the Word and work of God in your life. That gives you time and space to pray when the calendar fills up and the crowds press upon you.

Jesus used the margins of His life and ministry to escape the business of His schedule (Matt. 14:23); evade the futile accolades of men (Jn. 6:15); and select the twelve apostles (Lk. 6:12-16). Can you imagine what God might show you or what new *opportunities* might come to you from the margins of your life—assuming, of course, you have some margin? Evaluate your schedule, your budget, your specific family needs, your job, and your leisure and begin to build in some margin—some extra time, space, and money. Then you will be better prepared for every good work (Ti. 3:1).

> **Have you left any space in your life—any margins to your schedule, your finances, and your time?**

Lord, please show me how to build margins into my life so I can easily spend time with You in prayer and Bible study.

The Deacon and His Merit
Philippians 4:8

"Whatever is honorable . . . if there is any moral excellence and if there is any praise—dwell on these things."

Merit is usually thought of as "reward given for praiseworthy actions." It denotes actions of excellence. The servant of God must always remember the difference between human recognition and God's reward. Paul makes it clear in this text that moral excellence is produced by God's Holy Spirit working in and through us. It is His work. But it is His work in us. The ultimate glory and honor or praise for any moral excellence shown from our lives must go to God and God alone.

> We must be consistently and obediently willing to live under God's complete control.

There is, however, a serious role we are to fill in meritorious service. We must be consistently and obediently willing to live under God's complete control. We are not after man's applause. We are interested in pleasing God. And our reward for meritorious service is realized most completely in eternity. But the characteristics of moral excellence listed in Philippians 4:8 are to be dwelt upon and "practiced" (v.1). Our disciplined behavior must be a reflection of His moral excellence. It is very likely that you will receive some honor or reward for the service you render in the church. You may receive such recognition with sincerity and humility, acknowledging that it is God Himself who is "at work in you to will and to work for His good pleasure" (Phil. 2:13). You may wish to use the words of Paul from 1 Timothy 1:12 to express your appreciation to God. "I thank Christ Jesus our Lord, who has strengthened me, because He considered me faithful, putting me into service.

Lord, I am grateful that You have saved me and have called me to serve You. I deserve no recognition for this service but do acknowledge that it includes Your moral excellence in me. To You goes all the glory and honor.

The Deacon and His Music

Psalm 150:1, 6

"Praise God in His sanctuary . . . let everything that breathes praise the Lord."

All six verses of Psalm 150 are admonitions of praise and worship. The psalmist suggests where (v. 1), why (v. 2), and how (vv. 3-5) we are to worship. He identifies several instruments with which God can be worshipped, including trumpet, harp, lyre, tambourine, flute, strings, and cymbals. Verse six identifies the voice as an instrument of worship. Thus we worship God with our voices and with instruments.

Music has become a big part of most worship services. The servant-leader in the church should encourage and participate in worship through music. The music is merely a means to an end. The end is the worship of God. Thus, less emphasis should be put on the style of worship than on the hearts of those worshiping. It has too long been assumed that the church needs better song leaders or musicians when her greatest need has always been deeply devoted, heartfelt leaders of worship—literally leaders of people to worship God.

> **Music has become a big part of most worship services.**

Geoffrey Thomas captures this truth well: "In true worship men . . . have little thought of the means of worship; their thoughts are upon God."[10] Music, in and of itself, can be moral or immoral but never amoral. Even the melody, harmony, and rhythm need to be well-balanced in order to convey tranquility to one's spirit. To worship God in Spirit and truth (John 4:23), the believer must be filled (controlled) with the Holy Spirit of God. Spirit-led worshippers will be "speaking to one another in psalms, hymns, and spiritual songs, singing and making music to the Lord in your heart" (Eph. 5:19).

Deacons and other servant leaders in the church should promote the public worship of God. They should lead by example, and when so gifted, by conducting or presentation. Lead the church not merely to sing or play music. Lead your church to worship the true and living God. "Let everything that breath praise the Lord.

Lord, by Your enabling Spirit, empower me to worship You in spirit and truth whether vocally or instrumentally. I desire to praise You above all else.

The Deacon and His Mortality
Hebrews 9:27

"It is appointed for people to die once—and after this judgment."

Death is certain, and it is no respecter of persons. Martin Luther was right, "Every man must do two things alone: he must do his own believing, and his own dying."[11] There's absolutely nothing we can do to avoid dying, but there is much we can do to prepare for it. It is a mandatory appointment for which we must be ready. "Prepare to meet your God . . ." (Amos 4:12).

Most people live their earthly lives as if this is all there is. God's Word, the Bible, assures us that this life on earth is not all there is. In fact, this life is very temporal. "You do not know what your life will be like tomorrow. You are just a vapor that appears for a little while and then vanishes away" (Js. 4:14). Just about every person above sixty years of age would agree that the years go by like hours, and they see themselves living in the evening hours.

The servant of God in the church has an extraordinary opportunity to not only prepare himself but also to help prepare others for their mortality. Preparation for death begins not long after we are born. A child-like faith brings a person into a saving relationship with Christ. Spiritual rebirth assures us of a residence in heaven (Jn. 3:15-16). Spiritual growth and maturity assure us of a reward in heaven (1 Pet. 1:3-5). Thomas Chalmers said it well, "The character wherewith we sink into the grave at death is the very character wherewith we shall reappear at the resurrection."[12] Jesus said, "An hour is coming, in which all who are in the tombs will hear His voice, and will come forth; those who did the good deeds to a resurrection of life, those who committed the evil deeds to a resurrection of judgment" (Jn. 5:28-29).

> Until you are free to die, you will never be free to live.

Until you are free to die, you will never be free to live. Only those with a genuine relationship with Christ are free at all (Gal. 5:1). Be free. Live well. Die well.

**Dear Lord, please order my life in such a way
that I will be prepared to die
while helping others prepare to die.**

The Deacon's Commandments

A Deacon and His One True God

Exodus 20:3

"Do not have other gods besides Me."

This first of the well-known Ten Commandments makes very clear God's intent that we acknowledge Him and Him alone as God. Most Christians accept this command as exclusive. That is, every other so-called god must be excluded in favor of the one and only true and living God. A god is anyone or anything that attracts our attention, consumes our calendar, receives our resources, and calls for our commitment. We can give ourselves over to other people or material things and without intention allow them to become our god.

For God alone to be our God, we must deliberately and intentionally give ourselves—all of our attention, time, resources, and commitment—to Him. A theologian who taught Hebrew in a seminary would always speak of the prepositional phrase "besides Me" as having multiple applications, if not interpretations. He said it can mean "behind Me" or "ahead of Me" or "beside Me" or "instead of Me." Anything that is added to or replaces the true God in your life is a false god.

> For God alone to be our God, we must deliberately and intentionally give ourselves to Him.

You may have heard it said, "God is God, and I am not." That certainly is true. If you know that to be true, you should treat Him accordingly. He's not the "big guy in the sky" or "old man upstairs" or "master architect in the heavens." He is God! "The Lord has established His throne in the heavens, and His sovereignty rules over all" (Ps. 103:19). God rules and reigns in all of the universe and in all His creatures.

Thomas Brooks said, "There is infinitely more in God than the tongues of men or angels can express."[1] This is the God we know. This is the infinite, omniscient, omnipotent, omnipresent, immutable, independent, inscrutable, just, loving, sovereign God and Father of our Lord and Savior Jesus Christ. This is the God we serve.

> Dear Lord, help me never to try to substitute
> anyone or anything for You—especially myself.
> I acknowledge You as the only—my only—
> true and living God.

A Deacon and His "Idols"
Exodus 20:4

"Do not make an idol for yourself . . ."

A very popular television program at the beginning of the twenty-first century was *American Idol*. Contestants on this show would perform their talents in front of a panel of judges, mostly recording artists themselves, to be identified as the next "American Idol." An idol, according to *Webster's Dictionary* is "an image of a god used as an object of worship; any object of ardent or excessive devotion."[2] People can become idols in the minds of others (so-called fans), and they can become idols in their own minds. A. W. Tozer once said, "An idol of the mind is as offensive to God as an idol of the hand."[3]

> Jesus Christ, and He alone, should be the only one at the true center of your life.

People may also "create" or "concoct" an idol made out of some material substance. Clothes, automobiles, boats, motorcycles, houses, buildings, and any of hundreds of such material things can become idols to us. Have you ever heard a parent say of a precious child, "I just worship her!" or "My life centers around him!" Though God intends for us to love our children, He never intends for them to become idols to us. Jesus Christ, and He alone, should be the only one at the true center of your life. Generations are either blessed or cursed depending upon who your God is according to Exodus 20:4-6.

As an elected servant of God in your church, can you identify anything or anyone in your life that could be described as an idol—an object of such worth to you that it receives nearly all of your attention, time, resources, and commitment? Or can you honestly say today, "Jesus is my only Lord! My full allegiance goes to Him! He is the only object of my worship!"

> Dear Lord, please show me the unseen idols in my life and empower me by Your Holy Spirit to remove them from the place that You alone deserve.

A Deacon and God's Name

Exodus 20:7

"Do not misuse the name of the Lord your God . . ."

What's in a name? Maybe not much with some names given to babies these days, but not so in the Bible and particularly with the names attributed to God. The primary name God used to identify Himself to Moses was "I AM WHO I AM" (Ex. 3:14). This term conveyed something of His character. Thus, to know His name is to know God Himself. Perhaps the most important name for God is Jehovah or Yahweh, which, again, carries with it the idea "I am who I am" or "I will be who I will be."

The concise definitions of the names of God will lead the servant of God to a deeper devotion to Him:

Jehovah-Yahweh—The-Lord-IS (He will always exist in all reality.)
Jehovah-jireh—The-Lord-Will-Provide (He will provide for your needs.)
Jehovah-nissi—The-Lord-Is-My-Banner" (He will take up your battles and win.)
Jehovah-shalom—The-Lord-Is-Peace (He will give you His peace.)
Jehovah-shammah—The-Lord-Is-There (He will always be there for you.)
Jehovah-tsebaoth—The-Lord-of-Hosts (He will rule heaven in your favor.)
Jehovah-Eloke-Yisrael—The-Lord-God-of-Israel (He will possess your life.)

> To know His name is to know God Himself.

This has a rather significant meaning to us when we "call upon the name of the Lord" for our salvation (Rom. 10:13), in our worship (Eph. 5:20), in our daily lives (Rev. 2:13), and with our ultimate appearance before Him (Phil. 2:10). No believer, and certainly not a Deacon in the church, should ever use the name of the Lord in vain. We must use His name with the greatest of respect and reverence. We must attribute glory to His name. Elisha A. Hoffman worded it well in his 1878 hymn:

> Glory to his name, glory to his name:
> There to my heart was the blood applied; glory to his name.[4]

**Dear Lord, You are the only true and living God.
I acknowledge Your names as characteristic of
Who You are. May Your Name alone be praised in my life.**

A Deacon and the Lord's Day
Exodus 20:8

"Remember to dedicate the Sabbath day."

For the Jew in Moses'era, the *Sabbath* was the seventh day or Saturday. It was commemorated as the day of rest in light of God having created the world in six days (i.e., Sunday through Friday) and "resting on the Sabbath" (Gen. 2:13). With the life, death, and especially the resurrection of Jesus, the day of commemoration changed. Understanding Christ to be the "Lord of the Sabbath" (Mk. 2:28), His early followers began to worship Him particularly on Sunday, the first day of the week, the day of His resurrection (Matt. 28:1). Thus, the early church and subsequently the true church in the twenty-first century celebrate and worship Christ primarily on Sunday.

Nelson's Bible Dictionary says of the Lord's Day, "This was the day on which Jesus was raised from the dead; every Lord's Day, thereafter, is a weekly memorial of Christ's resurrection. Clearly the early church assembled for worship and religious instruction on Sunday, the Lord's Day (1 Cor. 16:2)."[5]

Is Sunday a special day for you and your family? Are you doing all you can to "keep it holy"? Do you remember it for what it is in light of the resurrection of your Savior?

> Take the Lord's Day seriously, and develop the habit of honoring the Lord on His day.

D. L. Moody once said, "You show me a nation that has given up the Sabbath and I will show you a nation that has got the seed of decay."[6] It is true that many in America have long since ignored any special day of the week. Even if employers allow them a day off on Sunday, in many cases, it is seen only as a day of leisure or a day to catch up on all the household chores. As a follower of Christ, and especially as a Deacon in the church, you ought to be very faithful in your Sunday school and worship service attendance. Take the Lord's Day seriously and develop the habit of honoring the Lord on His day.

> Dear Lord, I know that Your day, Sunday, is a day for me to acknowledge and honor You in worship and Christian instruction. Please empower me to develop consistency in this area of my life.

A Deacon and His Parents
Exodus 20:12

"Honor your father and your mother so that you may have a long life . . ."

The word *honor* means to "esteem highly or respect." It is the expression of genuineness in attributing value or worth to another. God's command shows He saw the need throughout history for each person to respect and honor his or her parents. Major interruptions in God's intended family structure—including polygamy and divorce—have led us to dishonor, rather than to honor, our parents.

Perhaps you are a Deacon who has come from a broken home because of divorced parents. You may find it hard to honor your birth father or mother. You may harbor resentment toward a step parent. You may find that your own children are watching you to discover how to "honor their father and mother." You must work hard on being a good example. The great commentator, G. Campbell Morgan, is right: "No service for God is of any value which is contradicted by the life at home."[7]

> No service for God is of any value that is contradicted by the life at home.

Though honoring our parents is usually initiated in childhood (Eph. 6:2), it is intended for adults, too. For example, Jesus said we "invalidate the word of God" when we fail to give to the needs of our parents (Matt. 15:4-6). Only wage-earning adults can fulfill this expectation.

This text—this fifth commandment—is "the first commandment with a promise" (Eph. 6:2). The promise is "that it may be well with you, and that you may live long on the earth" (Eph. 6:3). Honoring your parents is likely to result in a greater level of prosperity ("well with you") and longer, lasting posterity ("live long"). It is not merely a promise for you to have a longer life; it is assurance that your children will be blessed into future generations (Ex. 20:6).

> **Dear Lord, by Your Holy Spirit and the counsel of Your Word, please show me how to honor my parents and empower me to do so out of obedience to You and as an example to others.**

A Deacon Dealing With Anger
Exodus 20:13

"Do not murder."

The King James Version of this verse is "Thou shalt not kill." The word used for *kill* here and elsewhere in the Old Testament clearly means "murder." According to *Nelson's Bible Dictionary* it is "the unlawful killing of one person by another, especially with premeditated malice."[8] In our present legal system, we have penalties that differ for premeditated murder or accidental killing (involuntary manslaughter), etc. In the Bible, murder warranted the death penalty for the murderer (Num. 35:21). Accidental or involuntary manslaughter could be penalized by the offender's retreat to a City of Refuge (Num. 35:15), which we might refer to as incarceration.

> "Everyone who is angry with his brother shall be guilty before the court ..."

It is highly unlikely that, as a Deacon in the church, you have actually killed or murdered another person. But consider what Jesus said about this violation of God's law. "I say to you that everyone who is angry with his brother shall be guilty before the court . . ." (Matt. 5:22). This means that murder is rooted in anger and the person who is angry—filled with rage—is as guilty of *murder* in God's eyes as the one who actually killed another person. Murder begins in the heart—one's thoughts and meditations—and proceeds out of the heart (Matt. 15:19; Mk. 7:21). Of course, even murder can be forgiven (Matt. 12:31). But that does not give us the freedom to commit the sin of taking another person's life.

If anger is a problem in your life, it is imperative that you act aggressively and seriously to correct it. Your service for Christ and the church will be greatly hampered until you do.

> Dear Lord, please show me any anger or bitterness that may be in my life, and help me to repent of that. By Your Holy Spirit, please build into me Your own character.

WEEK 10   **DAY 3**

A DEACON DEALING WITH ADULTERY
Exodus 20:14

"Do not commit adultery."

Simply stated, *adultery* is a married person having sexual intercourse with another person other than their spouse. Fornication is a bit larger term, including sexual activity with someone to whom you are not married. For the servant of God in the church, this is a big and rather consistent temptation. It is not wrong to be tempted to commit adultery, but it is seriously wrong and sinful to give in to the temptation.

The Bible admonishes us to "abstain from fleshly desires that war against you" (1 Pet. 2:11). Abstain, of course, means "turn and run away" from fleshly desires. God, the Holy Spirit, empowers us to do this "because the Spirit's law of life in Christ Jesus has set you free from the law of sin and death" (Rom. 8:2). God will not allow you to be tempted "beyond what you are able" to resist with His power (1 Cor. 10:13).

> To commit adultery is to violate a covenant made between you and your spouse.

To commit adultery is to violate a covenant made between you and your spouse. A covenant made before God is not intended to be broken—ever. In most Christian marriage vows, we repeat the words, "and keep myself solely under her (or him) so long as we both shall live." This means we promise to remain morally faithful to our spouse. Every believer has this same responsibility, but the Deacons of the church are looked to for example in fidelity. Pastors and Deacons are to be "above reproach" in this area.

Fannie Davison, in the hymn "Purer in Heart, O God" captures the servant's prayer for moral purity:

> Purer in heart, O God, Help me to be;
> Until Thy holy face one day I see.
> Keep me from secret sin, reign Thou my soul within;
> Purer in heart, help me to be.[9]

**Dear Lord, please empower me by Your Spirit
to identify the temptations I face related to sinful lusts
and abstain from immorality in my life.**

WEEK 10 **DAY 4**

A Deacon and Stealing
Exodus 20:15

"Do not steal."

Most servants in the church do not intentionally and blatantly steal a material item from someone else. Seldom will you hear of a Pastor or a Deacon who is guilty of stealing a car or shoplifting. Nonetheless, the temptations to steal are real and subtle. For example, if a man takes a paycheck for work he did not do, is that stealing from his employer? Is cheating on your tax return whereby you receive more back from the government than you are actually owed called stealing? Can we steal other people's thoughts or knowledge by cheating on a test? There is a good likelihood that we have all been tempted to steal in these areas.

The writer of Proverbs 30:8-9 makes the appeal to God that every servant in the church should make:

> Give me neither poverty nor wealth; feed me with the food I need.
> Otherwise, I might have too much and deny You, saying,
> "Who is the Lord?" or I might have nothing and steal,
> Profaning the name of my God.

One of the keys in avoiding the temptation to steal is to "learn to be content in whatever circumstances I am; . . . know how to have a little, and . . . know how to have a lot . . . learn the secret of being content whether well-fed or hungry, whether in abundance or in need" (Phil. 4:11-12). Contentment is a blessed virtue for the servant of God. In whatever circumstances you find yourself, learn to be satisfied with what God has provided. It brings much more peace of mind than wanting more or wanting what someone else has.

> In whatever circumstances you find yourself, learn to be satisfied with what God has provided.

**Dear Lord, help me to see my life and circumstances as ordered and directed by You. Build into my spirit an attitude of contentment.
Be to me the all-sufficient God that You are.**

A Deacon and Lying

Exodus 20:16

"Do not give false testimony against your neighbor."

This falsehood is misrepresenting reality, breaking a trust, or being false in a personal relationship. *Richards Bible Dictionary* states that the Hebrew words for falsehood emphasize four aspects: (1) The false has no basis in reality. (2) The false is empty, unreal. (3) The false violates commitments. (4) The false is undependable.[10] We usually refer to this simply as "lying." Actually, it is a sin that includes deceit, misleading, lying, or promise-breaking.

Though we, as God's servants, may not intentionally lie, we certainly face many opportunities to mislead or misrepresent the truth. As a witness in a court of law, we are asked to "tell the truth the whole truth and nothing but the truth." As Deacons in the church, we are expected to both live the truth and tell the truth. Proverbs 19:9 states, "A false witness will not go unpunished and he who tells lies will perish." Ephesians 4:25 says, "Laying aside falsehood, speak truth each one of you with his neighbor, for we are members of one another.

The truth is vitally important to God—so much so that He referred to His Son as "the way, the truth, and the life" (Jn. 14:6). From God's perspective, it is better to tell the truth and face the consequences than to lie and face them. The next time you are tempted to lie or even "alter the truth" to cover up a deceit, pause and pray. Ask God to help you know the truth, live the truth, and always tell the truth.

> Though we, as God's servants, may not intentionally lie, we certainly face many opportunities to mislead or misrepresent the truth.

Dear Lord, please cause Your Holy Spirit who is in me to remind me when I am about to lie or mislead someone. Purify my thoughts, that I may know, live, and tell the truth.

A Deacon and Coveting
Exodus 20:17

"Do not covet . . ."

This command refers to a "desire for another person's possessions." *Richards Bible Dictionary* says, "We are not to look longingly on another's wealth or his wife."[11] In the text itself, the Word says, "Do not covet your neighbor's house, wife, slave [read: employee], ox or donkey [read: job, equipment, or means of livelihood] or anything that belongs to your neighbor." God has or will supply His servants with everything they need to live for Him and do His work.

Jesus warned us that we would never be able to serve two masters. He said, "You cannot be slaves of God and of money," (Matt. 6:24). Coveting usually takes place in us when we begin to change masters. We begin to give money and things—and especially the things others have that we don't—a greater place in our lives than God Himself.

> **God has or will supply His servants with everything they need to live for Him and do His work.**

Covetousness can quickly turn to greed and thus become idolatrous. The thing coveted becomes a god to us, determining the choices we make regarding it. This can contribute to risk-taking and gambling, both of which lead us astray from a genuine love and dependence upon God.

In its more serious form, coveting results in us not only wanting what others have but also wanting it so they can't have it. We think, *I deserve that more than he does!* Thus, we break the command of God, fall into sin, and render our so-called service to others null and void.

Let's take the words of the hymnist B.B. McKinney to heart:

> While passing through this world of sin
> and others your life shall view,
> Be clean and pure without within
> let others see Jesus in you.[12]

Dear Lord, please help me not to covet but to be clean and pure without and within for Your glory.

The Deacon's Common Ministry

A Deacon, a Saint?

Philippians 1:1

"To all the saints in Christ Jesus who are in Philippi, including the overseers and deacons."

This is the only Pauline Epistle that specifically identifies Deacons in the salutation. Deacons were obviously established as officers in the church by the time Paul wrote Philippians from a Roman prison cell around AD 61. And since he addresses this letter specifically to the Pastors and Deacons and refers to them as "saints in Christ Jesus," it only makes sense that we should evaluate what he said to them.

It would be a fair statement to say, "Whatever Paul says here to the Philippian church he is saying to the Deacons in that church." It would also be fair to say, "Whatever Paul said to the Philippian Deacons, he says to Deacons in the church today." Thus, we can embark upon a journey through Philippians that will give us keen insight into the intended character, service, and ministry functions of Deacons in the twenty-first-century church.

> A saint is merely a believer who has been set apart by the Lord in salvation for service.

At the outset, we see he is referred to as a saint. Not many churches refer to their members, much less their Deacons, as saints, mainly because of a misunderstanding of the term. A saint is merely a believer who has been set apart by the Lord in salvation for service. A servant in the church is one who has been set award from the world's system and wholly devoted to God's service. To be effective in serving the church, the Deacon must be consecrated or set apart unto God for that purpose. This was clearly the intent of the apostles in Acts 6:1-7. It should be the clear intent of the church today and is usually accompanied by ordination.

Dear Lord, as one who has been set apart for service in the church, I pray You would keep me spiritually strong and sensitive to the needs of others around me.

A Deacon By Grace
Philippians 1:2

"Grace to you . . . from God our Father and the Lord Jesus Christ."

Grace is God's "favor or kindness shown without regard to the worth or merit of the one who receives it and in spite of what that person deserves."[1] The servant of God has been saved by grace (Eph. 2:8-9), has been separated by grace (Rom. 5:20), and lives in the sufficiency of grace (2 Cor. 12:9).

It would be foolish for us to try to serve God apart from the unmerited favor of God supernaturally imputed to us by grace. Hymnist Julia H. Johnston penned the words to one of the greatest hymns ever written about God's grace. It reminds every servant of God that he has a reason and purpose for what he does:

> "Grace, grace, God's grace, grace that is greater than all our sin."

> Marvelous grace of our loving Lord,
> grace that exceeds our sin and our guilt,
>
> Yonder on Calvary's mount out-poured,
> there where the blood of the Lamb was spilt.
>
> Marvelous, infinite, matchless grace,
> freely bestowed on all who believe:
>
> All who are longing to see His face,
> will you this moment His grace receive?
>
> Grace, grace, God's grace, grace that will pardon and cleanse within;
>
> Grace, grace, God's grace, grace that is greater than all our sin.[2]

The grace of God was supremely revealed and given in the person and work of Jesus Christ. The one who would serve by grace will serve in the name and by the authority of Christ Himself. G. B. Duncan is right in saying, "A Christian never lacks what he needs when he possesses in Christ the unsearchable riches of God's grace."[3] As a servant of Christ and His church, you too have all you need by virtue of your possession of God's grace.

> **Dear Lord, remind me that I am saved by grace,
> set apart unto Your service by grace,
> and I have my complete sufficiency in You
> because of Your great grace.**

A Deacon and Relationships
Philippians 1:3

"I give thanks to my God for every remembrance of you . . ."

It is interesting to read into these words the apparent relationship that had been established between Paul and the Deacons at Philippi. In these opening verses he says, essentially, I think of you often (vv. 3-7); I long to see you again (v. 8); and I am praying for you (vv. 9-11). Have you ever received such a greeting from a friend or colleague in ministry? Building close relationships with other servants in the church is a vital part of God's purpose.

These relationships are especially important between a Pastor and the Deacons with whom he serves. Paul was more a missionary than a Pastor, yet he was the "founding Pastor" of several churches and likely an "interim Pastor" at Corinth (Acts 18:6) and Ephesus (Acts 20:31). With a Pastor's heart, Paul related to many servant-leaders in these churches.

What kind of relationship do you have with your Pastor and with fellow Deacons in your church? Do you pray regularly for them? This seems to be the kind of relationship God intends for His servants. Matthew Henry once wrote:

> **What kind of relationship do you have with your Pastor and with fellow Deacons in your church?**

We ought not to make any conditions of our brethren's acceptance with us but such as God has made the conditions of their acceptance with Him.[4]

Said another way, God accepts every one of His children for who they are and whom they may become in Christ. Our acceptance of our fellow servants should be based upon His acceptance and one's potential in Christ. Such relationships produce great fellowship, camaraderie, and service in the church.

Dear Lord, please show me how to relate to my fellow servants and others in the church. Help me to relate to them as You have graciously and lovingly related Yourself to me in Christ.

WEEK 11 **DAY 5**

A DEACON AND THE GOSPEL
Philippians 1:5

"Because of your partnership in the gospel from the first day until now."

The Deacons at Philippi were not only close friends to Paul; they were also fellow "ministers of the gospel." Every believer has a responsibility to participate in the church's primary task—taking the gospel of Christ to the ends of the earth (Matt. 28:18-20). The elected leaders assume a more exemplary role in fulfilling the Great Commission of the church. This assignment is given to us by Christ. Responsible leaders in the church will take it seriously and model it for the larger congregation.

There are numerous ways we can participate in the gospel. We can pray for the lost (Rom. 10:1), for missionaries and others who go to the lost (Acts 13:2-3), and for the resources needed to send the gospel. We can personally go and share the gospel with others (Acts 1:8). We can give money and other material resources to those who go.

> **Since 1925, Southern Baptists have utilized a method of mission support called cooperative program.**

Since 1925, Southern Baptists have utilized a method of mission support called cooperative program. This method calls upon churches to voluntarily designate a percentage of their offerings and channel those monies through convention agencies for appropriate distribution to the mission field. That is also participating in the gospel.

To what extent are you participating in your church's mission? Are you praying? Are you giving? Are you going? Are you sending others? All of these things seemed to be true of Paul and his fellow servants in Philippi. If William Gurnall was right, "The gospel is the chariot wherein which the Spirit rides victoriously when He makes His entrance into the hearts of men."[5] It is certainly something worthy of your participation.

Dear Lord, enable me to participate in as many ways as possible in taking the gospel of Christ to those who need to hear.

A Deacon Finishing Well

Philippians 1:6

"He who started a good work in you will carry it on to completion until the day of Christ Jesus."

It's true of both Pastors and Deacons, "How you start has everything to do with how you finish." Marathon runners know this principle. They know the secret to a good finish is starting at just the right pace and maintaining that pace for twenty-six miles. It should be no different for the servant of Christ in the church. If we have allowed God the freedom to begin His work in us—that is, if we have been saved by His grace, discipled by His Word, and filled with His Spirit—we may be assured that God will complete His plan and purpose for us. God is the one who gets us off the starting block, into the pace, and enables us to maintain the discipline necessary to finish well.

> "A faith that fails to finish was faulty from the first."

Paul wrote in his last letter to Pastor Timothy (and perhaps the Deacons at Ephesus), "I have fought the good fight, I have finished the race, I have kept the faith" (2 Tim. 4:7). He could only have said this at the end of his life because the one who had begun a good work in him was bringing it to completion. If Jesus could say (to God the Father) at the end of His life and ministry on earth, "I have glorified You on the earth by completing the work You gave Me to do" (Jn. 17:4), then should we not strive to complete our service?

It is true of all believers, certainly including deacons, that a faith that fails to finish was faulty from the first. Is your faith evidenced by faithful service that aims on finishing well? Are you allowing God's Holy Spirit, who began His great work in you, to complete it at His pace and in His place and with His purpose and for His pleasure? That is how you finish well!

Dear Lord, I desire to finish well. Please complete the work You have begun in me. Give me daily grace and order my steps to fulfill Your will even today.

A Deacon in Need of Prayer
Philippians 1:9-11

"And I pray this: that your love will keep on growing . . ."

One of the most valuable resources we have as servants in the church are the prayers of others. It is an unwise Deacon, indeed, who assumes he can do what is expected of him apart from the prayers of the church. In this text, the apostle Paul prays for this church and Deacons. His prayer includes a request of God that these men (and others) might grow in their love for God and one another (cf. Matt. 22:37-39), gain the knowledge and discernment they need to effectively serve (cf. 2 Tim. 3:17), determine what really matters and be pure and blameless in service (cf. Rom. 12:1-2), and be filled with God's Spirit (Eph. 5:18). They should exhibit the fruit of the Spirit or character (Gal. 5:22-23), the fruit of service or conduct (Phil. 1:11), and the fruit of souls or converts (Rom. 1:13).

> What a privilege to carry everything to God in prayer.

Would you not agree that you need others praying for you in this same way? You may know that Jesus is praying for you because "He always lives to intercede" for you (Heb. 7:25). He still is your greatest Friend in prayer. Joseph Scriven states it well in his great old hymn of the church:

> What a friend we have in Jesus, all our sins and griefs to bear!
> What a privilege to carry everything to God in prayer.
> Oh what peace we often forfeit, oh what needless pain we bear,
> All because we do not carry everything to God in prayer![6]

Perhaps you can identify with the chorus that says, "It's me! It's me! It's me, oh Lord, standing in the need of prayer." The servant of God must not only pray for others in need, but he must also depend on the prayers of others in his behalf.

Dear Lord Jesus, thank You for praying for me even today. Thank You for hearing and answering the prayers of others who are praying for me. Help me to forfeit no peace and bear no needless pain because of my prayerlessness.

WEEK 12 — DAY 3

A DEACON AWARE OF MINISTRY
Philippians 1:12-14

"Now I want you to know, brothers . . ."

In these verses, Paul makes a report to the Philippian church and to the Deacons regarding his present circumstances as a prisoner in Rome. It was important to him and valuable to them that such a report be brought. Several times during his missionary journeys Paul makes what could be seen as progress reports to the church (e.g., Acts 15:35, 18:22).

Deacons can play an important role in a church by staying personally informed and then informing the church about missions and missionaries. Some Southern Baptist churches have used a tool called "Missionary Moments." This includes several specific reports from missionaries regarding their work. Deacons can help communicate the reports to the church. We can also stay close to our local Pastor and other church leaders in our immediate community by receiving and sharing reports on their work.

> **Deacons can play an important role in a church by staying informed and informing the church about missions and missionaries.**

How informed are you about the work of your church or the missionaries with whom your church identifies? Do you know their names, locations, and kinds of ministry? Have you read or perhaps helped produce newsletters for missionaries? Are you as aware as you need to be of the work of your denomination? What do you know about your schools, hospitals, children's homes, retirement and nursing ministries, and other aspects of the ministry? These are all examples of how Deacons can be aware of and involved in a larger ministry.

Andrew Murray said, "Christian mission is the only reason for our being on earth."[7] Doesn't it just make sense that a Deacon in the church should be keenly aware of this mission purpose? Become aware! Become informed! Become involved! The church, and indeed the world, awaits your service.

Dear Lord, show me how to stay informed and how to best inform others of Your powerful work in and through Your church.

A Deacon Gaining Confidence
Philippians 1:14

"Most of the brothers in the Lord have gained confidence from my imprisonment."

It is amazing how much courage and sheer fortitude we can have simply by observing the commitment of others. Paul's imprisonment for Christ in Rome proved to be an occasion for gospel expansion. What others saw in Paul was a boldness that they needed. Deacons in the church can benefit greatly from observing and following other servants who are facing opposition for their faith. Paul says that because of his persecution most believers "dare even more to speak the message fearlessly" (v. 14b).

What effect does the persecution of others have on you? Does it make you regret that you are in such a state? Or do you want to compromise in some way for fear of experiencing your own persecution? Or does the persecution of others give you even greater faith and more boldness to fulfill your calling? It seems obvious from this passage that the Deacons in the church at Philippi were greatly encouraged to know that Paul was taking such a strong stand for the gospel. Apparently they believed they could do the same.

> What others saw in Paul was a boldness that they needed.

Peter and John experienced this confidence in Acts 4. After facing arrest and jail for the cause of Christ and finally being released, they prayed, were filled with the Holy Spirit, and began (actually, continued) to speak the Word of God with boldness. Matthew Henry said, "Christ's followers cannot expect better treatment in the world than their Master had."[8] And of course, he was right. Yet opposition and persecution can do one of two things to the servant of God. Either he will cower down, compromise, and retreat or he will stand up, boldly fulfill his duty, and face the consequences with the grace of God. What will it be for you today and in the future?

Dear Lord, please empower me by Your Spirit to withstand whatever persecution might come my way. Help me to be emboldened by the persecution I see others withstand.

A Deacon Getting the Gospel Out
Philippians 1:18

"Just that in every way . . . Christ is proclaimed . . ."

Paul announced to the Deacons at Philippi that they could be confident his imprisonment was for the greater expanse of the gospel. Every servant of Christ does well to learn this truth. Whatever it takes from us or from other servants in the church, Christ must be proclaimed. Even when some criticize and oppose the gospel, God has a way of using their negative motives to advance the message. In that we, too, may rejoice (v.18c).

> **What price are you willing to pay personally for the gospel to be taken to the nations?**

Every servant of God in every church has the supernatural power of God in him to face whatever he may in furthering the proclamation of the gospel. This was the reason Paul, to another church (perhaps to another group of Deacons) said, "I am not ashamed of the gospel, because it is God's power for salvation to everyone who believes . . ." (Rom. 1:16). Whether out of good times or bad and whether or not the message is accepted, we have the responsibility to get the gospel out.

How well are you doing at getting the gospel out? To what extent are you willing to take persecution and suffering for this great cause? Are there those in your sphere of influence who await your witness? These and similar questions are for every Deacon in the church to ask of himself.

It seems we have more who are willing to live for Christ than to die for Christ. After all, it is much easier to give lip service to the Great Commission than it is to be beaten for it. What price are you willing to pay personally for the gospel to be taken to the nations? We may not be able to bring the whole world to Christ, but we must do whatever it takes to bring Christ to the whole world. Be sure you are doing what you must do so that in every way Christ is proclaimed.

Dear Lord, please use me, whether by life or by death or both, to do what I must to get the gospel to the ends of the earth.

A Deacon by Life or by Death
Philippians 1:21

"For me, living is Christ and dying is gain."

Have you come to a place in your personal spiritual maturity that you find it hard to stay in this world, not because you are so depressed with your circumstances but because you have become so "homesick for heaven?" J. Sidlow Baxter, a great and wise preacher-theologian of the twentieth century often implied in his preaching that he had learned and lived with the Savior in such a way that he felt more like he was in Heaven than on Earth. The apostle Paul conveys a similar feeling in this passage.

> If I live on in the flesh, this means fruitful work for me; and I don't know which one I should choose. I am pressured by both. I have the desire to depart and be with Christ—which is far better—but to remain in the flesh is more necessary for you (1:22-24).

The central principle in this passage and a lesson every Deacon should learn is also wrapped up in Romans 14:7-8:

> For not one of us lives for himself, and not one of us dies for himself; for if we live, we live for the Lord, or if we die, we die for the Lord; therefore whether we live or die, we are the Lord's.

> "I'll consecrate my life to Thee, my Savior and my God."

Paul is encouraging the Deacons in Philippi and subsequently all the Deacons in the church today to live for Christ as long as you live and die for Christ whenever you are called upon to do so. After all, "whether we live or die we are the Lord's.

The last line of a great hymn by Ralph Hudson says, "O thou who died on Calvary to save my soul and make me free, I'll consecrate my life to Thee, my Savior and my God."[9] This is the kind of commitment that Deacons in the church are called upon to make. We must be committed to serve faithfully whether by life or by death or both.

Dear Lord, You have demonstrated to me what it is like to live and die for the sake of others. Please enable me to live for You in service to others, knowing that to die would be far better.

WEEK 13 **DAY 2**

A DEACON WITH A REPUTATION
Philippians 1:27

"I will hear about you that you are standing firm . . ."

Paul had high expectations for the Deacons at Philippi. In this verse he says, "Live your life in a manner worthy of the gospel of Christ." Their lives should reflect their Savior so that others would know who they were and for what they stood. Whether observed up close or from a long distance, their reputation would remain strong and true to the faith.

> "Be clean and pure, without within, let others see Jesus in you."

Paul identifies three characteristics of these servants' lives that he anticipated being reported to him: that they were standing firm in one spirit, thinking in like-mindedness and working side-by-side to present the gospel to others. Imagine a Pastor or missionary hearing such a report about you. One spirit means you have a positive attitude about Christ, His church, and your service that is compatible with others. Like-mindedness means you are very likely to think the same things, in the same way, about the same ministry decisions. Working side-by-side means you are not a "Lone Ranger" servant. You need others, and others need you.

B. B. McKinney, the well-known Baptist hymn writer, put this matter of reputation into perspective for every servant of God in the church:

> While passing through this world of sin
> > and others your life shall view,
> Be clean and pure without, within, let others see Jesus in you.
> Your life's a book before their eyes,
> > they're reading it through and through;
> Say, does it point them to the skies, do others see Jesus in you?
> Then live for Christ both day and night,
> > be faithful, be brave, and true,
> And lead the lost to life and light; let others see Jesus in you[10].

Dear Lord, I pray that You will so control my life that those who hear about me or the ministry in which I am involved will see Jesus in all His glory.

A Deacon Who Suffers
Philippians 1:29-30

"It has been given to you on Christ's behalf . . . to suffer for Him . . ."

When you were set aside and elected as a Deacon in your church, you probably were not asked, "Are you willing to experience serious suffering for your service?" And now, having tasted some suffering and realizing there will likely be more coming, you're not sure this is what you "signed up for." Of course, when you think and pray about it, you remember you didn't sign up for it. Rather, God chose you and directed the church to acknowledge His choice. And because God has placed you in service, you will suffer on one level or another for most of your life (cf. Matt. 5:10-12).

> **You may be assured that you will not suffer alone.**

You may be assured that you will not suffer alone. The Bible assures us, "If one member suffers, all the members suffer with it . . ." (1 Cor. 12:26). That may bring you little consolation. But remember, "The sufferings of this present time are not worth comparing with the glory that is going to be revealed to us" (Rom. 8:18). Night lasts for a little while, but joy comes in the morning. There is definitely a brighter day coming.

So, as a servant of God in the church, it is inevitable that you will experience suffering in your life. C. S. Lewis said it well:

> God whispers to us in health and prosperity, but being hard of hearing, we fail to hear God's voice in both. Whereupon God turns up the amplifier by means of suffering. Then his voice booms.[11]

Since this suffering "has been given to you on Christ's behalf," you may assume it with confident obedience. "For you were called to this because Christ also suffered for you, leaving you an example, so that you should follow in His steps" (1 Peter 2:21). Your life will be richer, your love will be purer, your compassion will be sweeter, your service will be more effective, and your reward will be greater because you "also suffer for Him.

Dear Lord, I thank You that I'll never suffer for Your service as You have suffered for my salvation. Grant to me Your great grace in whatever shall come.

A Deacon Bringing Joy to His Pastor

Philippians 2:1-2

"Fulfill my joy by thinking the same way, having the same love, sharing the same feelings, focusing on one goal."

"Pastor Paul" makes a beautiful appeal to the Deacons at Philippi. His desire is to experience joy in his heart as a result of the harmony and camaraderie seen in the church. As with Paul, so it is in the lives of many Pastors today. Their joy is made full when their Deacons are meeting the expectations identified in these verses. They think the same way. This literally means "to mind or think the same thing." A meeting of the minds would bring their petty squabbles to a logical, sensible, rational end. They share the same love. This means we relate to each other and to the world with a "God-like love"—love that is sacrificial in nature and puts the interests of the one loved ahead of the one expressing the love. They have the same feelings, spirit, or attitude. Servants in the church can bring great joy to their Pastor by maintaining and exhibiting a good attitude about the ministry. They focus on one goal or purpose. That purpose, of course, is fulfilling the Great Commission.

> **Are you bringing joy to your Pastor, or are you bringing him grief?**

The Deacons and others in the church are admonished by Scripture to "obey your leaders and submit to them, for they keep watch over your souls as those who will give an account. Let them do this with joy and not with grief, for this would be unprofitable for you" (Heb. 13:17).

Are you bringing joy to your Pastor, or are you bringing him grief? Are you seriously seeking to meet the expectations cited above? What might you need to do to show your Pastor that you love and support him? Are you willing to do that this week . . . today?

Dear Lord, please guide my attitude and actions as I seek to bring glory to You and joy to my Pastor.

A Deacon Exhibiting Humility
Philippians 2:3

"In humility consider others as more important than yourselves."

J. I. Packer, a well-known theologian at the turn of the twenty-first century, made a profound statement regarding the necessity of humility:

> Not until we have become humble and teachable, standing in awe of God's holiness and sovereignty . . . acknowledging our own littleness, distrusting our own thoughts, and willing to have our minds turned upside down, can divine wisdom become ours.[12]

When the apostle gives this directive to the Philippian Deacons, he does so with an experiential understanding of humility. Paul had spent several years of his adult life giving himself away to others. He humbled himself under the mighty hand of God (cf. Phil. 3:4-10) and saw his life and ministry exalted in due time (2 Tim. 4:7-8).

Many people have believed the lie that humility and meekness are inferiority and weakness. And there are some servants of God in the church who talk humility but live in arrogance. Genuine *humility* is "a freedom from arrogance that grows out of the recognition that all we have and are comes from God" (*Nelson's Bible Dictionary*).[13] There is absolutely no self-sufficiency for the humble servant of God.

How is humility being exhibited in your life and ministry? By the way, if it is not exhibited in your life, then you can forget about it showing up in your ministry, and you can certainly forget any future reward from God. "God resists the proud, but gives grace to the humble" (1 Pet. 5:5) and "humility comes before honor" (Prov. 15:33). Would you be willing to personally acknowledge any pride, arrogance, or self-sufficiency to God and ask Him to forgive you of that grave sin? Would you ask Him to develop His own humility in your life from this day forward?

> **How is humility being exhibited in your life and ministry?**

Dear Lord, I may be too prideful in my heart to even know what humility looks like to You. Please do a supernatural work in me and develop a spirit of humility in my life. I admit that only You can and that I need it badly.

WEEK 14   **DAY 1**

A DEACON LOOKING OUT FOR OTHERS
Philippians 2:4

"Everyone should look out not only for his own interest, but also for the interests of others."

Have you ever observed the circumstances of your Christian friends and thought, *I really care about that, but it's really none of my business.* Or maybe you've even been told by a fellow believer, "It's none of your business!" Most of the time we assume that the interests of others are none of our concern. Thus, to our neglect and theirs, we spend most of our time thinking about ourselves and ignoring the needs of Christian friends around us.

As a Deacon in the church, you have a unique opportunity to focus on the needs of others. This passage gives us Paul's challenge to the Deacons at the church in Philippi. John Phillips says, "To seek one's own advancement is worldly. To seek the prosperity, good and promotion of others is divine."[14] When the servant-leaders of the church serve the interests and needs of others, they are exhibiting the true nature of Christ (Mk. 10:45). During His earthly ministry, and more especially on the cross, He seemed to always have the interest of others on His heart (Lk. 23:34).

> When we fail to bear the burdens of others and ignore their needs, we are living a very narrow and selfish life.

When we fail to bear the burdens of others and ignore their needs, we are living a very narrow and selfish life. You'll live longer and you'll live stronger by putting others ahead of yourself. It gives you much more for which to live. Looking out for the interest of others and then applying yourself to intervene with prayer and deeds of service will give you great motivation to live. You will almost never be depressed since depression derives its meaning from self-interests and self-focus. Get outside yourself every day and in every possible way. You, your family, and yes, the church, will be the better for it.

Dear Lord, remind me at this time in my life how to put the interests and needs of my family, my church, my employer, and others ahead of my own.

A Deacon and Attitude Adjustments
Philippians 2:5-8

"Make your own attitude that of Jesus Christ . . ."

Philippians 2:5-11 is referred to as the *KENOSIS* passage of the New Testament. *KENOSIS* is the Greek word used in verse 7 for *emptied* when it says, "*He emptied Himself.*" *Ryrie Study Bible* notes on this word says:

> The kenosis (emptying) of Christ during His incarnation does not mean that He surrendered any attributes of deity, but that He took on the limitations of humanity. This involved a veiling of His pre-incarnate glory and the voluntary non-use of some of His divine prerogatives during the time He was on earth.[15]

> **As believers, we are to empty ourselves of ourselves.**

In following Christ's example, the believer is to develop such an attitude. The word *empty* literally means, "To set aside or make no use of."[16] As applied to believers, it suggests that we are to empty ourselves of ourselves—to make no use of the world, the flesh, or the devil in our intent to live for Christ. This, of course, requires great humility, the likes of which only God's Holy Spirit can produce. However, most of us, even as Deacons, often "think more highly of ourselves than we ought to think" (Rom. 12:3). John Calvin has stated it well, "God will never come to His right unless we are totally reduced to nothing, so that it may be clearly seen that all that is laudable in us comes from elsewhere."[17]

This is the attitude of Christ. This is our objective in the Christian life and especially as a Deacon in the church. Have this attitude in yourself that was also in Christ Jesus.

Dear Lord, help me to consider myself to be dead and Your Spirit to be alive in me that I might take on the attitude of Your dear Son from this day forward.

A Deacon and Exaltation
Philippians 2:9-11

"For this reason God also highly exalted Him . . ."

Most servants of God in the church, including Pastors and Deacons, enjoy a certain amount of respect. At times, members tend to put these leaders on a pedestal and elevate or exalt them before others. Though this is usually well-intended, it can result in the leader beginning to exalt himself.

The passage at hand is a clear explanation and illustration of what it means to humble rather than to exalt yourself. Jesus was certainly exalted by the Father. However, His exaltation did not precede His humiliation. Most servants today like the idea of being exalted but shun any notion of humility as a prerequisite. St. Augustine speaks in metaphorical terms of this necessary humiliation, "The proud hilltops let the rain run off; the lowly valleys are richly watered."[18]

Rather than taking the compliments of others too seriously and thus exalting ourselves, perhaps we should "humble ourselves under the mighty hand of God, that He may exalt us at the proper time" (1 Pet. 5:6). This is sometimes referred to as "deferring the praise." When someone compliments you, it is okay to say, "Thank you." However, if the compliments tempt you to exalt yourself, then defer the compliment. Give the Scriptures, the Holy Spirit, or another believer the credit for your success. Let it be clear that any effectiveness or success on your part has come only because of the investment of others in your life. In so doing, God will ultimately exalt you and reward you. And the church will be pointed past you to the Savior.

> **Give the Scriptures, the Holy Spirit, or another believer the credit for your success.**

Dear Lord, I pray that You would exalt Yourself in my life and that You will receive all the glory and credit for whatever "successes" may be attributed to me.

A Deacon Working Out His Salvation
Philippians 2:12

"Work out your own salvation with fear and trembling."

At just a mere glance, this text seems to hint at the idea that the Christian must work for his salvation for fear that he might somehow lose it. This, emphatically, is not the meaning. John Phillips captures well the intention of Paul's expression:

> We could liken the gift of salvation to the gift of a gold mine. If someone were to give you a gold mine of incalculable worth, you would have a treasure, but the gold would not do you any practical good unless you worked it out of the mine. Likewise, we need to get busy and set to work on our salvation.[19]

As genuine followers of Christ, and particularly as Deacons in the church, we carry the responsibility of working out (not working for) our salvation. Once we have been truly saved by grace alone through faith alone in Christ alone, we then have God's indwelling Spirit who seals our salvation for all eternity. We can "desire the unadulterated spiritual milk [of the Word], so that we may grow by it in our salvation" (1 Pet. 2:2).

> "God didn't save us to sit; He saved us to serve."

Though we are not saved by works, we are saved to work (Eph. 2:8-10). And James makes this very clear, "In the same way faith, if it doesn't have works, is dead by itself" (Jas. 2:17). God did not save us to sit, He saved us to serve. If our salvation doesn't result in service, then we may need to question whether we have actually been saved. Working out our salvation will inevitably result in some "fear and trembling" on our part, not because we might lose our salvation but because our relationship with Christ and our service will place us in situations of potential fear and uncertainty.

But work (serve) we must. Until Jesus comes for us or we go to Him, we are obligated to "work out our salvation." Serve today with your focus on others, even if that places you in a vulnerable position.

Dear Lord, empower me to work for You and serve You out of a heart of gratitude for Your great salvation.

A Deacon Serving to Please God

Philippians 2:13

"For it is God who is working in you, enabling you both to will and to act for His good pleasure."

God does not expect us to "work out" our salvation irrespective of His Holy Spirit "working" in and through us. We have a responsibility to be obedient. God assumes the responsibility to empower us. The work that God has begun in us, He will complete (Phil. 1:7). In this verse, two things become very obvious. One has to do with the source of our strength and the other has to do with the motivation for our work. God empowers us to serve Him and receives pleasure for Himself when we do.

> **God is pleased with your obedience to Him.**

Jesus said, "I do nothing on My own initiative, but I speak these things as the Father taught Me. And He who sent Me is with Me; He has not left Me alone, for I always do the things that are pleasing to Him" (Jn. 8:28-29). Jesus's motivation for doing the work that He did was to please his beloved Father. At the conclusion of His ministry on earth, He said to the Father, "I have glorified You on the earth by completing the work You gave Me to do" (Jn. 17:4).

We too are enabled by the Holy Spirit to work and act for His good pleasure. Your motivation to serve as a Deacon in the church should be, above all else, to please your heavenly Father. God is pleased with your obedience to Him. When you are led by God to serve the needs of another believer or anyone else and you willfully obey, then God is pleased. The apostle Paul offered a very special prayer for the church at Colossae in 1:9-10. He prayed, "That you may walk worthy of the Lord, fully pleasing to Him, bearing fruit in every good work and growing in the knowledge of God.

Would you determine from this day forward to bring pleasure to God through your service? Will you do the works of Him who sent you? Better, would you let Him work in you, enabling you to do His will?

Dear Lord, thank You for working in my life and enabling me to want to serve You. I pray that You will be pleased with my service and that I can finish the work You have given me to do.

A Deacon Who Shines

Philippians 2:15

"Be blameless and pure, children of God who are faultless in a crooked and perverted generation, among whom you shine like stars in the world."

There is little debate among Christian leaders in the church today that we are experiencing some of the darkest days of moral decline in American history. The Bible often refers to evil or sin as darkness and good or righteousness as light. It is said of Jesus, "In Him was life, and the life was the Light of men" (Jn. 1:4). "Light has come into the world, and men loved the darkness rather than the Light, for their deeds were evil" (Jn. 3:19).

Knowing that one's character is clearly discernable by others, Paul encourages the Deacons at Philippi to be blameless, pure, and faultless in the midst of a generation of unbelievers. Godly character in the lives of God's servants is like a bright light being turned on in a dark room. Church leaders should set an example for all believers on how to "let your light shine before men that they may see your good works and glorify your Father who is in heaven (Matt. 5:16).

> How effective are you at letting your light shine?

How effective are you at letting your light shine? Do your behavior and character unmistakably reflect the light of Christ? Stars, like the moon, have no light in themselves; they only reflect the light of the sun. Believers, and especially leaders in the church, have no light in and of themselves but are intended to reflect the light of the Son. When this is consistently true on a large scale in the church, then the words of H. Ernest Nichol become a reality:

> For the darkness shall turn to the dawning
> and the dawning to noonday bright.
> And Christ's great kingdom shall come on earth,
> The kingdom of love and light.[20]

Dear Lord, I pray You will so control my mind and govern my character that I might shine like a star in the world, giving light to the darkness around me.

WEEK 15 — DAY 2

A Deacon as a Living Sacrifice
Philippians 2:17

"I am poured out as a drink offering on the sacrifice and service of your faith . . ."

Clearly, the Deacons in the Philippian church were viewed, at least by Paul, as those who have presented themselves to God as living sacrifices (cf. Rom. 12:1-2). Every believer is expected to live sacrificially before God, but Deacons in the church are especially intended to set an example in this area. Service itself indicates some level of sacrifice. Toward the end of this epistle, Paul considers the monetary offerings of the church to be a "welcome sacrifice, pleasing to God" (4:18). In Romans, he refers to the believer presenting his body as a "living sacrifice, holy and pleasing to God" (12:1).

> What are you genuinely willing to sacrifice for the sake of the gospel?

Today we assume we are sacrificing if we have only two meals in a given day or if we have only one pair of shoes for each day of the week; or if we attend church services twice on a Sunday. We consider it a sacrifice to make a financial contribution to the church and can hardly imagine giving a tithe. God's idea of sacrifice is altogether different than ours since "He did not even spare His own Son, but offered Him up for us all . . ." (Rom. 8:32).

What are you genuinely willing to sacrifice for the sake of the gospel—your money? Your time? Your influence? Your family? Your life? God may or may not call upon you to sacrifice your life in physical death. But He calls upon all of us to be "living sacrifices" for Him. Would you agree with the words and make an intentional commitment with hymn writer Ralph Hudson? Make this your prayer of commitment . . . today!

> I'll live for Him who died for me,
>   how happy then my life shall be!
> I'll live for Him who died for me,
>   my Savior and my God![21]

Dear Lord, make of me a servant who will be faithful and true. Help me know what it means and be willing to sacrifice for the sake of the gospel.

A Deacon Given a Good Report
Philippians 2:19

"So that I may be encouraged when I hear news about you."

In this context, the apostle Paul intended to send Timothy, his young son in the ministry, to check in on the Deacons at Philippi that he might be encouraged when he heard news about them. Whenever a Pastor is away from his church and especially when he is away from his Deacons for a long period of time, he is anxious to hear a positive report about their service. Unfortunately, some Deacons in some churches don't have the best reputation, and their Pastor fears he might not be given a good report.

> We should live our lives and render service in such a way that others would know our Savior and see Him in us.

Just as Paul expected to be encouraged by the report from Timothy, would it not be commendable for the church to give a good report of you and your service? It really does matter not only what God thinks of your faithfulness but also what others think. After all, you are a model of ministry for the rest of the congregation.

Of course, a report that might bring real encouragement to a Pastor would be a report that Jesus is being proclaimed. But it is not the fellow servants in the church that should be expected to bring ultimate joy to the Pastor. You may have heard it said:

> If you wish to be disappointed look at others;
> If you wish to be disheartened, look at yourself;
> If you wish to be encouraged, look to Jesus.[22]

Yet we should live our lives and render service in such a way that others would know our Savior and see Him in us. If you have the opportunity, the next time your Pastor is away, serve the church with great intent and purpose so when he returns he will *"be encouraged when he hears news about you.*

> **Dear Lord, please help me to serve You, to serve Your church, and to serve Your undershepherd while I have the opportunity to do so.**

A Deacon of Kindred Spirit

Philippians 2:20-21

"For I have no one else like-minded who will
genuinely care about your interests."

Like Paul, most Pastors cherish the kindred-spirit relationship they have with other men. The word translated like-minded or kindred spirit is a word that literally means equal-souled. This is a relationship that connected Paul and Timothy to the point that he views Timothy as a son in the ministry. Of Timothy, John Phillips writes:

> Timothy was spiritually gifted and he was available. His natural way of caring for people enabled him to triumph in service, true service. A true servant is ready, able, and willing.[23]

Paul's desire for the Deacons and other believers at Philippi was that they "think the same way." The servant of God who has a kindred spirit with his Pastor and other spiritual leaders is very valuable to the church and to the kingdom. This does not mean that a man should have no ideas of his own, but it does mean that his ideas are in line with Scripture and honoring to Christ and His church. When two men are serving together and both are thinking the same things that God thinks about the same kinds of things then they share a kindred spirit.

> A true servant is ready, able, and willing.

Can you identify another man in your life—maybe your Pastor or another Deacon or someone else—with whom you have a kindred spirit? That kind of relationship is never forced. It just seems to be put together by God. Whether it's David and Jonathan in the Old Testament, Paul and Timothy in the New Testament, or you and your Pastor today, a kindred spirit is a great gift from God. Proverbs 27:17 says, "Iron sharpens iron, and one man sharpens another." Determine in your heart to discover and develop a kindred spirit with other servants in the church.

Dear Lord, show me the men with whom I should serve, and by Your Spirit, produce in me a kindred spirit with them. Let me develop those relationships for the greater benefit of the church and for Your glory.

A Deacon as a Fellow Worker
Philippians 2:25-26

"My brother, co-worker, and fellow soldier, as well as your messenger and minister to my need . . ."

What the apostle said of Epaphroditus in this passage could be said by many Pastors in regard to the Deacons in his church. This beloved servant was commended by Paul for several reasons. He saw him as a brother in Christ, as a colleague in ministry, and as a fellow soldier in the Lord's army. These are descriptions that should characterize every Deacon in the church today.

Of this man, Epaphroditus, John Phillip says:

> He was not only a brother in the family; he was also a fellow worker in the field. He was not afraid to roll up his sleeves and do a good day's work in the service of the Lord. Moreover he was a fellow soldier in the fight. He was not afraid to take on the enemy.[24]

God has called you to be a servant like Epaphroditus. You are where you are, with your fellow-workers, doing what you are doing because God has directed you. It is no accident that God has placed you where He has. You serve with others of like mind and strong, godly convictions. You will deliberately align yourself with and support your Pastor and staff. It will also be said of you by other Deacons in the church, "He is a messenger and minister to my need." For this, God has saved you. For this God has called you. For this God has placed you where you are.

> **You should never take your assignment lightly, and you should never retreat in the face of worldly, fleshly, or satanic opposition.**

You should never take your assignment lightly, and you should never retreat in the face of worldly, fleshly, or satanic opposition. For such whole-hearted commitment, you, like Epaphroditus, will be "held in high regard" (v. 29).

Dear Lord, I pray that You will supernaturally empower me to serve You and Your church with the passion and sincerity of Epaphroditus.

A Deacon on Guard

Philippians 3:2

"Watch out for 'dogs,' watch out for evil workers,
watch out for those who mutilate the flesh."

In this warning, Paul is challenging the Deacons and other servants at Philippi to keep their spiritual and theological guard up. The term "dogs" is used to refer to the Judaizers who taught that circumcision was necessary for salvation. It was a term that they themselves used for unbelieving Gentiles. "Evil workers" and "mutilators" referred to false circumcision—the practice of forcing unbelievers to mutilate the males who had never been circumcised, regardless of any real conversion to Christ.

There will always be a few false believers who will attempt to bring a false gospel or other false doctrine into the church. One of the practical functions of the New Testament Deacon was to watch for such persons, report their beliefs—and in some cases their teachings—to the apostles. Today, the Pastor has as one of his primary roles to "keep watch over the flock" (Acts 20:28). But the Deacons who stand with him in ministry can be of much help in keeping the church doctrinally pure.

> The Deacon who stands with the Pastor in ministry can be of much help in keeping the church doctrinally pure.

This is why you must be grounded in God's Word, infilled with God's Spirit, and embedded in the church. The genuine salvation of the lost, and certainly the spiritual maturity of the saved, will depend a great deal on your faithfulness. "Watch and pray" was Christ's charge to the disciples in the garden (Matt. 26:41) and should be seen as His charge to you as a Deacon in the church. Watch, pray, and keep your spiritual guard up! As you do, the Pastor will be more effective, the church will be more pure, and you will be blessed beyond measure.

Dear Lord, help me to keep my spiritual guard up. Help me to know Your truth so I can quickly recognize a lie. Empower me to stand for right, and encourage others to do the same.

A Deacon Serving Above the Flesh
Philippians 3:3

"For we are . . . the ones who serve by the Spirit of
God . . . and do not put confidence in the flesh."

The word *flesh* in this verse and in many of Paul's epistles refers to the lower, weaker, sinful element in human nature. In the believer it refers to the lower and temporary element that has become dormant in light of the new nature given us by the Holy Spirit. The flesh is intended to be considered or reckoned dead or inconsequential to the believer's life and service.

Deacons in the church will only be effective as they live and serve in the power of God's Holy Spirit. Clearly, "the flesh profits nothing" (Jn. 6:63). When you prepare to teach a Bible lesson, witness to an unsaved child, or deliver a covered dish of food to a needy family, would you rather have the mind of Christ and the wisdom of God or depend solely upon your natural instincts and human understanding? Obviously, you need God's Spirit to guide you. Put all your confidence in Him and none in yourself. Thus, you will provide service in which people will be blessed and God will be pleased.

> Deacons in the church will only be effective as they live and serve in the power of God's Holy Spirit.

If you find yourself being complimented for the deeds of service you are doing, that is quite all right. However, if you begin to expect those compliments or some other accolade and are disappointed when you don't receive them, then you may be serving in the flesh. Your service will bring deep satisfaction to your heart, but more important than anything, it will bring great glory to God.

Dear Lord, please help me in this day to serve others under the power and direction of Your Spirit. Guard me from putting confidence in my own abilities and understanding while disregarding Your Spirit's enablement.

A Deacon Serving Beyond Credentials

Philippians 3:4-7

*"If anyone thinks he has grounds for confidence
in the flesh, I have more . . ."*

In human terms alone, the apostle had every reason to flaunt his experience and credentials, proving to the Pastors and Deacons at Philippi that he could do this on his own. Of course, that is exactly the opposite of what Paul says. He discovered what we must all learn. Our ministry and acts of service are not dependent upon our credentials or even our past successes.

The apostle Paul cites his rite of circumcision, race as a Jew, religion as a Pharisee, record of religious activity, and reputation of blamelessness as potential reasons to depend upon himself. Yet, in a spirit of humility, he says, "Everything that was a gain to me, I have considered to be a loss because of Christ" (v. 7). Likewise, we, as servants in the church, must consider all of our self-motivated accomplishments as nothing compared to the Spirit-directed accomplishments of God. Religious reputation is but rubbish compared to a real relationship with the resurrected Redeemer. It is, in fact, "God who is working in you, enabling you both to will and to act for His good pleasure" (Phil. 2:13).

> Religious reputation is but rubbish compared to a real relationship with the resurrected Redeemer.

As a Deacon in the church, you have been given God's great grace to do what you do. You need never suggest to others and certainly not to God that any of it is of your own production. We must acknowledge and agree with Paul's statement made to the Corinthian church, "By God's grace I am what I am, and His grace toward me was not ineffective" (1 Cor. 15:10).

*Dear Lord, remind me today and each day hereafter
that I can never effectively serve You or Your
people while depending on my own credentials.
Empower me by Your spirit to minister to others.*

A Deacon Who Really Knows Christ
Philippians 3:10-11

"That I may know Him . . ."

There are two primary words in the New Testament translated *know*. One of those words is the word used here by Paul and carries with it the idea of "knowing experientially or coming to know, recognize or understand completely."[25] The apostle Paul had met Jesus and experienced the miraculous work of His Spirit. Yet, he still felt a need to know Him more thoroughly. He wanted a deeper, more complete knowledge of His person (v. 10a), His power (v. 10b), His pain (v. 10c), and His plan (v. 10d). Paul wanted to know Him in all of His fullness. For Paul, nothing on earth and no one on earth could come close in comparison to knowing Christ (3:8).

It is one thing to know of Christ or even know about Christ. It is quite another thing to know Him personally. One of the main goals for all believers and especially those who serve as Pastors or Deacons is to know Christ more personally and follow Him more perfectly. This was Paul's goal. It should be ours as well. John Phillips correctly says, "No one can live a holy life without utter dedication to the life-purpose of knowing Christ."[26] To know Him personally will mean we will love Him more dearly. The more we love Him, the more likely we are to serve Him faithfully.

> To know him personally will mean we will love Him more dearly.

How is it, practically, that a man comes to know Christ in this way? There are several ingredients. We must be certain that we have been born again from above (John 3:3); be faithful in praying and in Bible study (2 Tim. 2:15); be focused daily on the application of God's Word. (Jas. 1:22); be open to good, godly, biblical teaching as well as godly counsel from others (Jn. 13:15); and be observant of Christlikeness in the lives of other believers (Acts 4:13). It never hurts to associate with others who know Christ, but you'll only know Him personally when you spend time with Him.

> Dear Lord, I want to know You more personally, follow You more faithfully, and serve You more diligently. Please empower me to do so from this day forward.

WEEK 16   **DAY 5**

A Deacon Who Never Arrives
Philippians 3:12

"Not that I have already reached the goal, or am already mature, but I make every effort to take hold of it . . ."

John Phillips says of Paul's statement:

> If Paul had to make a statement like that, wherever do we stand? He did not feel he had arrived nor did he dare rest on his laurels. He was assessing his situation realistically in light of cold facts: the work of world evangelism was barely begun.[27]

Paul's testimony in chapter 3 of this epistle is clearly an admonition to the Pastors and Deacons in the Philippian church. In stating his own desires and position and condition, he is teaching these other servants to never see themselves as having arrived. They had not arrived in their personal spiritual growth, nor had they arrived in their ministry. For them, and for us, there was always room for improvement and always more ministry to undertake.

> **We are in a lifelong process of becoming more and more like our Savior.**

It is for this objective—pressing forward in ministry and missions—that Christ Himself has saved us and placed us in service. It is for this that we have been taken hold of by Christ Jesus. We must always remember that as long as we are in this flesh, living here on this earth, we will never reach absolute perfection. However, we must also see ourselves as in constant process. We are in a lifelong process of becoming more and more like our Savior. As believers, we are "predestined to be conformed to the image of His Son . . ." (Rom. 8:29).

Realizing that we will never reach the goal of full maturity in this life does not give us freedom to relax or resign our duties. We must press on toward the goal of full spiritual maturity. All of this requires discipline in each of us. It is for Deacons in the church to set the example and set the pace in this discipline.

> **Dear Lord, please show me where I am in my spiritual development and ministry and where You want me to go from here.**

A Deacon With a Vision
Philippians 3:13-15

"Forgetting what is behind and reaching forward to what is ahead, I pursue as my goal the prize promised by God's heavenly call in Christ Jesus."

D. L. Moody, a man of great vision and influence, used to say, "It is better to say, 'This one thing I do,' than to say, 'These forty things I dabble with.'"[28] The apostle Paul, at this stage in his ministry, having evangelized nearly half of the known world, decided there was only one thing to do: begin again as though nothing at all had already been accomplished. He purposed to put the past in the past with all its successes and failures. He envisioned an extraordinary opportunity for future ministry.

Many Deacons in the church today seem to focus more on past successes and present ministry than on what God may be directing for the future. Vision is not a really common word in Scripture. The word itself is not used in this passage. It is often connected with dreams. Prior to a closed canon of Scripture, God often revealed Himself to His servants in "visions and dreams" (cf. Acts 18:9). Nevertheless, the Lord had made it clear to Paul that he should "pursue" the future for which he had been prepared.

> You must not succumb to the temptation of basking in the past.

You may have experienced wonderful things, even miracles, in your service for Christ. But you must not succumb to the temptation of basking in the past. You must set behind you the experiences of the past and focus on your responsibilities and vision for the future. Don't forget the lessons God has taught you in the past, but don't spend all your time living in the past. For most of us, and probably for you, there is more future service (or at least effectiveness) ahead of you than behind you. Your goal, of course, is to glorify God by discovering and doing God's will for your life. Stay close to Him in prayer. Search His Word daily. Ask Him to show you His vision, and then commit yourself to follow it.

> Dear Lord, please help me know Your will and live close enough to You that Your vision will be clear and I will be enabled to follow You in it.

A Deacon and His Example
Philippians 3:16-17

"We should live up to whatever truth we have attained."

The New American Standard Bible translates this verse, "Let us keep living by the same standard to which we have attained." The admonition is clear. Paul wanted the Pastors and Deacons at Philippi to rise to spiritual maturity and continually live by the standards that accompany that maturity. We must all develop in our Christian lives. We do this by "coming to a knowledge of the truth" (2 Tim. 2:25), being set apart by God in the truth (Jn. 17:17), and daily applying the truth (1 Jn. 1:3-4). Of course, truth is both a Bible and a person. God's Word is truth (Jn. 17:17), and God's Son, Jesus, is truth (Jn. 14:6).

> "Our lives should be such as men may safely copy."

Therefore, to be a good example to others with whom and for whom you serve, you must live or abide in the Word. Let the Word of Christ richly dwell within you (Col. 3:16). "You have heard Him and have been taught in Him, just as truth is in Jesus" (Eph. 4:21). As you gain more truth from Scripture and as you abide in the one who is the truth, you will then be prepared to minister to the needs of others both by precept and practice.

Phillips Brooks, in charging other servants in the church, said, "Be such a man and live such a life that if every man were such as you and every life like yours, this earth would be a paradise."[29] This is our work. This is our challenge. We must diligently live up to the truth we have discovered. Charles Spurgeon put it another way, "Our lives should be such as men may safely copy."[30] Paul makes more of this in the verses to follow.

Determine in your heart today that you will keep living by the same standards of God's Word that you have come to know. Dwell on God's Word. Follow Christ's example. Live in the light of the truth you have.

Dear Lord, I thank You for Your Word. I desire to know it better and thus know You better. Guide me by Your Spirit to know and live Your truth.

A Deacon and His Enemies
Philippians 3:18

"Many live as enemies of the cross of Christ."

As Deacons in the church, we don't like to think of ourselves as having enemies. And we do need to be very careful who we refer to as such. But if Jesus charged His disciples to "love your enemies" (Lk. 6:35) and if James says, "whoever wishes to be a friend of the world makes himself an enemy of God" (Jas. 4:4), it seems that we do have some. For us, however, as servant-leaders, the primary enemy is spiritual, not physical. Ephesians 6:12 says, "For our battle is not against flesh and blood, but against . . . the world powers of this darkness, against the spiritual forces of evil in the heavens."

In spite of what you may feel at times, your enemy is not another believer and certainly not your Pastor or a fellow Deacon. Our arch enemy does work in the "sons of disobedience"—that is, those unbelievers who "deceive you with empty words" (Eph. 5:6). Satan does seek to control unbelievers and use them against the gospel, against the church, and against us. There are persons around us who, being under satanic, fleshly, or worldly influence, are to be viewed as "enemies of the cross of Christ." We must always love our enemies, but we must never compromise our *biblical convictions to please or appease them. They have merely been* blinded to the truth and subsequently resist the gospel (cf. 2 Cor. 4:3-4). They, too, are needy persons for whom Christ died.

> **The primary enemy is spiritual, not physical.**

So, how should you relate to or treat your enemies—that is, those who are enemies of Christ and His cross? You should love your enemies (Matt. 5:44), be good to your enemies (Lk. 6:35) and witness to your enemies (Rom. 5:10). This was Jesus' response and it should also be ours. In this world you will face spiritual enemy combatants but Jesus said, "Be courageous! I have conquered the world" (Jn. 16:33).

Dear Lord, help me know who my real enemies are, and help me to love them as You love them and as You loved me when I was an enemy of Your cross.

A Deacon and His Focus

Philippians 3:19

"They are focused on earthly things."

Of the "enemies of Christ" (i.e., unbelievers), the apostle says they focus their attention on their stomach or appetites and give no attention to the gospel of Christ. We expect this mindset from unbelieving enemies of the cross. We are not expected, as believers, to have such a focus. What is your mind set upon? Where you can next eat out? What delicacy you might consume? In what pleasure might you indulge? Who (or what) is your god? In a later passage in Philippians, Paul will charge these Deacons to give attention to godly, Christlike virtues and to "dwell on these things" (4:8). In Colossians 3:2, he said, "Set your minds on what is above, not on what is on the earth.

> The greater your focus on Him, the less you will focus on the world.

As a Deacon in His church, you should follow Paul's admonition. God has given you the extraordinary privilege of thinking and reasoning with Him (Isa. 1:18). In fact, you can truly "set your mind on Him" as you read and study His Word and pray to Him. And the greater your focus on Him, the less you will focus on the world. The more you think about heavenly and godly things, the less you will think about earthly and godless things.

It has been well said, "A man is not what he thinks he is, but what he thinks, he is." Proverbs 23:7 says, "As [a selfish man] thinks within himself, so he is." Even as a Deacon in the church, you will be tempted to think a lot about yourself and all the things this world can give you.

Fortunately, you have the power of God's Holy Spirit within you to resist this temptation (cf. 1 Cor. 10:13). You can set your mind daily upon Him. You can focus on His Word, His will, and His way. You can live and serve above the natural appetites of the flesh. You really can have victory in Jesus.

Dear Lord, please empower me by Your Holy Spirit to set my mind on You. Fill my spirit with Your Word even before You fill my stomach with food. Take control of my thoughts today so I might follow You more fully and serve You more faithfully.

A Deacon and His True Citizenship
Philippians 3:20

"Our citizenship is in heaven, from which we also
eagerly wait for a Savior, the Lord Jesus Christ."

Most of us are citizens of the country in which we were born. Some are citizens of a country by a process of immigration. Citizenship carries with it certain rights but also certain responsibilities. If you are a citizen of the United States of America, you have been given freedoms that some in other countries only dream of. The Constitution and Bill of Rights, as they are referred to, provide US citizens with "life, liberty and the pursuit of happiness." We cherish this citizenship. However, for the genuine Christian, there is a second and even higher citizenship.

Believers are citizens of heaven by virtue of our rebirth. We are not given this citizenship because we have filled out an application or learned a new language. We are citizens of heaven because we have been adopted and sanctioned by the King of heaven. Ironically, we are citizens of a land in which we've yet to reside. It is our homeland, but we have not yet lived there. We know much about it, and we learn more each day. Because of our new citizenship, we are provided freedoms of which some whose citizenship is limited to the countries of this world can only dream.

> **We are citizens of a land in which we've yet to reside.**

Your objectives as a Deacon in Christ's church are to model heavenly citizenship or be a good citizen, explain to other citizens the freedoms, benefits, and responsibilities of citizenship, and appeal to those who are outside this citizenship to come in total submission to the King of kings, the Lord Jesus Christ. After all, it is this King who does reside in heaven. It is the return of this King for which we wait that "where [He] is there we may be also" (Jn.14:3).

Dear Lord, thank You for causing me to be born again
into a new citizenship. Help me each day to learn more
of my homeland and live more there than here.

WEEK 18   **DAY 1**

A Deacon Anticipating a New Body
Philippians 3:21

"He will transform the body of our humble condition into the likeness of His glorious body . . ."

With the weaknesses of our present, physical bodies, we realize our need for transformation. The word used in this verse for *transform* is the word from which we get our English word metamorphosis. As in English, it carries with it the idea of "a marked or complete change of character, appearance, condition."[31] In biology it is what happens when a caterpillar turns into a butterfly. There is a complete, total transformation of one thing into another thing.

> **I am fearfully and wonderfully made.**

This transformation occurs in us spiritually when we are born again and supernaturally placed into the body of Christ. It is also a transformation that will occur in us physically when our present mortal bodies will put on immortal bodies (cf. 1 Cor. 15:35-50). At the second coming of Christ, He will not only receive us unto Himself (Jn. 14:3), but He will also supernaturally and instantaneously clothe our spirit with a brand new body like His own.

> In a human body some three billion cells die and are replaced every minute. The human brain contains some thirty billion cells; the skin has about a million cells per square inch; and in the veins some twenty trillion cells go about their business . . . That we should live at all is a miracle. That we should live again is a greater miracle. The God who made us once can easily make us again "according to the working whereby he is able even to subdue all things unto himself."[32]

Is it any wonder that the Psalmist said, "I am fearfully and wonderfully made" (Ps. 139:14)? We can only imagine how fearfully and wonderfully we will be re-made when we receive our new, glorified body, like unto His glorious body!

> **Dear Lord, thank You for creating me physically and re-creating me spiritually. Thank You for promising me a new, glorified body to go with my brand new regenerated spirit for all eternity.**

A Deacon: The Joy and Crown of His Pastor
Philippians 4:1

"My beloved brethren whom I long to see, my joy and crown . . ."

The Pastor's heart of the apostle Paul is seen in this opening phrase of chapter 4. He refers to the church and particularly to the Deacons as "beloved brethren." It is an expression used many times by Paul to affirm his love for his fellow servants and his kindred relationship to them. Paul wrote this letter from a Roman prison cell, having been separated from the Philippians for quite some time. Thus, he longed to see them again. He further referred to them as his *"joy and crown."* These are also expressions of endearment. However, these words imply Paul's investment in their spiritual lives. He believed that the fruit of his preaching—that is, the salvation of the lost and the building up of the church—would result in a crown of glory for him in heaven (2 Tim. 4:8).

> Great joy floods the heart of a Pastor who sees his Deacons faithfully growing and serving God.

Deacons in the church and especially those who have been led to the Lord and/or discipled by the Pastor become very close friends. A Christian love and bond is developed between them. Great joy floods the heart of a Pastor who sees his Deacons faithfully growing and serving God. They become, as it were, the *"crown"* or fruit of His labors (cf. 1 Thess. 2:19-20).

Robert Murray M'Cheyne once said, "Oh how sweet to work all day for God, and then lie down at night beneath His smile!"[33] Such should be the objective of every Pastor and every Deacon in every church. Our beloved brethren in the church can and should become for us a joy and reward for our ministry. May you work all day for God and lie down at night beneath His smile.

Dear Lord, create in me a love for my fellow servants in the church. Help me make an investment in the lives of others, resulting in joy for myself and my friends and glory for You.

A Deacon Standing Firm in the Lord
Philippians 4:16

"Stand firm in the Lord, dear friends."

This present tense verb for *stand firm* literally means keep on taking your stand in a willing subjection to Christ's authority. We too are to be willing to take a stand on issues facing the church. We are to do this based upon the clear teaching and authority of Scripture. The position we take should not be for any other reason—not because other church members disagree or so that we can "keep peace in the family." We stand firm *in the Lord*—that is, in the authority of the Lord.

As Deacons in the church, we are called upon to take a strong stand for the defense of the gospel (1 Cor. 15:1), for our freedom in Christ (Gal. 5:1), in resistance of the enemy (Eph. 6:11, 13), for the unity of the church (Phil. 1:27), in the assurance of God's will (Col. 4:2), for the grace of God (1 Pet. 5:12), and for the convictions of Scripture (2 Thess. 2:15). Having done everything we know to do and having clearly stated our position, we can stand firm (Eph. 6:13).

Are there areas in your life and ministry where you have not been willing to take a stand? If so, it may be because you don't know for sure what God's position is on the matter, in which case you should study and pray until you do. It may be because you are afraid of being misunderstood by others, in which case you should work hard at making your position clear by scriptural validation. It may be because you would really rather compromise than to potentially disrupt your fellowship with others, in which case you should confess your sin to God, maintain your stand and trust Him to restore any broken fellowship.

> "Stand up, stand up for Jesus, ye soldiers of the cross."

In the words of George Duffield, Jr., "Stand up for Jesus, Ye soldiers of the cross; Lift high His royal banner, it must not, it must not suffer loss."[34] Stand firm in the Lord, dear friend, and you will gain the approval of God and the respect of the church.

> Dear Lord, help me to take a firm stand for the right things and to never compromise Your Word. Help me to do so in an attitude of gentleness and love.

A Deacon Resolving Conflict
Philippians 4:2-3

"I urge Euodia and I urge Syntyche to agree in the Lord . . . help those women . . ."

Even in a church as Christ-centered and generous as Philippi, there were some who did not always agree or get along. So, after eighty-two verses, Paul finally names two ladies who apparently posed a conflict. We don't know exactly what their disagreement was about, but we do know there was dissension between them. And the dissension had led to a disruption in the fellowship.

Paul appeals to his "true companion" or "partner" at Philippi to intervene in the situation and help resolve the conflict. This partner was likely either the current Pastor of the church or a Deacon who could easily and lovingly confront these ladies about the problem. It was extremely important in the mind of Paul that these ladies, and in fact the entire church, "live in harmony in the Lord." It is no less important that the church in which you serve live in harmony in the Lord. Occasionally, disciplinary action is required to maintain that harmony.

> It is extremely important to live in harmony in the Lord.

You probably have been called upon to intervene in some conflict in the church and help bring resolution. What do you do with such a request? Do you try to pass it off to another Deacon or maybe one of the staff members? Or do you assume your responsibility and deal with it head-on? Matthew 18:15-20 is a good passage to use in applying church discipline. Sometimes the best way you can serve your church is to help carry out this kind of discipline. It is always done with a view to forgiveness and reconciliation, not criticism and excommunication. In most cases the conflicts can be resolved, and the unity of the church is preserved. You can be used of God to help make that happen.

Dear Lord, I pray that You would grant to me the wisdom I need to confront conflict and lovingly bring resolution.

A Deacon Experiencing Joy

Philippians 4:4

"Rejoice in the Lord always. I will say it again: Rejoice!"

Paul calls for joy many times in this epistle (1:4, 25; 2:2, 17, 18; 4:1). Clearly, joy is an emotion—"a feeling of gladness, happiness, great pleasure or delight."[35] Joy for the Christian comes from the Holy Spirit. Galatians 5:22 says, "The fruit of the Spirit is . . . joy . . ." Even in the midst of trials and personal struggles, we can "greatly rejoice with joy inexpressible and full of glory" (1 Pet. 1:8). There is a distinction to be made between human happiness and Spirit-produced joy. Happiness depends on happenings, while joy depends on Jesus.

Paul says, "Rejoice always." We are challenged to know how to do that when we are in the midst of hurtful, disappointing circumstances. Ironically, the two shortest verses in the New Testament are "Jesus wept" (Jn. 11:35) and "Rejoice always" (1 Thess. 5:16). These represent the two ends of the emotional spectrum—weeping and rejoicing. We experience both, and we minister to others who experience both. Sometimes we are called upon to minister to multiple people who are experiencing both emotions at the same time. Thus, we are admonished by Scripture to "rejoice with those who rejoice, and weep with those who weep" (Rom. 12:15). You may find yourself rejoicing in the morning with a young couple's delivery of a new baby and weeping in the evening with a couple whose son was just pronounced dead by suicide.

> Happiness depends on happenings, while joy depends on Jesus.

Even through the trials of ministry, always remember, "The joy of the Lord is your strength" (Neh. 8:10). So, in this day will you follow Paul's admonition and say with the psalmist, "This is the day which the Lord has made; let us rejoice and be glad in it" (Ps. 118:24)?

Dear Lord, I desire to live in Your joy. I want to rejoice in You, regardless of the circumstances. Would You please fill me with Your Spirit, so the fruit of joy might be exhibited through me?

A Deacon Who Is Gracious

Philippians 4:5

"Let your graciousness be known to everyone. The Lord is near."

The word used in this verse for *graciousness* may be translated gentle spirit, forbearing spirit, or gentleness. It carries the idea of forbearance or yielding. John Phillips says, "The word speaks of selflessness, of a spirit ready to yield in anything that is simply of self—for the Lord's sake."[36] With the added "The Lord is near," Paul is reminding these Philippian Deacons that God is watching and listening to every act and word.

When others in the church and outside the church watch you in your servant role or listen to you counsel, do they think, *Now there is a gentle giant of a Christian!* They may never use the words "forbearing spirit," but do they know that you have virtues and qualities in your life and servanthood that Christians should have? Whether we demonstrate gentleness in our service is a telling statement of whether we are bearing the fruit of the Holy Spirit. Gentleness is a fruit of God's Spirit (Gal. 5:22) intended to be borne out in us.

Admittedly, it is not always easy to be gentle or to treat obnoxious people with grace. You may have heard it said, "To live up above with saints I love, oh that will be glory. But to live here below with saints I know; now that's another story!" Jesus did not say it would be easy. As a matter of fact, He clearly taught that it would be impossible apart from His infilling Spirit. But with God's Holy Spirit infilling you, controlling you, and directing you, you can let His graciousness in you be known to everyone. You can serve others with a gentle spirit and a sincere heart. They will certainly be watching, and so will the Lord, who is near.

> Gentleness is a fruit of God's Spirit intended to be borne out in us.

Dear Lord, I pray that You would so control me by Your Holy Spirit that Your gentleness, graciousness, and forbearance would be evident in my life. Please let Your graciousness in me be known to everyone around me for Your glory.

A Deacon Who Worries

Philippians 4:6a

"Don't worry about anything . . ."

The New American Standard Version and a few others translate this phrase, "Be anxious for nothing . . ." Williams translates, "Stop being worried about anything . . ." The point is clear. Christians in general, and Deacons in particular, do not need to worry about anything. We know this principally, but we struggle to apply it practically. How do you not worry when your child is sick or when you are sick or when you run out of money before you run out of bills? Can anyone actually live a "worry-free" life?

We know from the words of Jesus Himself that we are not to worry. In His "Sermon on the Mount," Jesus strongly admonished His hearers not to worry. In Matthew 6:25-34, three times Jesus says, *"Do not worry!"* Actually the literal rendering of His statement is, "You are worrying. Stop it!" This is a rather harsh, but needed, reprimand. His admonition was not only very clear and very forceful but also very pointed. He said, in essence, don't worry about where your next meal will come from (v. 25), don't worry about your wardrobe or what style of clothing you will wear (v. 31), and don't worry about what tomorrow may bring (v. 34). These are very practical admonitions for us today. "Who of you, by being worried can add a single hour to his life?" (v. 27). The truth is, long-term worry will seriously shorten your life.

> "A day of worry is more exhausting than a week of work."

John Lubbock said, "A day of worry is more exhausting than a week of work."[37] So rather than spend your time worrying about anything, why not spend your time and energy focusing on the service you can give to others? The more you focus on others and the less you focus on yourself, the less likely you will be to worry. So, don't worry, trust the Lord, focus on the needs of others, and everything is going to be all right.

> Dear Lord, help me to know why I worry and by Your Spirit enable me to trust You consistently and completely to meet all the needs in my life. Allow me to live in You, worry-free.

A Deacon Who Prays
Philippians 4:6b

"In everything, through prayer and petition with thanksgiving, let your request be made known to God."

John Phillips says of this passage, "God arranged prayer to encourage us to come to Him. He longs for us to come, come often and linger long. He longs for us to talk to Him, tell Him all about our troubles and make our requests known to Him."[38] Prayer is a wonderful privilege for the believer. In prayer we have immediate and direct access to the God of the universe. We are often taught in our churches that there are four aspects to prayer, which normally follow the acrostic A.C.T.S. Prayer allows us to, "**A**—Acknowledge God for who He is and what He has done for us"; "**C**—Confess our sins to God receiving His instant and gracious forgiveness"; "**T**—Thank God for His provisions, be they physical, material, spiritual, financial, or otherwise"; and "**S**—Supplicate or request of God what we believe to be a legitimate need in our lives." All of these aspects of prayer are alluded to by Paul in this verse.

> **Prayer certainly does change things.**

Prayer certainly does change things. But more importantly, prayer certainly can change you. It can change your marriage, your family, your job, your church, and your ministry but never before, or unless, it changes you. This could hardly be better stated than by Joseph Scriven who, in 1855, wrote the poem, "What a Friend We Have in Jesus":

> What a friend we have in Jesus, all our sins and griefs to bear!
> What a privilege to carry, everything to God in prayer!
> Oh what peace we often forfeit,
> Oh what needless pain we bear,
> All because we do not carry everything to God in prayer![39]

Rather than study any further about it, perhaps you would now pray. Pray earnestly, pray often, pray aright, and you will see God do great and mighty things in you and in your church.

Dear Lord, please build into me a disciplined prayer life. Teach me to pray, and help me know for what to pray. Thank You for hearing and answering my prayers.

A Deacon with Peace of Mind
Philippians 4:7

"And the peace of God, which surpasses every thought, will guard your hearts and your minds in Christ Jesus."

Hardly anything means more to the Christian, and certainly to a Deacon in the church, than having peace of mind. Most people want it. Few people have it on a regular basis. The apostle clarifies in this verse that the greatest answer God can give to the prayers of His children is peace—peace of mind and heart. What could be more valuable? And what could be more miserable than living without it?

The peace *of* God only comes to those who have peace *with* God. Peace *with* God only comes when we repent of our sins, place our faith in the Prince of Peace—the Lord Jesus Christ—and surrender our very lives to His Lordship. With the intention of leaving the earth, going back to the Father in heaven, and providing His Holy Spirit to permanently indwell every believer, Jesus said, "Peace I leave with you; My peace I give to you; not as the world gives do I give to you. Do not let your heart be troubled, nor let it be fearful" (Jn. 14:27). Paul said to another church on another occasion, "We have peace with God through our Lord Jesus Christ" (Rom. 5:1). The prophet Isaiah said, "The steadfast of mind You will keep in perfect peace" (Isa. 26:3). Is there any question as to the source of this peace?

> The peace of God only comes to those who have peace with God.

John Bunyan, author of *Pilgrim's Progress*, said, "If we have not quiet in our minds, outward comfort will do no more for us than a golden slipper on a gouty foot."[40] How true that is. Without the peace of God in our hearts, our minds will deceive us into believing that all manner of things and pleasures will relax us when they never will. As you pray, surrender all your anxieties and fears to the Lord Jesus "for He Himself is our peace" (Eph. 2:14). Then begin to observe how your thoughts and feelings change. Don't be surprised if things that used to really upset you hardly bother you at all anymore.

> Dear Lord, having received You as my only Lord
> and Savior, I know I have peace with You.
> Please help me to think and feel and live and serve
> in Your perfect tranquility.

WEEK 19   **DAY 5**

A DEACON DWELLING ON TRUTH
Philippians 4:8a

"Whatever is true . . . dwell on these things."

For the Pastor and Deacons in any Bible-believing church, truth is of utmost importance. When the apostle John described Jesus's coming in the flesh, he referred to Him as "the only begotten from the Father full of grace and truth" (John 1:14). When Jesus was praying His high priestly prayer in John 17, He asked that the Father might "Sanctify them in the truth; Your word is truth" (v. 17). Jesus is the truth, and the Bible is the truth and if "you know the truth . . . the truth will make you free" (John 8:32).

> Let the word of Christ richly dwell within you.

    Is it any wonder that Paul charges the Philippian church leaders to dwell on the things that are true? It's easy enough to believe a lie. In fact, some over the years have tried to "exchange the truth of God for a lie . . ." (Rom. 1:25). So how do we know if something is true or false—if it is to be believed or rejected? This is an age-old question that is answered in the Bible. On one occasion Jesus said to Pontius Pilate, "Everyone who is of the truth hears My voice. Pilate said to Him, What is truth?" (Jn. 18:38).

    Richards Bible Dictionary defines truth, as used throughout the New Testament, "Something in accord with reality and therefore accurate, reliable and, in the case of God, trustworthy . . . God's unveiling of reality through natural and special revelation . . . Reality that can be experienced."[41] Of course something can only be experienced as true when it is compared to that which is false. Thus, there must be an absolute standard of true and false or right and wrong. For Christians, and really for every person, that standard is God's word—the Bible (Jn. 17:17).

    So, if you intend to heed this appeal in Philippians 4:8 made by Paul to "dwell on whatever is true," then you must dwell on God's Word. Colossians 3:16 states, "Let the word of Christ richly dwell within you." Be "sanctified in the truth.

> **Dear Lord, by the power of Your Holy Spirit, please guide me into the truth and enable me to dwell on the truth. I desire to live by the truth and serve You and worship You in Spirit and in truth.**

Week 20 — **Day 1**

A Deacon Who Is Honorable
Philippians 4:8b

"Whatever is honorable . . . dwell on these things."

Webster defines honor as "high regard or great respect given, received or enjoyed."42 Richards Bible Dictionary says it means "to be elevated in the eyes of others on the basis of rank, reputation, status or character: to show respect to a person in appropriate ways."43 In the verse cited, Paul is encouraging the Deacons and overseers at Philippi to think seriously and regularly about doing those acts of service that would be genuinely deserving of honor or commendation. A good biblical example of this is 1 Timothy 5:17 where, "The elders who rule well are to be considered worthy of double honor, especially those who work hard at preaching and teaching." In this particular verse, an argument could be made for such hard-working leaders to receive "double honorará" or double pay. Honor does and should have its benefits. But such benefits should not be selfishly exploited.

> We should sincerely defer all the honor and praise that might be directed toward us to Him.

Therefore, honor is not to be assumed or expected by any church leader merely because of his position. A person should dwell on noble service and do honorable deeds but not particularly for man's reward. It is God's reward that we seek. It is His approval of our service that really matters. We should sincerely defer all the honor and praise that might be directed toward us to Him. And we should be willing to receive honor from God. In John 12:26, Jesus said, "If anyone serves Me, the Father will honor him." That is what Jesus says about you.

If you will serve Him, the heavenly Father will honor you. He will elevate you in the eyes of others. He will cause you to be respected by others. He will develop in you righteous character. Your honorable life and service will bring great glory to Him and much good to the church.

Dear Lord, I pray that You will receive all glory and honor from my life. Help me defer compliments back to You. You alone are worthy of honor!

A Deacon Who Is Just

Philippians 4:8c

"Whatever is just . . . dwell on these things."

The *New American Standard Bible* translates *just* with the word "right," as does the *New International Version*. In Greek it "denotes righteous, a state of being right or right conduct, judged by God's standards."[44] Since right actions or right living is always a result of right thinking, then dwelling on just things becomes very important for God's servants.

It is said of Joseph of Arimathea, the man who offered his own grave to entomb Jesus, that he was "a good and righteous [just] man" (Lk. 23:50). John the Baptist was referred to by his enemy, King Herod, as "a righteous [just] and holy man" (Mk. 6:20). Close friends of Cornelius informed Peter that "Cornelius, a centurion, [was] a righteous [just] and God-fearing man" (Acts 10:22). This term, right or just, is used of many in the Bible who did the right thing because they believed the right thing and dwelled on the right things.

> Dwelling on just things becomes very important for God's servants.

According to God's standard, the Bible, there are moral absolutes. That is, there are some things that are distinctively right and some things that are distinctively wrong. We don't get to decide which is which. We do get to discover from prayer, Bible study, and practical living what God has pre-determined to be right and wrong. We do receive by faith the spiritual capacity to know the difference and choose what's right.

God has given you, as a Deacon in the church, the capacity to not only think what's right but to also do what's right. Right actions flow out of right conduct, and right conduct flows out of right character, and right character flows out of a genuine, personal, intimate relationship with Christ. Dwell on the things Christ dwelt on, and do the things Christ did. You will live a more holy and just life and bring righteousness and justice to the people of God.

Dear Lord, help me to think right. Help me to dwell on the right things so I will be faithful to do the right—the righteous—things.

A Deacon Who Is Pure

Philippians 4:8d

"Whatever is pure . . . dwell on these things."

Purity is not a word that is used very often to describe Christian men, especially Pastors and Deacons in the church. Maybe smart, devoted, educated, capable, slick, busy—but seldom do we think of our ministers as pure. Yet the apostle Paul charges these servants in Philippi to dwell on things that are pure. Clearly the implication is to live a morally pure life before God and before others.

The term pure may mean different things to different people. But our concern is what it means to God and what it should mean to us. The Greek word means "pure from defilement, not contaminated."[45] Richards Bible Dictionary says, "in a moral sense, characterized by blamelessness; a habit of making right and good choices . . . in a spiritual sense, characterized by a whole-hearted commitment to God."[46]

> **Often the Bible connects purity with the heart.**

Often the Bible connects purity with the heart. In Psalm 51:10 David prayed, "Create in me a clean heart, O God." Jesus said, "Blessed are the pure in heart, for they shall see God" (Matt. 5:8). And in 1 Timothy 1:5 Paul says to Pastor Timothy, "The goal of our instruction is love from a pure heart . . ." Again, Paul warned Timothy, "Flee from youthful lusts and pursue righteousness . . . with those who call on the Lord from a pure heart" (2 Tim. 2:22).

So many impurities in life are as a result of what we put into our minds. What you put into your mind will work its way into your heart and eventually out in everyday living. Hebrews 5:14 says, "Solid food is for the mature, who because of practice have their senses trained to discern good and evil." Wherever you find yourself in the next several days, observe what you are seeing, touching, tasting, hearing, and then thinking. Begin, or continue, to dwell on whatever is pure at all times in all places!

> **Dear Lord, I pray that You will remind me as often as necessary of my impure thoughts and actions. Empower me, by Your Holy Spirit, to dwell on whatever is pure so I might more closely reflect the purity that You have.**

A Deacon Expressing Love

Philippians 4:8e

"Whatever is lovely . . . dwell on these things."

Lovely is yet another word that is almost never used to describe a Christian man. Perhaps it might refer to a Christian woman, but not a man. This is probably because of a misunderstanding of the term and the way it is used in contemporary society. We think of flowers or trees or mountains as being lovely—not men and certainly not "real men." But Paul uses this word to charge these Philippian Deacons and others to dwell on "lovely things" or "things that point toward love." By the way, this is the only occurrence of this word in this form in all of the New Testament, which makes it a bit intriguing, to say the least.

Webster defines *lovely* as "those qualities that inspire love, affection or admiration in others; qualities that are morally or spiritually attractive, precious."[47] So, we are hearing Paul charging the Philippians to think about and practice the kinds of things that draw themselves and point others to God's love. As an adverb, lovely always modifies a verb, an adjective, or another adverb. For example, a believer may "lovingly express his sympathy to a hurting person."

> **What is your primary motivation for serving God?**

He is actually expressing sympathy, but how he does it is "lovingly." Your act of service may often be viewed by others as a "lovely thing to do." That is, it has shown an expression of genuine love by a particular act of service. The deed is the service. The motivation for the deed is love.

This, of course, begs the question, "Why do you do what you do?" What is your primary motivation for serving God? Second Corinthians 5:14 says, "The love of Christ compels us . . ." If genuine Christian love is your motivation to serve, then dwell on "whatever is lovely"—whatever will express the love of God to others and point them to Jesus.

Dear Lord, please show me the lovely things in my life—the things that I can embrace and express to others. Help me dwell on and share the lovely things that picture Your love in and through me.

WEEK 20 **DAY 5**

A DEACON WHO IS COMMENDABLE
Philippians 4:8f

"Whatever is commendable . . . dwell on these things."

Some versions of the Bible translate the word *commendable* as admirable, of good repute, high-toned, and appealing. *Webster* defines *commend* "to put in the care of another; entrust; to mention as worthy of attention; recommend; to express approval of; praise."[48]

The apostle is appealing to the Philippian church leaders to think about the things in their lives that they could freely and unapologetically recommend to others. They could always commend to others the Lord and His Word. Paul did this with the Ephesian elders, "I commend you to God and to the word of His grace, which is able to build you up . . ." (Acts 20:32). Paul discouraged commending himself (1 Cor. 5:12) but did think about and practice the commendable qualities of love and clear-mindedness (1 Cor. 10:12).

> When you look at your life and ministry what do you see that is truly commendable?

When you look at your life and ministry, what do you see that is truly commendable? What are you doing that is worth the attention of the church? And what are you doing that is of good repute in the eyes of the world? There are several things identified in Scripture that are commendable in the eyes of the Lord and "when a man's ways are pleasing to the Lord, He makes even his enemies to be at peace with him" (Prov. 16:7). For example God commends us when we live under His Spirit's control (Rom. 8:8), when we excel in moral purity (1 Thess. 4:1ff), when we love our neighbors and treat them as we would want to be treated (Rom. 15:2-3), and when we trust God without reservation for all the needs in our lives and in the church (Heb. 11:6). Set aside some time to dwell on these things.

> We have to make deliberate choices to think profitable thoughts. Our minds will not automatically drift into these channels.[49]
> (John Phillips)

Dear Lord, please help me to dwell on these great virtues cited in Philippians 4:8. I desire to exhibit all of these qualities in my life.

WEEK 21 — **DAY 1**

A DEACON WHO FOLLOWS A GOOD EXAMPLE
Philippians 4:9

"Do what you have learned and received and heard and seen in me . . ."

On the surface, this sounds like a boast by Paul, somehow indicating superiority over his fellow-servants at Philippi. But at a closer look, we see that the apostle is merely charging them to practice the "things" mentioned in verse 8. Paul had disciplined himself to not only teach these principles of excellence but to practice them as well. He had already admonished these believers to "follow my example, and . . . walk according to the pattern you have in us" (3:17). It is this pattern of behavior that best exhibits our principal beliefs.

Charles Spurgeon said, "Our lives should be such as men may safely copy."[50] This is not to imply that we have it all down and are perfect examples of Christian servanthood. But as Pastors and Deacons, we certainly have an obligation to set a Christlike example. Thus, it is important whom we follow and emulate. First and foremost, we must follow Christ. He is our ultimate example of servanthood (Mark 10:45). It is also important that we have other men of God in our lives we may follow. Clearly, Timothy had Paul; John Mark had Barnabas; Peter had Andrew; and Nathanael had Philip. These are only a few of many biblical examples of men who followed the example of others who were following Jesus.

> As Pastors and Deacons, we have an obligation to set a Christlike example.

We cannot expect others to follow us in every single way. But as long as we are patterning our lives and character after Christ, we can legitimately expect others to follow that example. Our lives, like theirs, should look and act more and more like Christ's. You will be a much better example to others when you follow those who are beautiful examples of Jesus.

Dear Lord, I pray that You will guide me to those who are really good examples of Christian servanthood. Help me to become a more faithful example to others.

A Deacon Who Cares for His Pastor
Philippians 4:10

> "I rejoice in the Lord greatly that now at last
> you have renewed your care for me."

The apostle Paul, a Pastor at heart, had found himself in a Roman prison, arrested for proclaiming the gospel. He had prayed for the Philippian believers and especially the Pastors and Deacons (1:3-5). Out of deep love and concern, Paul sent Epaphroditus, possibly a Deacon out of the Philippian church who had come to visit him in jail, back to the church with a report on his ministry. Epaphroditus almost died from an illness in his attempt to complete this communication (2:25-27). Nonetheless, eventually Paul received a significant offering from the Philippian church (4:18) and wrote this epistle in response.

> You have both the influence and the responsibility to care for your Pastor and his family.

It seems that the leaders in the church, especially the Deacons, looked to Paul as a major influence in their spiritual lives. Therefore, they made a sacrificial contribution to him. They revived their concern for him. They realized anew that it was as much their responsibility as any other to support their leaders. Whether it's a local Pastor, ministry staff member, or missionary, the church is uniquely responsible for their support (1 Tim. 5:17-18).

Most Southern Baptist churches contribute a percentage of their undesignated receipts to the cooperative program. This is a program whereby hundreds of millions of dollars are pooled together and distributed to over ten thousand North American and international missionaries. It is a proven means of expressing our concern for mission support.

As a Deacon in your church, you have both the influence and the responsibility to care for your Pastor and his family. Take this responsibility seriously, and do all you can to "renew your concern" for him. He will be better for it. You will be better for it. The church will be better for it. The Kingdom of God will be the better for it.

> Dear Lord, I pray that You will renew my concern for
> the needs and ministry of my Pastor.
> Help me support him as he fulfills his ministry.

A Deacon Who Is Content
Philippians 4:11

"I have learned to be content in whatever circumstances I am."

A Deacon was asked by a Pastor how he was doing today. The Deacon replied that he was doing fine, under the circumstances. The Pastor responded "So what are you doing under there?" Perhaps you, too, are living your daily life not merely surrounded by your circumstances but controlled by them. How many times have you either heard someone say or even said yourself, "I'll just have to wait and see what tomorrow holds"? This may be an indication that tomorrow is in the hands of your circumstances and not in the hands of God!

> The key to victorious living is not found in the circumstances of your life.

There is a sense in which we "take no thought for tomorrow" (Matt. 6:34), but there is also a sense in which we "sit down and calculate the cost" (Lk. 14:28). The key to victorious living is not found in the circumstances of your life. The key is in your relationship to the God of your circumstances. Are you at complete peace with yourself and God? Are you fully trusting in His grace this hour? Or are you at the mercy of your circumstances?

The word for *content* primarily signifies "to be sufficient, to be possessed of sufficient strength, to be strong, to be enough for a thing."[51] Webster defines *content*, "to appease the desires, to limit (oneself) in requirements, desires or actions."[52] This means we are to be at peace with God and completely satisfied with His will—and circumstances—for our lives. Perhaps you would do well to learn and earnestly pray the "Serenity Prayer" of Dr. Reinhold Niebuhr:

> God, grant me the serenity to accept the things that I cannot change; The courage to change the things I can. And the wisdom to know the difference.[53]

According to the words of this text, contentment is learned. Would you be willing to spend some focused time studying, learning, and applying contentment in your life? Invite God to change you—your mind, heart, attitude, and will—if He never changes your circumstances.

**Dear Lord, teach me to be content with
Your will for my life and ministry.**

A Deacon Living on Little
Philippians 4:12

"I have learned the secret [of being content]—whether well-fed or hungry, whether in abundance or in need."

The *New American Standard Bible* translates the early part of this verse, "I know how to get along with humble means . . ." Living on little is seemingly impossible for some in the American church today. Certainly there are exceptions. But for the most part, the church is made up of people who are very discontent with their living and quite focused on getting more.

Paul's focus was on mission and ministry, not money or material things. He knew that he needed some money and some material things. But these were not, for him, status symbols or a show of success. These were merely a means to an end—the end being the fulfillment of God's call to the Great Commission. Thus, Paul could live on much or he could live on little, but he would live for Jesus no matter the cost.

> **Paul's focus was on mission and ministry, not money or material things.**

These words from 4:12 of this epistle are both informative and challenging. They are intended to inform the Deacons at Philippi of Paul's position and condition and lessons learned. But they were also intended to challenge the other servants in the Philippian church to make a similar surrender to service. And of course, the challenge to us is obvious. Are we willing to live with much or live with little in order to fulfill God's purpose for our own lives and for our church?

Joseph Pearce has stated it well, "Nothing less than a living sacrifice is demanded. Not a loan, but a gift; not a compromise, but a sacrifice; not our poorest, but our best; not a dead but a living offering."[54] Paul knew and practiced this truth. He essentially charged the Philippian Deacons to do the same. And of course, he brings the same challenge to you today. Will you serve God and His church faithfully whether with little or much?

> **Dear Lord, please help me to be content with what I have. Help me focus on my mission and ministry and trust You for the money and materials.**

A Deacon Who Can Do Anything

Philippians 4:13

"I am able to do all things through Him who strengthens me."

This must be one of the most often-quoted verses in this epistle. It is an affirmation of the power of God to do everything He wants to in and through the surrendered servant. A Deacon is a servant to the church. He cannot do every single thing that others expect of him. He cannot be all things to all people all the time. But he can do anything that God calls upon him to do. He is enabled by God to not only know what to do and how to do it but also to appropriate the power with which to do it.

> You have the capacity to do anything and everything God intends for you to do.

As John Phillips put it, "Christ, living His life in Paul, made all the difference. Paul commended this secret to his friends in Philippi and to us wherever we are today."[55] As an elected servant in your church, you, like Paul, have the capacity to do anything and everything God intends for you to do. You do not do it in your own strength. You do it by the infilling and enablement of the Holy Spirit in you. Stephen Curtis Chapman wrote a short chorus several years ago that states the truth of Philippians 4:13:

> His strength is perfect when our strength is gone;
> He'll carry us when we can't carry on.
> Raised in His power, the weak become strong;
> His strength is perfect, His strength is perfect.[56]

The next time a task or mission is placed by God in front of you, would you be willing to accept it and enter into it with abandonment to the flesh? Rather than convincing yourself that you can't do it, would you pray for God to so transform your mind that you can and will do it? God will never give you an assignment of any kind without giving you the spiritual, mental, emotional, and physical strength to carry it out. You really are "able to do all things through Him who strengthens you." So, go for it!

> Dear Lord, I know You have, by Your Spirit, enabled me to do everything You intend for me to do in service to Your church. Please remind me of this each time a task or assignment is given to me—even in the task before me today.

Week 22 — **Day 1**

A Deacon Who Has Done Well

Philippians 4:14

"You did well by sharing with me in my hardship."

Paul expressed his sincere appreciation to the Deacons and others in the Philippian church who had sent a generous gift to him at Rome (4:15). He states clearly that they had done well by sharing with him as they had. Notice what they did, they did well. Many times in today's church we think about how little we can give, how little we can get by on, or how little we can pay the Pastor. Though Paul was more than willing to live on little, the church at Philippi and particularly the Deacons in that church, saw to it that "he received everything in full and had an abundance" (4:18). Thus, Paul commended them for doing well by him.

John Phillips highlights a very special character quality in Paul that should be true of Pastors and Deacons in many contemporary churches:

> Under normal conditions when funds dried up, Paul had a simple remedy: work! Paul scorned the idea of sending out urgent appeals for money. He went back to making tents. He did not stop his soul-winning, church planting, and disciple-training activities; he simply added secular work to his evangelistic activities.[57]

The Deacons saw to it that "he received everything in full and had an abundance."

Some Pastors are bi-vocational. That is, they pastor a church as well as work at a second job to help pay their expenses. Most Deacons are fully employed by a company apart from the church. This only gives them greater resources to share with others—especially Pastors, missionaries, chaplains, etc. It also provides financial support for the mission and ministries of their churches. Do well by your Pastor and staff!

Dear Lord, please provide for me in such a way that I might do well in sharing with others who are more intricately involved in ministry than I. Help me know of the hardship of other servants, and let me be a blessing to them, however You see fit.

A Deacon Supporting Missions

Philippians 4:15-16

"When I left Macedonia, no church shared with me in the matter of giving and receiving except you alone."

Though the missionary had established churches in Philippi, Berea (Macedonia or northern Greece), and Thessalonica, when he moved to Athens and Corinth (southern Greece), he found himself in great need for food and shelter. Of course, he also had need of some resources to pay other ministry expenses. Paul would willingly have starved to death for the cause of Christ, but he was glad that the Philippian aid came when it did. It seems the Deacons and other servants in the church were unusually conscientious of the need for mission support. They would have had to track Paul's journey and ministry by receiving periodic reports to know where he was, what he was doing, and what resources he needed.

Likewise, Pastors, Deacons, and others in today's church—even your church—should conscientiously support missionaries. There are many from our churches who are called of God and commissioned by the church (sometimes through a denominational agency like the International Mission Board [IMB] of the Southern Baptist Convention) to leave their "Macedonia" and travel to their "Athens." In so doing, they may find themselves in great need of support.

> Pastors, Deacons, and others in today's church should conscientiously support missionaries.

As a Deacon in your church, you will want to help your congregation to regularly identify, track, and support these missionaries. Most Southern Baptist churches will do this through Cooperative Program Mission Support and the IMB. You can play a vital role in promoting this mission support in your church. Follow the admonition of Charles Gabriel, "We have heard the Macedonian call today, and a golden offering at the cross we lay, Send the light!"[58]

Dear Lord, allow me to see missions and missionaries from Your vantage point. Enable me to promote, support, and participate in missions through my church.

A Deacon Growing His Eternal Account
Philippians 4:17

"Not that I seek the gift, but I seek the fruit that is increasing in your account."

Though Paul was very appreciative of the gift sent to him by the Philippian church, he was much more interested in the investment in souls made by this church. The money sent to the missionaries is not merely so they will have food and shelter. It is so they will have the strength to win souls, make disciples, plant churches, and fulfill the Great Commission. The "*fruit*" mentioned by Paul was undoubtedly the fruit of converts (cf. Rom. 1:13). He knew that mission support had come to him for a bigger purpose than mere life sustenance. The support was for the advancement of the Kingdom of God.

> Your mission offerings are resulting in an accumulation of souls that will be eternally saved.

There is a sense in which your mission giving is seen by God as "increasing your account." That is, your offerings to missions are resulting in an accumulation of souls that will be eternally saved as a result. This does not mean that we give so we can brag to others about the size of our account. But it does mean that we can humbly "store up for ourselves treasures in heaven . . ." (Matt. 6:20). The Word of God and the souls of men are the only two things that will be treasured in heaven. Thus, our investment here and now must be in those things that will be there then. It would be very wise if we were to make more and larger deposits.

There is also a sense in which you will give an accounting of your mission support when you stand before Jesus. The noun here translated *account* is the word that means "a word or saying." It carries the idea of "an account which one gives by word of mouth."[59] You may never be asked by your church how much you gave to missions. But you will declare it before the Lord one day.

So, give faithfully to missions through your church—not just because the missionaries need the money but because you need to grow your eternal account.

Dear Lord, I pray that You will enable me to give sacrificially to the work of missions at home and abroad. Help me to always see my offerings as given to You for Your use in world evangelism.

A Deacon Giving an Abundance
Philippians 4:18

"I have received everything in full, and I have an abundance . . ."

The offering Epaphroditus delivered to Paul on behalf of the Philippian church was more than expected and even more than needed at the time. The generosity of the Deacons and others was a gift that not only supplied the needs of the missionary, but it also pleased God. They must have made the assumption it would be better to give too much than too little.

In the book of Exodus, chapter 36, we read of the people of God bringing their contributions to Moses for the construction of the tabernacle. In verse 5 it says, "The people are bringing much more than enough for the work." And then in verses 6 and 7, an amazing thing happened, "The people were restrained from bringing anymore. For the material they had was sufficient and more than enough for all the work, to perform it." Do you know of any time in your church when the congregation was restrained from giving because they had given more than was needed?

> Their generosity not only supplied the needs of the missionary but it also pleased God.

This was apparently the attitude of the Philippian church. They knew they could never out give God, so they gave an abundant offering, a welcomed sacrifice, pleasing to God. With this sacrificial mission offering, Paul was able to bring the gospel to Athens, Corinth, and southern Greece and then complete his second missionary journey. The following is a paraphrase of a statement once heard in a sermon, which emphasizes the point of Philippians 4:18:

> Your money can make you an overseas missionary without ever leaving your home town, an evangelist without ever mounting a platform, a broadcaster without ever entering a studio, a Bible teacher without ever writing a book. All you have to do with your money is give it away.

Dear Lord, I pray that You will make of me a generous giver, that the Pastor and staff and all the missionaries will have more than enough for their work.

A Deacon's Source of Provision
Philippians 4:19a

"My God will supply all your needs . . ."

This one verse (19) is filled with multiple truths having to do with God's provision for this generous church. In essence, Paul says, "Because you have obeyed God and provided an abundance for mission causes, God will multiply it back to you out of His inexhaustible resources." Think of this verse in terms of the *source* of your provision, the *supply* for your provision, the *scope* of your provision, and the *Savior* who has provided for you.

The Creator God of the entire universe is our ultimate source of provision. The Bible says, "Every generous act and every perfect gift is from above, coming down from the Father of lights; with Him there is no variation or shadow cast by turning" (James 1:17). This verse (4:19) begins "And my God . . ." These words speak volumes about God being both a personal source (my) and a powerful source (God). The Bible speaks with reference to us as God's people, "I will be their God and they shall be my people" (2 Cor. 6:16). He is a personal God who identifies your personal need and provides for that need personally. The name used here for God is *THEOS*, which is the name for the Creator-God (cf. Gen. 1:1). It only stands to reason if He created the world and all that is in it, then He is powerful enough to supply all of your needs.

> The Creator God of all the universe is our ultimate source of provision.

So, you have both a personal and powerful source for all the provision you will ever need for life and service. You need not turn to any other for your provision. You have a source who has your personal welfare and well-being constantly on His mind. He is an inexhaustible source able to meet every one of your needs. He is your God. You are His servant. You can trust and depend on Him without reservation.

Dear Lord, please help me see You and You alone as my ultimate source. By Your Spirit, illumine my mind to understand Your provision. Help me to trust in You alone for all my needs.

A Deacon's Supply for Ministry
Philippians 4:19b

"And my God will supply all your needs . . ."

The word used here by Paul for *supply* means "to fulfill or complete," the idea being, "God will fully and completely supply 'all your needs.'" The word is used two other times in Philippians. In 1:19 it refers to the "provision" of the Spirit of Jesus Christ. In 2:30 it refers to Epaphroditus risking his life to "complete" what was deficient in the church's service to Paul.

Clearly, Pastor Paul is saying to the Deacons at Philippi, "God will fully and completely supply every need you have for finishing your work of service." When the other words, "according to His riches in glory," are attached to the verb "will supply," we see both the absolute supply of God and the abundant supply of God. It is absolute in the sense that "God will" supply it. It is abundant in the sense that it comes out of "His riches in glory" . . . a limitless supply.

> The same Lord provides, from the same source, each and every thing you need for your life and for your ministry.

Jesus said, "Seek first the kingdom of God and His righteousness, and all these things [i.e., basic life necessities] will be provided for you" (Matt. 6:33). The same Lord provides, from the same source, each and every thing you need for your life and for your ministry. God does not lack supply. If we do, it may be because we have depended on what man alone can provide or because we are serving in a way that is outside of God's will for us. God provides for the ministry He orders. He may not provide for ministry that we order. But He will fully and abundantly and faithfully supply each and every need you have for your personal life sustenance and life service.

Dear Lord, please increase my faith so I may enter only those works You intend for me to do and for which You intend to provide. And help me to trust You for supplies that I may not be able to see beforehand.

A Deacon's Personal Needs

Philippians 4:19c

"God will supply all your needs . . ."

What needs might Paul have been referring to with this statement? We may assume from the overriding theme of this epistle that the Deacons at Philippi needed a new joy in their lives. Forms of the noun joy and the verb rejoice occur fifteen times in this short letter. Of all Paul's letters, this one most extensively defines and describes joy. Of course, for genuine joy to characterize our lives, other needs must be met.

> We need a personal and intimate knowledge of Christ that includes His person, His power, His pain, and His plan.

As with the Philippian Deacons, we need God's righteousness (1:11; 3:9) not only imputed to us in our salvation but also exhibited in our daily lives. We need genuine humility like that of Christ depicted in 2:5-11. We need to develop a sincere heart of gratitude for Christ, His people (the Church), His Word, and His great grace. We need a personal and intimate knowledge of Christ that includes His person, His power, His pain, and His plan (3:10-11). We need a fortitude and tenacity to press on in the service of Christ in spite of obvious opposition and setbacks (3:12-21). We need to live daily in the peace and contentment that only Christ can give us (4:10-13). We need to trust God and God alone to provide for both our personal and ministry needs (4:15-19). In short, we need a personal, consistent, intimate, genuine relationship with Christ.

To what extent do you experience the joy of Jesus in your own life? Would your wife or children or grandchildren describe you as a person who is filled with joy? How well are you applying God's Word for the needs described in this letter? What adjustments do you need to make in order to begin—or continue to live in His joy? And what is it that you really have need of that God has not supplied?

> **Dear Lord, I acknowledge that one of my greatest needs is Your joy and the peace of mind and heart that come with that. Please show me how to adjust my thinking as well as my actions in order to live and serve with Your joy.**

A Deacon Bringing Glory to God
Philippians 4:20

"Now to our God and Father be glory forever and ever."

Nelson's Bible Dictionary defines the term *glory* as:

> Beauty, power, or honour; a quality of God's character that emphasizes His greatness and authority. The word is used in three senses in the Bible: (1) God's moral beauty and perfection of character, (2) God's moral beauty and perfection as visible presence, and (3) the honor and audible praise which God's creatures give Him.[60]

In this verse at the end of Philippians, Paul seems to be using the word in this third sense but with a clear understanding of all the senses.

Pastor Paul uses "our God" to reiterate the personal nature of God and the personal relationship that he had—and that we can have—with God. Our God is Jehovah, the I AM GOD who is to us and for us everything we need Him to be. Our God is "Father," the intimate, personal, relational God and Father of our Lord Jesus Christ. Likewise, He is heavenly Father God to each and every one of His born-again children. To you, a child of God who has been born again into His family, He is your heavenly Father.

> All creation and all created things exist for the glory of God.

We also notice in this phrase the apostle says this glory, honor, majesty, greatness, and absolute authority is to be attributed to God alone "forever and ever." There has never been a time in eternity past nor will there ever be a time in eternity future when our God will not receive glory. All of creation and all created things that have ever existed or will ever exist are for the glory of God.

The well-known hymn writer, Fanny Crosby, blind from childhood, captured this text beautifully:

> To God be the glory great things He hath done;
> So loved He the world that He gave us His Son.
> Who yielded His life an atonement for sin.
> And opened the life-gate that all may go in.[61]

**Dear Lord, please empower me by Your Spirit
to bring glory and honor to You.**

A Deacon "Greeting the Saints"
Philippians 4:21-22

"Greet every saint in Christ Jesus. The brothers who are with me greet you."

Webster's Dictionary defines *greet* "to address in a friendly and respectful way: welcome."[62] The Greek word used here was used for a military salute as well as a salutation to begin a letter or speech. What was Paul saying when he encouraged his fellow servants at Philippi to "greet the saints"? We must remember that Paul was writing this letter from a prison cell in Rome. He sent the letter to the church and particularly to the Deacons by Epaphroditus, who may have been a Deacon himself. In this statement, Paul is asking the leaders in the church to bring greetings to the Philippian church in his behalf.

In some of Paul's letters, he actually names several saints to whom he sends greetings (cf. Col. 4:10-18). And he often sends written greetings from the saints at his current ministry location. Though this was a common thing, even as it is today, the thing that made it special for Paul and the church was that the greeting was "in Christ Jesus." It is one thing to greet another person on the street or in a crowd. But it is quite another thing to greet a fellow follower of Christ in the context of the local church.

> A greeting to the saints in Christ Jesus carries with it a unique love, affection, commonality, and kinship.

A greeting to the saints in Christ Jesus carries with it a unique love, affection, commonality, and kinship. We are often overjoyed when we see a fellow believer after being separated for a long while. We may even hug a brother as an expression of greeting because of our common bond in Christ. It is perfectly fitting and proper that we do this. After all, we are admonished to "love the brethren" (1 Jn. 3:14).

The next time you meet a fellow servant whom you've known and for whom you have prayed but from whom you have been separated for a long while, greet him with sincere love and enthusiasm. And make it a practice to greet fellow believers and welcome those who visit your church.

Dear Lord, please remind me regularly to greet other believers in Christian love.

A Deacon Whose Spirit Is Filled with Grace
Philippians 4:23

"The grace of the Lord Jesus Christ be with your spirit."

Pastor Paul is giving a blessing as it were to the Deacons and others in the Philippian church. In such a blessing, the apostle essentially says, "May the grace of the Lord be with you." It had become obvious by this time in his ministry that he could do nothing apart from the grace (unmerited favor) of God empowering his human spirit. The Spirit of God had borne witness to his spirit that he was a child of God (Rom. 8:16). His spirit had not only been regenerated (Titus 3:5) but infilled and empowered by God so that he could live and serve in a Christ-like manner.

> May the grace of the Lord be with you.

Another way of stating this blessing might be, "May the unmerited but manifold favor that has come to you in your reception and surrender to Jesus Christ as Lord be evident in your attitude and demeanor toward others." When your human spirit is filled with God's Holy Spirit, then your perspective changes greatly toward yourself, your church, and your community. You will "walk in a manner worthy of the Lord, to please Him in all respects" (Col. 1:10). But you will also walk "not as unwise men but as wise, making the most of your time, because the days are evil" (Eph. 5:15-16).

Julia H. Johnston penned these words, which we have come to love when we think of the grace of the Lord Jesus:

> Grace, grace, God's grace,
> Grace that will pardon and cleanse within;
> Grace, grace, God's grace,
> Grace that is greater than all our sin.[63]

With your spirit filled with the Spirit of God and with God's great grace keeping you clean and ready, you can serve Him and His church all the days of your life. Serving well as a Deacon, you will obtain for yourself a high standing and great confidence in the faith that is in Christ Jesus (1 Tim. 3:13).

> **Dear Lord, thank You for Your free and unmerited gift of grace in my life. I humbly accept Your blessing of grace and pray that I may always serve with Your favor.**

The Deacon's Relational Characteristics

A Deacon's Respect for Others
Leviticus 19:11

"You must not act deceptively or lie to one another."

A favorite verse in the New Testament for many is Matthew 7:12, "Therefore, whatever you want others to do for you, do also the same for them . . ." This is commonly referred to as the Golden Rule. It is not likely that you would want someone else to disrespect you by deceiving you or lying to you. Nor should you disrespect others. Even if a person is an unbeliever who may not want anything to do with you or your God, he still deserves your respect as another human being. You don't have to agree with everything (or anything) a person may say about you, God, the Bible, or church in order to show respect toward him. You can be polite and courteous to others with whom you may disagree.

> As a Deacon in a local church, you are to "consider others as more important than yourself."

In fact, Jesus instructs us to "love your enemies, do good to those who mistreat you" (Lk. 6:27). The apostle Paul told the church at Rome, "Do not repay anyone evil for evil. Try to do what is honorable in everyone's eyes" (Rom. 12:17). As you pay respect to others, they will usually pay respect to you in return. But even if they don't, you are still obligated to respect others and show genuine Christian love toward them.

Respect is especially important among fellow believers in the church. As a Deacon in a local church, you are to "consider others as more important than yourself" (Phil. 2:3). What are you currently doing to show respect for others? Are your prayers sincere? Are your thoughts above reproach? Are your words encouraging? Are you complimentary of others? Do your actions match your words? Your respect of others may lead them to respect you, and it may also lead them to have a greater respect for God and His Word.

Dear Lord, please help me to have genuine respect and consideration for others, knowing that they, too, need Your great grace and forgiveness.

A Deacon's Compassion for Others
Zechariah 7:9

"Show faithful love and compassion to one another."

You probably have heard the familiar saying, "Others will not care how much you know until they know how much you care." This could not be truer than with the servants of God in a local community. Most Deacons in a church usually have established a fairly solid belief in Christ, the Bible, the Church, and the Christian life. Many are very interested in sharing what they believe with others. This is certainly what Jesus commissioned us to do. How effective we are at sharing our faith hinges on how effective we are at living our faith.

The apostle John wrote, "Little children, we must not love in word or speech, but in deed and truth" (1 Jn. 3:18). Genuine concern for others is observed in what we do long before we say anything.

> When did you last find yourself so moved by the pain and suffering of someone else that it brought you to tears?

Compassion is what makes a person feel pain when somebody else hurts. When Jesus walked on this earth, He spent much of His ministry watching and listening to the pain and sufferings of others. And then He would act out His compassion in service. Whether it was toward a large people group that was starving (Matt. 15:32), two blind men who needed healing (Matt. 20:34), a lone leper who was an outcast from society (Matt. 1:41), or a widow whose son had died (Lk. 7:13), Jesus was always moved with compassion. Their pain became His so much so that He gave of His time, energy, influence, and resources to help them. His first reaction to their pain was His service.

When did you last find yourself so moved by the pain and suffering of someone else that it brought you to tears? And when you felt such strong emotion, did you seriously look for a way in which you could serve the needs of another?

> Dear Lord, by Your Holy Spirit, please produce a Christlike compassion in my heart for others in need. Then enlighten and empower me to serve their needs.

A Deacon as a Peacemaker
Mark 9:50

"Be at peace with one another."

In the early church, one of the reasons for the selection and election of the first Deacons was so they might restore peace. Acts 6:1 says, "There arose a complaint by the Hellenistic Jews against the Hebraic Jews that their widows were being overlooked in the daily distribution." There was a great need for resolution and peace within the body. So the apostles led the congregation to select seven godly men who would perform the service needed to bring peace. Among other important assignments, these early Deacons became peacemakers.

> Jesus intends for the entire church in which you serve to live alongside one another in a bond of love and peace.

Jesus intends for all the members of the church in which you serve to live alongside one another in a bond of love and peace. Just before His crucifixion and resurrection, knowing that He would soon be back in heaven with His Father, Jesus said to His disciples, "Peace I leave with you. My peace I give to you" (Jn. 14:27). You are serving in a role that includes keeping the peace . . . in your heart, in your family, in your church, and in the larger Christian community.

A. W. Pink, scholar and preacher of the last century, said, "Few things more adorn and beautify a Christian profession than exercising and manifesting the spirit of peace."[1] You can have this kind of peacemaking ministry. Most of the time it will not require many words at all. You may simply need to show up and act to fill a certain need. Your service alone will often settle emotions and prompt reconciliation. Never underestimate how God may use you to bring His peace to the heart of another. You need only to be spiritually prepared and practically available.

*Dear Lord, please help me know
how to maintain Your peace in my own life
and bring that same peace into the lives of others.*

A Deacon With a Servant's Heart
John 13:14

"So if I, your Lord and Teacher, have washed your feet,
you also ought to wash one another's feet."

In the context of John 13, Jesus is demonstrating His own servant's heart by gathering His disciples for the Last Supper. They sat around the table in the upper room with dusty, dirty feet. There had been no servant awaiting them at the door with a basin and towel.

> So [Jesus] got up from supper, laid aside His robe, took a towel, and tied it around Himself. Next, He poured water into a basin and began to wash His disciple's feet and to dry them with the towel tied around Him (Jn. 13:4-5).

In doing this, He demonstrated the kind of service we should render toward other believers. This is not to say that we should include an organized plan for "foot-washing services" or that we should assume this as a third ordinance in the church, along with baptism and the Lord's Supper. We should simply apply the principles of humble service toward each other day in and day out.

> If God has given you a servant's heart —a Deacon's heart— then serve you must.

It may be a job nobody else would ever do . . . or ever think to do. You may be prompted to clean a floor, take out trash, aid a handicapped worshiper, or help a sick child. You may find yourself surrounded by rather self-focused people whose pride would resist your service. Apparently Jesus was (Jn. 13:8). But if God has given you a servant's heart—a Deacon's heart—then serve you must. Know in your heart that Jesus "did not come to be served, but to serve and to give His life a ransom for many" (Mk. 10:45). Thus, you also have come to your present place of ministry not to be served but to serve and to give your life "washing dirty, dusty, stinky feet," as it were.

> Dear Lord, thank You for Your beautiful example of servanthood when You washed the disciples' feet. Please help me to be a sensitive servant among my fellow church members even as You were among the Twelve.

A Deacon Who Genuinely Loves Others
John 13:35

> "By this all people will know that you are My disciples, if you have love for one another."

It is often said among church members who know each other fairly well, "We have such a loving church!" From their perspective, they really do feel that way. But in this context, Jesus was not saying that the church members' love for one another is only evaluated by one another. He said our love for one another is evaluated by "all people." Though our love for one another does demonstrate a sincerity in the church, we must also ask, "How do those outside the church view us?" Are they able to observe genuine Christian love to the degree that it is obvious we are His disciples?

Unfortunately, in some churches there is more strife, disagreement, disrespect, conflict, and carnality than genuine love. In observing such churches, the unbelieving world rightly assumes that we are not faithful followers of Christ at all. In fact, to many outsiders we are only hypocritical churchgoers who believe, live, act, dress, talk, and conduct our business in pretty much the same way they do. To them, the only difference is we go to church and they don't.

> Unfortunately, in some churches there is more strife, disagreement, disrespect, conflict, and carnality than genuine love.

The Savior had many negative things to say about hypocritical, pretentious religious leaders in His day, referring to them on one occasion as a "Brood of vipers" (Matt. 3:7). He expects a much different reflection of Himself from you. He wants you, as His servant in the church, to know and exercise genuine Christian love for others. When you do, you will not only be observed by unbelievers as being a true disciple of Christ, but you will also become the recipient of God's love (cf. Jn. 14:21).

> Dear Lord, I pray that You will produce Your own love in me and demonstrate it through me. Help me resist the temptation to muster my own kind of love instead of allowing Your love to flow through me.

WEEK 25 — DAY 1

A Deacon Who Shows Affection Toward Others
Romans 12:10

"Show family affection to one another with brotherly love."

The city of Philadelphia, Pennsylvania, was named after two Greek words. One word is *phileo,* meaning love and the other is *adelphos,* meaning brother. Thus, it is "the city of brotherly love." This is the same construction used in this text to refer to the kind of family affection believers are to have toward one another. It is different from the God-like love produced by His Spirit (Gal. 5:22) in us, yet it is intended to be an extension of His love borne out in our hearts toward others (cf. Rom. 5:5).

The Great Commandment given us by Jesus is, "Love the Lord your God with all your heart, with all your soul, and with all your mind [and] . . . Love your neighbor as yourself" (Matt. 22:37-39). It only stands to reason that the apostle Paul would charge us to show this love to one another. Not only should your fellow church members and other Deacons be the recipients of God's love, but they should also receive your love. They should become some of your very closest friends.

> It is possible for us to have a greater affection for another believer than even our own blood-related family.

It is quite possible for us to have a greater affection for another believer than even our own blood-related family members. This is most likely when your family member is not a believer. As a Deacon in your church, you should love your fellow servants with a God-honoring tenderness and fondness that only His Spirit can produce. You may find it quite encouraging to receive a big hug or a kind pat on the back. You may give or receive this brotherly love by participating in sports, traveling together, or just studying together. Look for such opportunities to show family affection to one another. After all, you are in the same family.

Dear Lord, I pray that You will show me how to express Christlike affection toward my fellow church members. Help me to bring honor to You with the highest of integrity in my relationships.

A Deacon Who Agrees with Others
Romans 12:16

"Be in agreement with one another . . ."

To *be in agreement* in this context means to "be of the same mind toward one another." In 15:5 of this epistle, the apostle amplifies the thought. "Now may the God who gives perseverance and encouragement grant you to be of the same mind with one another according to Christ Jesus." We are not expected to agree on every imaginable subject or interest, but we are expected to agree with the Bible and develop the "mind of Christ" within our own minds (cf. 1 Cor. 2:16). We are expected to agree with Christ.

The key to believers agreeing with each other is in each believer agreeing with Christ. Someone once said of the Bible, "God said it, I believe it and that settles it!" To this statement someone else added, "God said it and that settles it, whether you believe it or not." If God's Word is, in fact, settled in heaven (Ps. 119:89) and we have committed ourselves to it, then we'll have no trouble agreeing with those who agree with Him.

> The key to believers agreeing with each other is in each believer agreeing with Christ.

But what about having an understanding attitude toward those who disagree with you? Can you disagree agreeably? Or agree to disagree? The answer is *yes!* However, we must never compromise our core values in order to merely get along. You can have deep convictions about certain things, and you should. You may never agree with those who disagree with those things. But remember the further words of Paul to young Pastor Timothy, "If anyone advocates a different doctrine and does not agree with sound words, those of our Lord Jesus Christ . . . he is conceited and understands nothing" (1 Tim. 6:3-4, NASB).

Genuine love agrees to disagree, but genuine love never gives in to deceit. Within the church, you should be ready to agree with those who agree with God's Word and graciously disagree with those who don't.

Dear Lord, allow me to know those things with which I can agree and let me learn how to disagree agreeably.

A Deacon Who Compliments Others

Romans 14:13

"Let us no longer criticize one another."

Here Paul is speaking of the believer's responsibility to be slow to criticize another believer just because he sees certain practices differently. Charles Ryrie, in his Study Bible notes, says of this verse:

> The stronger Christian who allows himself certain liberties must be careful that his lifestyle does not place a stumbling block (something that leads to sin) or an obstacle (something to trip over in the Christian walk) in the path of another believer.[2]

> Rather than be critical of another believer's perspective and assume your perspective to be right, be complimentary.

You may think you have a right to act a certain way or freely practice a certain thing because you are living under grace and not law. In some things, you may be right. But that doesn't mean you should always feel free to do so. What you think is okay for you to do or okay for you to wear or okay for you to say may be the very thing that will prohibit someone else from wanting to follow Christ. You may become a stumbling block to someone and not even realize it.

Rather than be critical of another believer's perspective and assume your perspective to be right, be complimentary. Express appreciation to your brother for his willingness to share his perspective. Allow God the complete freedom He deserves to work in the hearts of others and in your own heart. You will usually be received much better by merely sharing your perspective in love than by criticizing your fellow believer's position. So determine in your mind and heart that you will criticize less and compliment more.

> Dear Lord, please enable me to understand my liberty in Christ and rest in Your grace while I also give consideration to a spiritually weaker brother.

A Deacon Who Is Accepting of Others
Romans 15:7

"Accept one another, just as the Messiah also accepted you."

Hardly anything is harder to experience than rejection. Perhaps you have experienced this in your own life. Many of us had a difficult time growing up because we felt rejected as a child. Teenagers often feel rejected by their parents, their siblings, their teachers, or their friends. Unfortunately, many people don't come to church because they feel rejected by church members.

> We as servant leaders in the church should accept one another in the same way Jesus has accepted us.

In this verse, the apostle is appealing to us to accept others just as Christ accepted us. We often accept people who look like us, sound like us, think like us, and live like we live. We tend to shun, if not outright reject, those we perceive to be different from us. Jesus accepted us into His family even while we were still sinners and looked nothing like Him (cf. Rom. 5:8). In the church, it is essential that all of us, but especially Pastors and Deacons, follow Jesus's example.

This is not to say that God never rejects us, because apart from repentance of sins and a personal surrender of our lives to Jesus Christ, ultimately He will (cf. Matt. 7:23). But it does mean that every believer is accepted by God and welcomed into the family of God. Therefore, we, as Deacons in the church, should accept one another in just the same way Jesus has accepted us. We cannot wait for them to measure up to our standards or expectations before we accept them. We cannot hold back our genuine love and consideration just because we think they have not yet deserved our acceptance. We love and accept each other in spite of our weaknesses. Let this be the pattern of your life and service for Christ.

> Dear Lord, please help me better understand Your acceptance of me as Your child. And help me to show by my words, attitude and actions that I truly accept others as my brothers and sisters in Christ.

A Deacon Who Gives and Receives Instruction

Romans 15:14

"You are able to instruct one another."

The word here for *instruct* is also translated *admonish,* which carries the idea of imparting positive truth or sometimes warning. This may result in encouragement in what is right or correction for what is wrong. We are free in our relationship with other believers to warn them of sin's consequence in their lives. We are free to hold each other accountable before God and before the church (cf. Matt. 18:15-18).

As a Deacon, you may find yourself helping the Pastor carry out discipline in the church. You must be mature enough and spiritually minded enough to instruct or admonish others when called upon by God to do so. Of course, you will never be able to admonish others effectively unless you have personally experienced the admonition of God. We can only give the instruction we have received.

> You will never be able to admonish others effectively unless you have personally experienced the admonition of God.

You have a special opportunity if you teach a Sunday school class or lead a small group in your church to instruct others. You will want to be as prepared as possible to do this. Spend much of your time gaining from the instruction of others more mature than yourself. Remember "All Scripture is . . . profitable for teaching, for reproof, for correction, for training in righteousness" (2 Tim. 3:16, NASB). When you instruct others by explaining and applying Scripture, you will render a great service to the body of Christ. Giving and receiving instruction is one of God's great blessings to His Church. Do it and do it well.

> Dear Lord, I ask that You instruct me. Admonish me in Your truth that I might live in obedience to Your Word and teach others also.

A Deacon Greeting Other Believers
Romans 16:16

"Greet one another with a holy kiss. All the churches of Christ send you greetings."

In twenty-first-century America, this verse sounds a little strange. However, in AD 58 in the Roman world of the early church, this was a customary greeting, especially between Christ-followers. It would be a little like a firm handshake between men and perhaps a gentle hug between women in the American church today.

This kind of greeting should never be given with improper motivation. It should not be done out of obligation or routine. It should be done out of sincerity and genuine love and appreciation for the other person. Sending and receiving greetings is something Deacons do with regularity. You may be a "greeter" at your church on Sundays. One of your jobs is to greet both regular members and newcomers to your worship services. The next time you greet someone at the door, be prepared to speak a word of encouragement. Rather than just handing out a bulletin, you could also provide a warm handshake and say, "Welcome, I hope you and your family have a blessed experience today!"

> **The next time you greet someone, be prepared to speak a word of encouragement.**

Pray and pick your own words. But greet others with sincerity, and let them know how much God loves them and how genuinely interested you are in them. In doing this, you will be rendering service to Christ and His church. What an opportunity! What a blessing!

Dear Lord, by Your Holy Spirit, please heighten my sensitivity to other believers so I might greet them with sincere appreciation and genuine Christian love.

A Deacon Who Patiently Waits on Others
1 Corinthians 11:33

"When you come together to eat, wait for one another."

This is a principle of servanthood that is beautifully illustrated in the Lord's Supper or Communion Service in the church. As a Pastor or Deacon, you very likely lead the church in the observance of this ordinance. There are so many deep truths illustrated in this observance that we usually miss this one: "Wait for one another!" It is more than mere courtesy. It is an illustration of considering others as more important than yourself (cf. Phil. 2:3). It shows a picture of oneness and unity. It also pictures the discipline to be exhibited by us when it comes to fleshly appetites. So, we normally distribute the elements of the Lord's Supper to each believer and once everyone is served, we then all eat or drink at the same time.

> "Patient waiting is the highest way of doing God's will."

Few Christians—even few Deacons—are gifted with patience. Not many of us, especially men, enjoy waiting on others. It seems easier to prefer ourselves above or ahead of others. That's why we jockey for position at the gas pumps, parking lots, checkout lanes, or food lines. Oh, we force ourselves to wait when we're at a church meeting or function, but deep in our hearts, we'd rather be first. Jeremy Collier said, "Patient waiting is often the highest way of doing God's will."[3]

So the next time you are tempted to step ahead of others or cut in some proverbial line, remember, as a servant of God, you must set a Christlike example. Take on the form of a bondservant and humbly wait on other believers. Then one day you, too, will be highly exalted with Him.

Dear Lord, please build Your patience into my life so I will more naturally wait on others and put their needs ahead of my own.

A Deacon Who Serves Out of Love

Galatians 5:13

"Serve one another through love."

This is a very often used "one another" verse in the Bible. Jesus said that all people will know whether or not we are Christians by the way we love—not primarily by the way we love them but by the way we love each other. Most men can join a civic club and participate in service projects. For that they will often be rewarded by other men. Some men join the church and participate in similar service projects out of obligation or maybe for some human recognition. It is obvious from this and many other passages of Scripture that God is more interested in our motivation for service than He is in the service itself.

Service grows out of love more than love grows out of service. Richard Braunstein said, "It is possible to give without loving, but it is impossible to love without giving."[4] Genuine love—the love of Christ—compels us to serve. As a Deacon in the church, you are an identified servant of others. Unless you have a genuine love for God and a sincere love for other believers (cf. Matt. 22:37-39), your motivation for service will wane over time. You will grow frustrated and may even want to resign. You may still be going through the motions of service, but you've lost your zeal. You have little or no passion to serve as you once did. You have left your first love.

> Service grows out of love more than love grows out of service.

Fortunately, this love that motivates us to serve is a product of the Holy Spirit who lives inside us. Confess your weaknesses. Acknowledge your need. Ask God to re-invigorate you with His love. He has promised to do so. Then His love in you and through you will demonstrate godly service to others.

Dear God, please restore the love that Your Spirit has placed in me. Move me from being dormant to serving vigorously through love.

A Deacon Who Shows Kindness to Others
Ephesians 4:32a

"Be kind and compassionate toward one another."

Every moment is the right one to be kind. And there are a thousand ways in which kindness can be expressed. The word used in this verse for *kind* carries with it the idea of serviceable, good or pleasant. When used of God, it refers to His "royal love and favor toward His people."[5] In the New Testament, the word relates to grace—the unmerited favor or kindness of God—by which we have been saved (cf. Eph. 2:8-10).

> We do not determine our kindness based on the merit or response of those to whom we may express it.

So, we are not to be kind to others just when, and if, they are kind to us. We do not determine our kindness based on the merit or response of those to whom we may express it. Actually, it is not a matter of others at all; it is a matter of kindness in us. Kindness only comes out when kindness is within. If kindness is in you by virtue of the Holy Spirit's fruit (cf. Gal. 5:22-23), then it follows that He will be kind to others through you. If His Spirit is not in you or if He is quenched, then kindness may not be expressed through you at all.

Compassion is what makes a person feel pain when somebody else hurts. How do you feel when you see a brother or sister dying before your very eyes? How do you feel when you witness a couple going through a messy divorce? Do you "rejoice with those who rejoice, and weep with those who weep" (Rom. 12:15, NASB)? Every believer, and especially Deacons, should be kind and compassionate toward one another.

As you walk in God's Spirit and allow Him to produce and reflect His own spiritual fruit in you, you will be more kind and compassionate than you ever thought you could.

Dear Lord, cause Your kindness, which is produced by Your Spirit who indwells me, to be evident in my daily service to others.

A Deacon Who Forgives Others

Ephesians 4:32b

"Forgive one another, just as God also forgave you in Christ."

The great preacher, D.L. Moody, said: "Those who say they will forgive but can't forget, simply bury the hatchet but leave the handle out for immediate use."[6]

Few would argue that there is a huge need in the church for forgiveness. No one is guiltless, and no one is exempt. We've all offended others and have been offended, and we've all felt anger and bitterness toward the one who offended us. The question is not "Will I be offended?" or "Will someone sin against me?" The question is, "How will I respond and what will I do about it?

> Deacons have a special role in the church that gives them the opportunity to not only teach the precept of forgiveness but to exemplify forgiveness.

Deacons have a special role in the church that gives them the opportunity to not only teach the precept of forgiveness but to also exemplify forgiveness. Perhaps you are dealing with your feelings toward a fellow believer who has offended you or one of your family members. You know he was clearly in the wrong even though he does not realize it. What will you do? Will you live in unforgiveness, waiting for him to say he's sorry? Will you let your feelings toward him adversely affect every other area of your life and service? Or will you take your unforgiveness to God and acknowledge your need to forgive—in your heart—before Him? You may or may not ever receive an apology. But that cannot prevent you from living and serving as a forgiven sinner. Sometimes reconciliation can happen because of our forgiveness, not because of an apology from another person.

**Dear God, thank You for forgiving all of my sins—
my offenses against You. Please help me to forgive
others just as You have forgiven me.**

A Deacon Who Sings With Others
Ephesians 5:19

"Speak to one another in psalms, hymns and spiritual songs."

We are encouraged in Scripture to sing praise to God. This verse indicates we are also to sing to one another. This does not mean we are to worship each other but that we are to encourage each other—in song—to worship God. Let's consider the hymn, "Let Him Have His Way with Thee" by Cyrus S. Nusbaum:

> Would you live for Jesus and be always pure and good?
> Would you walk with Him within the narrow road?
> Would you let Him bare your burden, carry all your load?
> Let Him have His way with Thee!
> His power can make you what you ought to be.
> His blood can cleanse your heart and make you free.
> His love can fill your soul and you will see
> 'Twas best for Him to have His way with thee.[7]

There are a large number of Deacons in the church today who have never sung that hymn. Some have never sung a chorus or hymn that was written to "speak to one another." You can and should sing with the church great praise choruses and other hymns to the Lord. But don't do that to the neglect of singing to one another. We all need these challenges and encouragements from each other.

> We sing praise to Him and sing truth to one another.

Consider such songs as *Brethren, We Have Met to Worship*, *Let Others See Jesus in You*, *Tell It Out With Gladness*, *There Is Power in the Blood*, or *We've a Story to Tell to the Nations*. We sing praises to Him and sing truth to one another.

Go to church this Sunday prepared to worship! And regardless of your vocal ability, you can certainly "make a joyful noise" unto the Lord. It may be one of your best opportunities to sing your testimony to others, challenging them to follow Christ more faithfully.

> Dear Lord, help me to live with and for You daily
> that I might have in my heart a song of praise
> to You and a song of truth for others.

A Deacon Who Submits to Biblical Authority

Ephesians 5:21

"Submit to one another in the fear of Christ."

God has established orders of authority within the institutions of family, church, government, and employment. These lines of authority are designed to mature us as Christians and bring peace and safety to the society.

In the family, there is specific authority entrusted to the man, and the wife is to willingly submit to his loving leadership (cf. 1 Cor. 11:3). In the church, there is specific authority entrusted to the Pastor(s). Other church members, including Deacons, are to submit to his godly and biblically based leadership. In the government, the president (or kings or heads of state) are in authority, and citizens are to respect and submit to that authority. Likewise, employers carry specific responsibility and authority toward their employees (cf. Eph. 5:22-6:9).

> We as Christians and servant-leaders in the church have a clear mandate to submit foremost to God.

Of course, we as Christians and servant leaders in the church have a clear mandate to submit foremost to God. This means we are willing to line up under His Word, obey His commands, and follow His leadership. But in the course of lining up under His Word, we find that He commands us to "submit to one another in the fear of Christ." Dr. Ryrie in his *Study Bible* says, "This subjection is to be mutual and based on reverence for God. The differing responsibilities, if followed, bring harmony, but, if ignored, they bring difficulties."[8]

Submission to God's established authorities in your life will not limit you but will instead free you to serve Him and His church with great peace. Purpose today to submit to God and to others. God will honor your obedience and reward you accordingly.

> Dear Lord, I pray that You will show me those persons of authority in my life to whom I should submit. Help me live in mutual submission to other believers around me.

A Deacon Who Believes and Tells the Truth
Colossians 3:9

"Do not lie to one another, since you have put off the old man with his practices."

According to the polls reported by *USA Today*, Americans lie—and are lied to—much more than we realize. Citing statistics from the book *The Day American Told the Truth*, the newspaper reported 91 percent of Americans lie routinely. It is hard to imagine, but a good number of that 91 percent are Christians. Some are even Pastors or Deacons in the churches. A rather literal rendering of Colossians 3:9 is "You are lying . . . stop it!" Apparently, as healthy as the Colossian church seemed to be, the apostle still was compelled to tell them to stop lying.

> A lie has become a common, tactical, strategic statement that puts the person making the statement in a favorable light.

One reason we do it and don't realize it is because we have changed the definition. A lie used to mean, "A false statement purposely put forward as truth: *falsehood*. Something meant to deceive or give a wrong impression."[9] It has become for many a common tactical, strategic statement that puts the person making the statement in a favorable light—something that "everyone does." Ignoring any absolute truth, we assume since everyone does it, it becomes acceptable. The question then becomes, "Who can tell the most consistent lies and get by with it?"

Church leaders, such as Pastors and Deacons, should daily "put off the old man with his practices." That is, we must consider ourselves dead to the sins of lying and deceit and alive to the truth (Jn. 17:17). Jesus is truth (Jn. 14:6). You can know the truth and tell the truth—and the truth will make you free (Jn. 3:32).

Dear Lord, since You know my every thought, please remind me in advance when I am about to lie. And enable me by Your Spirit to speak the truth.

WEEK 27 — **DAY 4**

A Deacon Who Admonishes Others
Colossians 3:16

"Teach and admonish one another in all wisdom."

You may be one of many Deacons in the church who also teaches a Bible study or Sunday school class. If so, you've been given a great gift and a great big responsibility. You have the opportunity to teach others what God has said and encourage them to learn what God would have them do. Of course, you must teach with the wisdom of God in your mind and on your tongue.

According to *Nelson's Dictionary,* wisdom is the "ability to judge correctly and to follow the best course of action, based on knowledge and understanding."[10] The first principle of biblical wisdom is that a man should humble himself before God in reverence and worship, obedient to His commands. Apart from God's Holy Spirit illuminating your human mind unto His Holy Word, you have no wisdom and nothing to teach.

By the end of his life, Dr. Oscar Loury, who once thought he could never remember a verse of Scripture, had learned over twenty thousand verses, and he could locate each by chapter and verse without his Bible. His life was full of joy, his mind full of wisdom, and his heart on fire for the souls of men. With such wisdom, he could effectively teach and admonish others. You can do this too. Hear, read, study, meditate, and memorize God's Word and you will have no trouble admonishing others.

> Of course, you must teach with the wisdom of God in your mind and on your tongue.

Most churches have those members who are gifted to teach and who are used greatly by God to pass on His wisdom to others. As a Deacon in your church, you may be one of those teachers. Or you may be one who helps identify such teachers and support them in their ministry. Either way, admonish one another!

Dear Lord, I ask that You would so control my mind that I might gain and maintain enough of Your wisdom to effectively teach Your Word.

A Deacon Who Encourages Others
1 Thessalonians 5:11

"Encourage one another and build each other up as you are already doing."

Encourage is a beautiful word. Webster defines it "to inspire with hope, courage, or confidence: *hearten*."[11] The word used in this text means "to urge forward, persuade, exhort or stimulate to the discharge of the ordinary duties of life."[12] One of the responsibilities you have as a Deacon is to encourage other believers. No doubt you have been the recipient of someone else's encouragement. You must assume the responsibility of encouraging others.

There are some practical ways you can encourage others. Pray for them and let them know you are. Communicate with them—listen carefully to what they say and ask good questions about their needs and only offer advice that you know to be scriptural. Compliment them regularly on their achievements. Become sensitive to tangible needs in their lives that God may use you to meet. Regularly introduce them to other believers whom you know to be encouragers. As you do these things, you will not only be an encouragement to someone else, but you will also find great encouragement for yourself by knowing you have helped another. The church should be a community of encouragement.

> One of the responsibilities you have as a Deacon is to encourage other believers.

As a servant of God's people, you can join the Barnabas group. His name literally means, "Son of Encouragement" (Acts 4:36). He was a great encouragement to Paul and later to John Mark and no doubt to hundreds of others. You can be too!

Even as you go through your day today or this next weekend, make a conscious effort to encourage someone—maybe your spouse, your children, your grandchildren, your neighbor, your fellow church member, your Pastor or staff, or another Deacon. Encourage someone soon. He or she may need it . . . and you need to give it.

> Dear Lord, please encourage my heart
> and use me to be an encouragement to others
> in my church and on my job.

WEEK 28 **DAY 1**

A DEACON WHO CARES ABOUT OTHERS
Hebrews 10:24

"Be concerned about one another in order to promote love and good works."

We are taught in God's Word to care about others. Numerous times in the Old Testament history of God's people, He showed His care for them. He cared when Adam hid himself in the Garden of Eden (Gen. 3:10). God cared when Cain killed Abel (Gen. 4:9ff). He cared when Noah and his family found grace in His sight (Gen. 6:8). He cared for His people by raising up a leader, Abraham (Gen. 12:1-4). He showed His care by providing the patriarchs, judges, kings, and prophets for His people.

Of course, there has never been a greater expression of care for God's people than when He sent His only Son to die on the cross for our sin (cf. 1 Pet. 3:18). Because He cares for us, we can cast all our cares on Him (cf. 1 Pet. 5:7). Being on the receiving end of God's care compels us to care for others.

As a Deacon in your church, personify care and service for all of God's people. Someone once said, "People won't care how much you know until they know how much you care." You probably have found this to be true in your own life. This would be a good time to seek God's compassion and concern not only for His people but for unbelievers too. Be genuinely concerned about others, and don't merely look out for yourself (cf. Phil. 2:3-4). They need you!

> Be genuinely concerned about others and don't merely look out for yourself.

When you meet a lost person, show him that you care about his salvation. When you visit sick or dying people, show them that you care about their recovery or their comfort. When you see a brother or sister in need of money or some other resource, show him or her you care by meeting that need. Others really do need you!

Dear Lord, help me to develop a sincere concern for those with whom I live and serve. Show me how to care like You do and how to help others care.

A Deacon Who Deals With Complaints
James 5:9

"Brothers, do not complain about one another."

Very early in the first-century church the apostles called upon the congregation of believers to select seven men to assist them in ministry. These seven became the prototypes of the first Deacons (cf. Acts 6:1-7). One of the big reasons these men were enlisted was to deal with complaints within the church. "As the number of the disciples was multiplying, there arose a complaint by the Hellenistic [Greek speaking] Jews against the Hebraic [Hebrew speaking] Jews that their widows were being overlooked in the daily distribution of food" (Acts 6:1).

Most men who serve as Deacons understand that part of their responsibility is to help keep peace in the family. In order to do this, a man must not be a complainer himself. We are all tempted to complain—that is "to express feelings of dissatisfaction, resentment, or pain."[13] Some churches have multiple complainers. These have a tendency to point their fingers and criticize the opinions and actions of others. Deacons are needed to intervene for peace and reconciliation, especially when the Pastor becomes a target for complainers. They are to be part of the solution, not contributing to the problem.

> Most men who serve as Deacons understand that part of their responsibility is to help keep peace in the family.

The next time a complaint arises and you hear about it, what will you do? Will you meet with the complainer, and from a scriptural and godly perspective, attempt to deal with it? You can, and you should. There will always be those who resist reproof or correction. But that should not prevent you from intervening and trying to bring resolution. In the process you can be a good example of how not to complain.

Dear Lord, when I am tempted to complain about someone or some activity in the church, please remind me of my responsibility. Help me to be a part of the solution and not contribute to the problem.

A Deacon Who Admits When He's Wrong

James 5:16

"Confess your sins to one another and pray for one another . . ."

Little teaching has happened in the church on the subject of confessing our sins to one another. And there is good reason for this. There may be a tendency in a testimony to pour out some details about our sin to others. But we have assumed that confessing our sins to God alone is usually enough. And so far as God's forgiveness is concerned, it is enough (cf. 1 Jn. 1:9). However, in order to receive the forgiveness of others or in order to forgive ourselves, we may need to literally confess some sins to one or more other believers.

> Concealed sin prevents us from experiencing blessings.

Proverbs 28:13 says, "He who conceals his sins will not prosper, but he who confesses and forsakes them will find compassion." Most Christians, especially Pastors and Deacons, want to prosper in ministry. That is, we want to gain the blessing of God on what we do. Concealed sin prevents us from experiencing these blessings. Confession of sin puts the soul under the blessing of God.

Don't be afraid to admit your sin. You don't have to use every service or class to do it. In fact, confession of sin to other people may be a rare occurrence in your life. But when God prompts you to do it and you know that it is the right thing to do, then do it. Mature believers who hear your confession will understand and pray for you. And God can use your humility to bring conviction and growth in the less mature. It's more than okay to admit when you're wrong; it is essential.

> Dear Lord, I again acknowledge my sin before You.
> I confess that I have sinned. Please show me the
> sins I must confess to You and especially
> those I may need to confess to others.

A Deacon Who Shows Hospitality to Others
1 Peter 4:9

"Be hospitable to one another without complaining."

To be *hospitable* is to be "cordial and generous to guests."[14] It is the practice of entertaining strangers graciously. In the New Testament, the Greek word translated as hospitality literally means "love to strangers."[15] This virtue is to be generally characteristic of all Christians and especially of Pastors and Deacons (cf. Ti. 1:8; 1 Tim. 3:2).

When W. A. Criswell was ten years old, a preacher came to their church to hold revival services. Anna Criswell, his mother, lodged and fed the evangelist, who took an interest in W. A. Rev. John Hicks led the lad to Christ. This happened as a result of the hospitality of Anna Criswell and her husband.[16] We never know when we express hospitality to someone what long-range impact it may have. W. A. Criswell became the most powerful Southern Baptist preacher of his generation. He spent over seventy-five years in gospel ministry, the last fifty years as Pastor of the First Baptist Church, Dallas, Texas.

As a Deacon, you, along with your wife, can show hospitality to others and allow God the use of your life to influence them for His kingdom. You may never know in this life the total impact you'll have. But if you don't show any hospitality, you'll have no impact at all by that means. Start by entertaining your Pastor and staff. Then expand your guest lists to Deacons, your Sunday school class, senior adults, or youth groups. And don't forget your family. They need your hospitality too! Be hospitable to others and don't complain. Ultimately, it will bring great joy to your life and great good to God's people.

> **Be hospitable to others and don't complain.**

Dear Lord, please show me ways that I can show hospitality to others around me, and develop in me a desire to do this so I won't see it as a burden.

A Deacon Who Is Humble Toward Others
1 Peter 5:5

"All of you clothe yourselves with humility toward one another . . ."

Humility is one of the most important virtues in the Christian life and certainly in the life of a Pastor or Deacon. It was the virtue in Jesus that resulted in His exaltation (cf. Phil. 2:7-9). It is a virtue that is desperately needed in the church today—especially among church leaders. *Humility* is "a freedom from arrogance that grows out of the recognition that all we have and are comes from God."[17] True humility does not produce pride but gratitude—gratitude to God, since He is our Creator and Redeemer. We owe our very existence to Him.

> **God thinks most of the man who thinks least of himself.**

To clothe ourselves in humility is just another way of saying we need to cover our lives with this virtue. We need to think, speak, and act in humility. Humility is akin to meekness. And meekness is not weakness. It is the power of God under the Holy Spirit's control. God thinks most of the man who thinks least of himself. A. Lindsay Glegg said, in humility:

> If there is one thing I would like to have said of me by those who are left behind when I have gone into the glory land, it would be just this—that the overflow hid the vessel![18]

Only from a life of humility will such a legacy result. Humility always precedes honor, and honor always follows genuine humility.

As a selected Deacon in your church, you can develop a life of humility. Keep your focus on God and His Word and daily place the needs of others ahead of your own. If you do that consistently and faithfully, you will exhibit a life of humility. Others will notice, and you won't have to convince them.

> *Dear Lord, please develop in me an attitude and heart of humility. Show me the selfish pride of my life and remove it from me. By Your Holy Spirit, clothe me with humility toward others.*

A Deacon Who Is a Friend to Others
1 John 1:7

*"If we walk in the light as He Himself is in the light,
we have fellowship with one another . . ."*

Ralph Waldo Emerson said, "The only way to have a friend is to be one."[19] God expects us to have friends and particularly Christian friends. We might modify Emerson's statement in light of the glorious gospel of Christ that has shined unto us (cf. 2 Cor. 4:4) and say, "The only way to have a Christian friend is to be a Christian friend." Genuine friendship grows out of genuine love. Jesus said, "Greater love has no one than this, that one lay down his life for his friends" (Jn. 15:13). Proverbs 17:17 says, "A friend loves at all times . . .

Christian friendships are made by God more than by us. It is God who has befriended us. It is God who loves us and loves through us. It is God who orders our steps to the persons who will be our close Christian friends on earth. It is God who matches kindred spirits so we have those with whom we can share true fellowship and friendship, as well as ministry.

> **Christian friendships are made by God more than by us.**

It may be a fellow Deacon, a Pastor, a colleague in ministry, a teacher, or an employer. God knows the friends you need and the friend you need to be. So, conduct your life and discipline your behavior in light of God's truth. And let Him show you over time those persons who will become your lifelong friends.

Today some of our churches still sing the world-famous hymn of John Fawcett:

> Blest be the tie that binds our hearts in Christian love. The fellowship
> of kindred minds is like to that above.[20]

You will become a friend to many, but you will become a kindred-friend with other Christians whom God will put into your life. Cherish them all your life! They are gifts from God.

**Dear Lord, show me how to be a friend. Place
in my life those whom You know need to be my
friends. And help me to love them all my life.**

The Deacon's Giftedness

A Deacon Who Supernaturally Proclaims Truth

Romans 12:6

"If prophecy, use it according to the standard of faith"

According to Scripture, every believer has been given one or more spiritual gifts (cf. 1 Cor. 12:11). There are hundreds of thousands of Deacons in American churches who teach the Bible to others. Many of these are lay-preachers as well. They proclaim the truths of Scripture in obedience to their call and their giftedness. A great many Pastors who preach the gospel multiple times a week were at one time Deacons in churches. They prayed and studied. They visited the sick and the lost. They attended to the bereaved and the poor. Then, with their faithfulness, God planted a call into their hearts to preach. And now they do. They do not preach to the neglect of their other ministries, but they have now added preaching and in many cases have become vocational Pastors.

> A great many Pastors were at one time Deacons in churches.

Henry Wilkinson said, "An ignorant minister is none of God's making, for God gives gifts where He gives a calling."[1] It may very well be that God is calling you at this stage in your life to preach. If so, you will know. God will make it known to you. If there is a shortage of preachers today, it is not because God has not been calling. More likely, it is because we have not been answering.

Of the seven chosen in Acts 6—originally as Deacons—at least two of them became preachers of the gospel. Stephen lost his life shortly after his first sermon (cf. Acts 6:8-7:60). Phillip became a preaching evangelist and actually baptized one of his converts (cf. Acts 8:26-40). Perhaps this would be a good time for you to listen very carefully to the still small voice of God in your heart and see if there is a call you've not yet answered.

Dear Lord, as Your servant, I want to be obedient to Your call and direction in my life. Please speak to my heart and help me to know what I should do.

WEEK 29 — DAY 3

A Deacon Who Supernaturally Serves Others

Romans 12:7

"If service, in service . . ."

The spiritual gift of serving or service is a blessed gift from God to His church. It stands to reason that almost all Deacons should have the spiritual gift of service. Acts 6:1 indicates clearly that the early church Deacons were chosen to help serve food to widows. They literally served tables. This gift is given in order for the church to effectively do what Jesus did. "For even the Son of Man did not come to be served, but to serve, and to give His life a ransom for many" (Mk. 10:45). We may not find ourselves merely serving tea and coffee at the church dinner. Our form of service has grown with the needs of God's people. There are numerous ways for today's Deacon to serve the church:

> There are numerous ways for today's Deacon to serve the church.

- Spend focused time in prayer regularly for your Pastor and the church.
- Open and close the building around worship and meeting times.
- Help people find parking, seating, nurseries, and restrooms.
- Network with others in visitation to the sick, the lost, the poor, and the needy.
- Be available to the Pastor and staff to assist them in their respective ministries.

These are just a few ways you can serve your church. You may be doing all of these and more. Be sure you serve for the right reason and with the right motivation. "Whatever you do, do your work heartily, as for the Lord rather than for men" (Col. 3:23).

> Dear Lord, I acknowledge that my primary role as a Deacon is to bring glory to You by serving other believers. Show me week-by-week what I should do to be a better servant in and through my church.

A Deacon Who Supernaturally Teaches Others

Romans 12:7

"If teaching, in teaching . . ."

The spiritual gift of teaching is the capacity to instruct students or impart knowledge and information. As seen in the New Testament, the concept of teaching usually means instruction in the faith. Teaching is distinguished from preaching or the proclamation of the gospel to the non-Christian world. Teaching in the Christian faith was validated by Jesus, who was called "teacher" more than anything else.

A very large number of Deacons are gifted to teach. They are often used to teach Bible study classes or lead discipleship groups. These gifted men find a great deal of satisfaction in exercising this gift. They love to see the light come on for those being taught.

Teaching may be something you do. If so, be diligent and take the responsibility seriously. James 3:1 says, "Let not many of you become teachers, my brethren, knowing that as such we will incur a stricter judgment." We must not decide from this verse that since we will be judged more strictly that we just won't teach at all. We must remember that if God has called us and gifted us to teach, we have no recourse—unless we wish to blatantly disobey God. The "stricter judgment" is not harsh punishment. It is an accounting of our discipline in preparation, delivery, application, and accuracy.

> **Consider your gift of teaching a wonderful gift from God.**

Consider your gift of teaching a wonderful gift from God. You will either love it or you never had it to begin with. It is God's gift to be discovered, developed, and used for His glory in the church. If you know you've been gifted to teach, then go for it!

Dear Lord, I ask that You would make clear to me whether I am gifted by You to teach. If so, empower me by Your Holy Spirit to do it well.

A Deacon Who Supernaturally Exhorts Others
Romans 12:8

"If exhorting, in exhortation . . ."

Exhortation is a message of warning or encouragement designed to motivate persons to action. The apostle Paul often exhorted his fellow Christians to live out their calling as ministers of the Lord Jesus and exercise this gift regularly in the church. There has never been a day when the people of God have needed exhortation any more than today. Pastors and Deacons are expected to lead the way for the congregation in delivering this gift to the larger body. Fred Catherwood has rightly pronounced, "The church should be a community of encouragement."[2]

> There has never been a day when the people of God have needed exhortation any more than today.

It only makes sense that what the church needs, God supplies. If it's preaching, He provides preachers. If it's serving, He provides servers. If it's teaching, He provides teachers. And if it's exhortation or encouragement, He provides exhorters. You may very well be gifted to exhort the church. You may find yourself regularly encouraging other believers and challenging them by precept and practice. You tell others what to do while at the same time show them what to do in order for them to faithfully live out their calling.

The legendary coach of Alabama's Crimson Tide, Bear Bryant, once said, "I'm just a plowhand from Arkansas, but I have learned to hold a team together. How to lift some men up, how to calm others down, until finally they've got one heartbeat together, a team. There are just three things I'd say to encourage them:

- If anything goes bad, I did it.
- If anything goes semi-good, then we did it.
- If anything goes real good, then you did it."

Dear Lord, I want to be an exhorter to those members of my church who need encouragement. I pray You will teach me how to exhort others to love and good works.

A Deacon Who Supernaturally Gives

Romans 12:8

"Of giving, with generosity . . ."

All believers are the recipients of God's great gift of salvation. No one has ever given more than God gave when He "spared not His own Son, but delivered Him over for us all" (Rom. 8:32). In our giving, we are not trying to somehow pay God back for His gift to us. Rather, we give out of a heart of love and gratefulness to God. We give to acknowledge God's complete provision for our lives.

The spiritual gift of giving is provided by God to those with whom He can trust His resources. It is a spiritual gift that exceeds the tithing and giving expected of all Christians. We seldom ever know who has this gift because they never want to be recognized or honored for their giving. Nevertheless, it is a gift sorely needed in the church today. Statistics show us that professing Christians give less than 2.5 percent, on average, of their incomes to the Lord's work.

Pastors and Deacons have an obligation to preach and teach about giving, and they need to model it as well. No man should even be considered for a pastorate or the deaconship if he's not a tither. J. Oswald Sanders once said, "The basic question is not how much of *our* money we should give to God, but how much of *God's* money we should keep for ourselves." John Wesley said, "Whenever I get any money I get rid of it as quickly as possible lest it find a place in my heart." Stephen Olford said, "God demands the tithe, deserves the offerings, defends the savings and directs the expenses."[4]

> The spiritual gift of giving is provided by God to those with whom He can trust His resources.

We all can and should tithe and give to the Lord's work through our church. Some among us are uniquely gifted to give much more. If you are gifted to give, then do so generously with a cheerful heart (2 Cor. 9:7). Allow God's Holy Spirit to show you how, where, when, and how much to give. You will be richly blessed for your faithfulness.

Dear Lord, I pray that You will place both a desire and a will in me to give as I should to Your work. Help me to generously give far above the tithe and help me to start this month.

A Deacon Who Supernaturally Leads

Romans 12:8

"Leading, with diligence . . ."

There is the mistaken notion among some well-meaning believers today that servanthood is not leadership and that the leadership is left to the Pastor or staff of the church. The greatest Leader who ever lived on this earth, one who has gained multiplied billions of followers, was the one who said, "The greatest among you shall be your servant" (Matt. 23:11). "For even the Son of Man did not come to be served, but to serve . . ." (Mk. 10:45). And because He was the humble, sacrificial Servant, He could say to His disciples, including all of us, "Follow Me, and I will make you fishers of men" (Matt. 4:19). He was the great "Servant-Leader" who calls upon us to follow His example.

> **Servants are attracted to leaders who also serve.**

Deacons are church officers who have the special opportunity to model Jesus's kind of leadership—leadership out of servanthood. Servants are attracted to leaders who also serve. When you step out first and take on the task and then invite others to join you, you are leading. When you show another person how to do a certain thing and then mentor him and encourage him to do it on his own, you are leading.

With leadership comes responsibility. If you lead a Sunday school class or department, you assume responsibility for your students. If you facilitate a small discipleship group, you are responsible for those you lead. If you lead a mission team, you are responsible for the outcome in the lives of the missionaries. Are you being directed by God to lead others in a certain area of ministry? Do you desire to do it? Do you will to do it? Then lead! The followers await.

Dear Lord, show me how to follow You so that I will know how to lead others. Help me to lead by service and set a good example for those who will follow my leadership.

A Deacon Who Supernaturally Shows Mercy
Romans 12:8

"Showing mercy, with cheerfulness."

Mercy is the aspect of God's love that causes Him to help the miserable. They may be miserable either because they have broken God's laws or because of circumstances beyond their control. In a more specific sense, mercy is God withholding His judgment and giving us ample time to repent of our sin and surrender our lives to Him. Likewise, when we show mercy, we postpone personal judgment as to why those needing mercy are in their predicament. We want to give them time to change.

As servants of God in His church, we must express sincere mercy to those who have broken God's law (i.e., disobeyed His commands) and those who are sick, blind, lame, or otherwise handicapped for no apparent reason. Since we have been shown the mercy of God when He saved us (cf. Ti. 3:5), we must all show mercy to other believers who are hurting.

This is a supernaturally endowed gift provided for many in the church so that those who are distressed and downcast will have a sympathizing Savior presented to them. You may be one of God's servants who has this gift. You see the hurts of others early. You speak words of encouragement to them regularly. You identify actions that can be taken to help them, and you work with others to take those measures. You care sincerely. You desire to help others in real tangible ways. Your heart goes out to the needy.

> Since we have been shown the mercy of God, we must show mercy.

We will always meet unmerciful people. It is our responsibility to show mercy, even when others show little or no mercy toward us. This is next to impossible unless the Holy Spirit is being allowed absolute freedom in us to exercise His own mercy (cf. Gal. 5:23-24). This is exactly what Jesus did when He showed mercy. This is showing mercy—with cheerfulness. How are you doing?

Dear Lord, I ask that You produce the virtue of mercy in me to others. If You have specially gifted me this way, let me excel in mercy, that You might receive glory for Yourself from my life.

The Deacon's Caregiving Ministries

A Deacon Who Listens Well

Proverbs 23:19

"Listen, my son, and be wise: keep your mind on the right cause."

A wise Deacon will listen as much or more than he speaks. It is important for you to listen to God, to other believers and lost people. Listening to God will give you the truth. Listening to other more mature believers will re-enforce the truth. Listening to unbelievers will give you insight into their need for the truth.

"When you are in distress and all things have come upon you (ever feel like that?) . . . you will return to the Lord your God and listen to His voice" (Deut. 4:30). It would be better if we listened to the voice of the Lord regularly—throughout every day. But when we don't and we come under stress and strain, we can return to our Bible and our prayer closets and listen to God. We need to listen well to God.

We also need to listen to other believers. Proverbs 11:14 says, "In an abundance of counselors there is victory." Undoubtedly, God has placed one or more persons in your life to whom you should listen carefully. One of them may be your wife. One of them may be your Pastor or another Deacon. It may simply be a very close friend. But you are wise to listen to good, godly counsel from other Christians.

> **Return to the Lord and listen to His voice.**

You may find listening to unbelievers a little more difficult. Most of them do not think like you or talk like you. But listening to them can be very revealing. Those conversations will help you better understand their great need for spiritual truth. You will need to discipline your hearing so you do not allow Satan an opportunity to plant impure or godless thoughts in your mind. Always be prepared "to make a defense to everyone who asks you to give an account for the hope that is in you, yet with gentleness and reverence" (1 Pet. 3:15). Listen well!

Dear Lord, thank You for speaking to me through Your Word, by Your Spirit, and through Your people. Please help me to be a good listener. Help me to listen with discernment so I may distinguish between truth and falsehood.

A Deacon Who Loves Sincerely
1 John 3:14

*"We know that we have passed from death to
life because we love our brothers."*

You may have wondered for yourself or for others, "How can I really know if I'm saved?" A superb answer can be found for this question in the Bible. Actually, there are many ways to know, but one excellent way is to evaluate your love and interest in the lives of other Christians. Have you noticed, since you were saved, a great desire to go to church, to be around other Christians, and to develop relationships with believers?

One of the evidences that we have been genuinely saved is that we genuinely love other Christians. There should be no doubt in the church but that you, as a Deacon, are truly saved. If you are developing true Christian love and friendship with other believers, the church will know that you are saved and that you desire to serve them in love. If, on the other hand, you have no affection for God's people, little compassion or concern for their welfare, or resistance to building close friendships, you may need to resign as a Deacon and "examine yourself to see if you are in the faith" at all (cf. 2 Cor. 13:5).

> **One of the evidences that we have been genuinely saved is that we genuinely love other Christians.**

Sincere love for others is not something that we muster or arbitrarily assume just because we are Deacons. This kind of love is God's love. It is a specific fruit of the Holy Spirit produced in you and through you for other people. God's Spirit only indwells true believers. Therefore, you will know you are saved if you love others with God's kind of love, and you will love others when you know you are saved.

A. W. Tozer said, "Perfect love knows no because."[1] Sincere love never loves to get. It always loves to give. It is the binding power that holds the body of the Christian church together. Is this the kind of love that is exhibited from your life?

> Dear Lord, I know I'm saved because You have given me a deep, sincere love for Your people. Help me to excel still more in Your love—and for Your glory.

WEEK 31 — DAY 1

A Deacon Helping Those With Uncertainty
1 Kings 17:12

> "I have only a handful of flour in the jar and a bit of oil in the jug. I am gathering a couple of sticks in order to prepare it for myself and my son so we can eat it and die."

The great prophet of God Elijah is a wonderful example of one who helped others through their uncertainty and hopelessness. This text shows us how we, as servants in the church today, can also help others with their uncertainties. There are many reasons for people to feel uncertain, scared, and hopeless. For example, thousands of single mothers are in this situation. If they were widowed, it would be expected that the church would help them. Such was the case with Elijah and this widow from Zarephath. But what about all those unwed and divorced mothers who are overwhelmed with uncertainty and hopelessness? That really complicates the ministry of the church and particularly the ministry of the Deacon.

> The best thing we can do for those dealing with severe uncertainty and hopelessness is to bring them to Jesus.

For the helpless mom who is in such a state, there is hope in Jesus. And those are more than just words. God, through the mouth of His servant, made a powerful appeal to this destitute single mother. First, He said, "Give me your bread and I will multiply it!" (17:11). Second, He said, "Give Me your son and I will resurrect him!" (17:19). Third, He said, in essence, "Give Me your trust and I will give you My help! (17:24). Essentially, He said, "Give Me your life, and I will give you Mine.

Obviously, the best thing we can do for those dealing with severe uncertainty and hopelessness is to bring them to Jesus. Once they know Him, they will, over time, begin to exchange their faithlessness for faith, their resistance for embrace, their hatred for love, their bitterness for forgiveness, and their very life for His. This is how you can help those dealing with uncertainty. God will show you how. You will need to simply obey Him and serve.

> Dear Lord, I desire to minister to those in need of certainty and hope. Please help me to live with faith and hope so that, through me, You can give faith and hope to them.

A Deacon Who Can Be Trusted
Proverbs 20:6

"Who can find a trustworthy man?"

Have you ever heard a Pastor say of one of his Deacons, "I can trust this man with my life . . . and my wife"? The indication, of course, is that the Pastor could not only trust the Deacon to die for him but also to live in purity and integrity with him. This is an example of a trustworthy man.

At the selection of the first-century Deacons, the apostles were looking for trustworthy men who were "of good reputation, full of the Spirit and wisdom," to whom they could entrust the ministry. (cf. Acts 6:3). They found seven such men and set them aside for that purpose. Because these men were available, the apostles could delegate specific ministry to them. When they did, "the Word of God kept on spreading . . ." (Acts 6:7).

> You must be a man of God whom God can trust.

This all sounds quite simple. However, God is the one who defines *trustworthy*. He is the one—and only one—who decides who is and who isn't trustworthy. To God, this means He knows exactly how we will think and what we will do with that which He entrusts to us, and He entrusts it to us still. God has entrusted His Son to us—what will we do with Jesus? God has entrusted His Spirit to us—how will we respond to His prompting? God has entrusted His Word to us—will we believe, receive, and apply His truth? God has entrusted His gospel to us—will we be faithful (trustworthy) to proclaim it to the nations?

As a Deacon in the church, you must be a man of God whom God can trust. Others you serve should view you as a trustworthy man.

> Dear Lord, though I feel woefully inadequate,
> I pray that You will build my character to conform
> with Yours. I pray that You will find me trustworthy
> for the ministry in which you have placed me.

A Deacon Helping Others Overcome Fear
Isaiah 41:10

"Do not fear, for I am with you; do not be afraid, for I am your God."

William Gurnall said, "The chains of love are stronger than the chains of fear. We fear men so much because we fear God so little."[2] Numerous times in both the Old and New Testaments, we are admonished not to fear. Yet, we do fear and some of us live in habitual fear.

Americans, in general, have a number of phobias or fears. There are those who don't drive for fear of having an accident. Some refuse to see a physician for fear their symptoms might mean they have cancer. Many breadwinners become workaholics for fear they will have too little money to pay their bills. Then there are those who have hidden fears of wars, violence, natural disasters, and innumerable conflicts with others.

> The only thing we can do to help others overcome their fears is to introduce them to Jesus.

You may need to do an honest assessment of your own life regarding your fears. Ask yourself what you obviously fear and then search a little deeper for fears that may be less obvious. Then, entrust your fears to the Lord, Who has promised to help you!

The only real, substantive thing we can do to help others overcome their fears is to introduce them to Jesus. Once His Holy Spirit resides in them, He gradually but inevitably removes the fears from their minds. They need not be afraid of anything or anyone. Even when entering the valley of the shadow of death, they will fear no evil because God is with them. With God, there is really no need to fear (Ps. 23:4).

> Dear Lord, please help me to daily live in freedom from fear. Allow me to help others know Your freedom from fear. Thank You for Your absolute, sovereign control over my life.

A Deacon Helping Others Overcome Discouragement

Deuteronomy 31:8

"The Lord is the One who will go before you . . . Do not be afraid or discouraged!"

To be *discouraged* is to be "deprived of confidence, hope, or spirit . . . to be devoid of courage or boldness."[3] The word in the New Testament means "to be disheartened or dispirited." Discouragement is common to all of us since it is an emotion prompted by circumstances—usually negative circumstances. This feeling of discouragement, though common, need not capture us. It does not have the right to take over and defeat us, or worse, depress us.

Victory over discouragement, especially as it is viewed in God's people, is dependent upon the Lord God going before us. Whenever we feel discouraged, we must quickly remember that God, who has the whole world in His hands, also has all our circumstances in control. It does not appear so when we focus on the circumstances themselves. But it is clear when we focus upon Him, commune with Him, listen to Him, and identify some of His purpose for the circumstances. How could we be encouraged if we were never discouraged? How could we find victory if we have never known defeat? God really does have the power and intention "that all things work together for good to those who love God, to those who are called according to His purpose" (Rom. 2:28).

> **Discouragement need not capture us.**

John Newton, former slave trader and eventual author of the hymn, *Amazing Grace*, once said:

> There is many a thing which the world calls disappointment, but there is no such word in the dictionary of faith. What to others are disappointments are to believers intimations of the way of God.[4]

In your ministry, always point the discouraged ones back to the sovereign one. Let them know that the Lord is the one who will go before them, and they need never be discouraged—because He never is!

Lord, thank You for every encouraging word You give me from Scripture. Help me to live victoriously and assist others to do the same.

A Deacon Helping Others Learn Patience

James 5:10

*"Brothers, take the prophets who spoke in the
Lord's name as an example of patience."*

Jesus said:

> Blessed are you when people insult you and persecute you, and falsely say all kinds of evil against you because of Me. Rejoice and be glad, for your reward in heaven is great; for in the same way they persecuted the prophets who were before you (Matt. 5:11-12).

It is not likely that we, as servants in the church today, will be spared from persecution. The great need is for us to be patient when wronged.

This kind of patience is not merely a human exercise in fortitude or a courageous stand to the end. It is a quality of God Himself reproduced in every Spirit-filled follower of Christ. The fruit of the Spirit, among other things, includes patience. The word literally means "to abide under." That is, to abide in Christ under the worst of conditions. It is "forbearance under suffering and endurance in the face of adversity."[5] The only way to experience the patience of God is to give your very life to the person of Jesus Christ and yield all your faculties to the power of His Holy Spirit who lives in you.

> **Patience is a quality of God Himself reproduced in every Spirit-filled follower of Christ.**

Every servant of God in the church must learn to live in patience. This is never easy and always costs us both time and devotion. Our natural instinct is to want all of God's patience all at once. It never happens that way!

Patience waits. It waits for God to speak. It waits for God to act. It waits for God to empower. Patience waits upon the Lord and in the end, finds that which man intended for evil to be the greatest victory we could ever know.

Dear Lord, by Your powerful Spirit, embed patience into my spirit. Cause me to know forbearance and endurance even when I cannot yet see the outcome.

A Deacon Ministering to the Lonely
Psalm 25:16

"Turn to me and be gracious to me, for I am alone and afflicted."

There's hardly anything in the human experience more difficult than being alone. When God created man, one of the first things He said was, "It is not good for the man to be alone . . ." (Gen. 2:18). Though centuries have come and gone, that principle has never changed. It is still not good for man to be alone.

Webster defines lonely, "Without companions, marked by aloneness, unfrequented by people, isolated, solitary."[6] Man was created to belong. He was created to belong to God. He was created to belong to one wife. He was created to be part of a society and therefore, is a social being. It is good for man to have companionship. It is not good for man to be alone.

As a Deacon, you can minister to those who are lonely by visiting them, by reading to them, by playing a simple game with them, or by introducing them to others. Of course, this takes time—time that you may feel you don't have to spare. But what if you were the lonely one? Would it be your hope and prayer that someone—anyone—would make the time for you?

> Man was created to belong.
> He was created to belong to God.

Aside from ministry to those who have no family or companionship, there are innumerable persons who feel alone, separated from the very one who created them. Apart from a genuine relationship with Christ, there will always be a feeling of aloneness and separation. With a true relationship there is a feeling of His abiding presence. The Lord said, "I will never desert you, nor will I ever forsake you, so we can confidently say, the Lord is my helper, I will not be afraid" (Heb. 13:5-6).

Consider the chorus of a great old hymn (written anonymously), "No, never alone, No never alone, He promised never to leave me, never to leave me alone."[7] And He never will!

> Dear Lord, thank You for never leaving me alone.
> Please use me to minister to others so they,
> too, will no longer feel alone.

WEEK 32 **DAY 2**

A Deacon for Those Who Need Healing
Proverbs 16:24

*"Pleasant words are a honeycomb; sweet to
the taste and health to the body."*

A caregiver is not the "Healer." God is the one who heals. We do have the great privilege of presenting the Great Physician (Jesus) to those who are ill. We may be able to read Scripture to them and pray with them. Encouraging words are good for most patients who are conscious and alert enough to understand them. When a patient cannot hear or understand encouraging words, then the caregiver can pray. The effective prayer of a servant of God can penetrate the heart of the one in need. We must never underestimate the power of prayer.

Though there are certain things we can and should do in our ministry to the sick, we must never out-step the bounds of Scripture, and we should never play the role of the medical doctor or the Lord.

A Deacon can bring an encouraging word to those who are sick. These may be words from the Psalms or Proverbs. They may be words from Jesus out of the gospels. In speaking about encouraging words, the writer of Proverbs said, "Do not let them depart from your sight; Keep them in the midst of your heart. For they are life to those who find them and health to all their body" (Prov. 4:22-23). It is miraculous what God's Word can do for the body. Proverbs 3:7-8 says, "Fear the Lord and turn away from evil. It will be healing to your body and refreshment to your bones.

> **God may have a specific purpose for some sickness.**

God may have a specific purpose for some sickness. Of Lazarus, who was on his deathbed, He said, "This sickness is not to end in death, but for the glory of God, so that the Son of God may be glorified by it" (John 11:4). Jesus healed a young man born blind "so that the works of God might be displayed in him" (John 9:3). Visit, share Scripture, encourage, pray, and leave the healing to God.

Dear Lord, please prepare me to minister to those who need Your healing. Help me know what to say and do as well as what not to say and do that You may be glorified.

A Deacon Comforting Those in Pain

2 Corinthians 1:4

"He comforts us in all our affliction, so that we may be able to comfort those who are in any kind of affliction, through the comfort we ourselves receive from God."

The word for *comfort* or *comforter* in the New Testament is an intriguing word. It is actually made up of two words, one that means "beside" and one that means "to call." Together the idea is "a calling to one's side." It translates "exhortation, consolation, or comfort."[8] In the study and practice of pastoral ministry or pastoral care, professors always remind their students to never forget or neglect the ministry of presence. You may not have much you can say, but you can show up and put a hand in a patient's hand or on a shoulder and pray. It is amazing the comfort that presence brings.

It becomes much easier to comfort the afflicted when we, ourselves, have received the ministry of the Great Comforter—the Holy Spirit of God. Speaking to His disciples, Jesus said, "I will ask the Father, and He will give you another Comforter, that He may be with you forever; that is the Spirit of truth . . ." (Jn. 14:16-17). The Holy Spirit has many functions in the life of the believer. One of those is to bring comfort to us in times of pain. When you appeal to Him on behalf of another believer, He also brings comfort to them.

> **Never forget or neglect the ministry of presence.**

The next time you are called upon to comfort someone in pain, just keep in mind the comfort that you yourself have received. Pray and ask the Divine Comforter to precede you to the side of the patient, and then—just show up!

Dear Lord, I want to thank You for bringing such comfort to my life. You have come beside me in times of pain. Help me come beside others so You might provide that comfort by Your Spirit in me.

A Deacon Helping One Who Is Dying

Job 14:5

*"Man's days are determined and the number
of his months depend on You . . .
You have set limits he cannot pass."*

When ministering to someone who is surely dying, there are several things to keep in mind. First, we need to understand the person's capacity to listen or communicate. As concerned as you might be for someone's soul, you will need to find a time when he or she can actually comprehend what you are saying. Second, you will try to determine, either from the patient or from a close family member, if he or she has truly received Christ as his or her personal Lord and Savior. If the person has, you can console him or her with the great promises of God regarding the resurrection. If he or she has not, you can tenderly share God's plan of salvation and lead him or her in a prayer to receive Christ. Third, you can provide comfort and support to surviving loved ones who may be with the person during his or her final days or hours on earth.

> **Death comes easier for the Christian, though it may not be painless.**

Death really does come easier for the Christian, though it may not be painless. God's grace prepares the spirit to "let go" of the body, and in so doing, relieves some of the emotional trauma of death. The Lord said in Revelation 14:13, "Blessed are the dead who die in the Lord from now on! Yes, says the Spirit, so that they may rest from their labors, for their deeds follow with them." In death, God transfers our spirit from this body, which literally dies, and takes our spirit immediately to be with Him (cf. 2 Cor. 5:6-8). Then at the time of His Second Coming, He will provide a brand new, glorified body that will become the residence of our saved, transformed human spirit. We shall spend eternity in that state with the Lord (cf. 1 Thess. 4:13-18). You may console others with those words.

Dear Lord, thank You for Your assurance of my salvation. With that, I know you will use me to help those who are dying. Please grant to me both clarity of thought and compassion of heart as I care for the dying.

A Deacon for the Emotionally Distraught
Psalm 34:18

"The Lord is near the broken hearted; He saves those crushed in spirit."

Jeremy Taylor said, "It is impossible for that man to despair who remembers that his Helper is omnipotent."[9] When you come to the aid of one who is emotionally distraught, deeply discouraged, and despairing of hope, you must turn to the Divine Comforter and as best you can, turn him to the Divine Comforter. Your presence alone will not be sufficient in this case. God's presence and power are absolutely essential to transform a disturbed mind. You will precede the meeting with sincere, fervent prayer. You will be prepared to quote God's Word and appeal to God's Spirit to expel any evil spirit or influence. You will have gained the prayer support of others as well.

> God's presence and power are absolutely essential to transform a disturbed mind.

If the distraught person is, in fact, a believer, then you will proceed to bring God's promises of peace and tranquility. Jesus said in John 14:27, "Peace I leave with you; My peace I give to you; not as the world gives do I give to you. Do not let your heart be troubled, nor let it be afraid." Let the person know that Jesus is his peace. You might even help him memorize this or a similar verse. We know that "the steadfast of mind You will keep in perfect peace, because he trusts in You" (Isa. 26:3). Get him into God's Word, and get God's Word into him as quickly as possible. In it he will find great peace of mind and renewed emotional stability.

You may feel that, though you are a Deacon, you are not qualified to deal with a person who is emotionally wrung-out. The truth is, you are not. But no one else is either—except God, the Holy Spirit who indwells you. God does the work. He simply has you "with flesh on" to be His hands, His feet, and His voice. You are not the Healer. He alone is the Healer. But He will use you as an instrument of peace in another person if you will just make yourself available.

Dear Lord, I do want to be available to You, as Your servant, to be an instrument of peace in the lives of those who need it. I just now re-commit myself to You for this service.

A Deacon for the Bereaved

John 11:37

"Couldn't He who opened the blind man's eyes also have kept this man from dying?"

In the account of Jesus ministering to Lazarus, Mary, and Martha, we discover some wonderful truths about ministry to those who are grieving. God knows everything there is to know about death and dying and grieving. So, as we find ourselves trying to help those who have lost a loved one, we can learn from Jesus's encounter with this family from Bethany (cf. Jn. 11).

When Jesus heard of Lazarus's condition and knew that he was dying, He did not come to him immediately. That sounds strange to those of us who have been taught to go quickly. Jesus was on a mission trip with His apostles but after two days was able to head back to check on Lazarus. By that time, Lazarus had died, and his family was a little upset with Jesus (11:21, 32). There will be times—hopefully not many—when you simply cannot be with a family when they bury a loved one. But you can follow up and help them cope with the loss.

> Bring to the grieving family not only loving words but loving deeds.

Once Jesus arrived, He responded to their need with a precious love (11:5) and a promise of life (11:25). These are the two crucial elements for a Deacon to bring with him on a visit like this. Express love! Bring to the grieving family not only loving words but loving deeds (cf. 1 Jn. 3:18). Then share with them, as you have opportunity, promises from God's Word that will assure them of a resurrection (cf. Col. 2:12). If they and their deceased loved one are true believers, then they can be assured of seeing their loved one again in heaven (cf. 2 Sam. 12:23). If they or the deceased are not believers, you can still show the love of Christ and without references to the dead family member, lovingly share the gospel (cf. 1 Cor. 15:1-11).

> **Dear Lord, remind me regularly of Your own love for me and my own hope of resurrection. Then help me as I minister to those who are grieving to bring Your precious love and promise of life to them.**

A Deacon Assisting with Funeral Arrangements

Luke 23:53

"Taking it [Jesus's body] down, he wrapped it in fine linen and placed it in a tomb . . ."

Joseph of Arimathea was a religious Jew who had been converted and saved under Jesus's ministry (cf. Jn. 21:38). Nicodemus, another religious Jew who was saved by Jesus, joined Joseph, and they both made Jesus's funeral arrangements (cf. Jn. 21:38-39). These men did what many Pastors and sometimes Deacons are called upon to do. We learn a lot from reading what Joseph and Nicodemus did.

Once Jesus was pronounced dead on the cross (Jn. 19:33), Joseph got permission from the local authorities to move His body, as we might from a coroner or other medical professional (Lk. 23:52). He then enlisted Nicodemus to assist him, as we might enlist a mortician or funeral director (Jn. 19:39). They then arranged for Jesus's body to be appropriately prepared for burial, as we might request embalming and dressing (Jn. 19:40). Joseph arranged a gravesite by offering a new tomb that he had previously prepared for himself, as we might reserve a grave in a designated cemetery (Matt. 27:60-61). They actually placed Jesus' dead body in the tomb, as we, or pallbearers, might place a casket in a grave (Matt. 27:60). They left the tomb having provided, with dignity, a proper burial for their friend—and their Savior.

> **Prepare and serve!**

Fortunately, we have many people in the church and community who can help us in making funeral arrangements. But as a Deacon, you will want to be as familiar as possible with the process. You will be there not only to grieve with those who grieve but to assist in making decisions that the bereaved family may not know how to make. Prepare . . . and serve!

Dear Lord, I thank You for the biblical example of Jesus's funeral. Please help me to be sensitive to bereaved families so I can serve them sincerely in love.

A Deacon Helping Others Overcome Anger

James 1:20

"Be slow to anger, for man's anger does not accomplish God's righteousness."

Secular psychologists have built seminars, lectures, and therapeutic methods for anger management. Yet society continues to arrest and jail criminals whose anger brought them to their wit's end. The Bible, again, becomes our sourcebook when we are attempting to help others who have a serious problem with anger.

Proverbs 29:11 says, "A fool always loses his temper, but a wise man holds it back." Someone once said, "People who fly into a rage always make a bad landing." Anger is an emotional, verbal, and sometimes physical response or reaction that we have when faced with criticism, opposition, rudeness, or judgment of others—especially toward us personally. Since it is an emotion first, it can be controlled. It is not wrong to be angry for the right reasons as long as you "do not let the sun go down on your anger" (Eph. 4:26). It is wrong to be angry and harbor anger in your heart. This soon results in resentment and bitterness and ultimately revenge. The apostle Paul warned the church at Ephesus, "Let all bitterness and wrath and anger and clamor and slander be put away from you, along with all malice" (Eph. 4:31).

> **People who fly into a rage always make a bad landing.**

When speaking with one who wishes to resolve his anger problem, you will want to guide him through a few steps:

(1) Give him a biblical definition and example of sin and its consequences. (You might use Cain as an example—Gen. 4:6-8.)
(2) Share any victories you may have personally gained over anger.
(3) Ask him to admit his problem as sinful (cf. Ps. 66:18).
(4) Lead him to confess (daily, if necessary) his anger to God and to accept, by faith, God's forgiveness (cf. 1 Jn. 1:8-10).
(5) Follow up on him and you, or others, hold him accountable for at least a year.

Dear Lord, please empower me by Your Holy Spirit to control my own feelings of anger. Remind me of the Scriptures I need to help others. Give me the right words to say to them.

A Deacon Helping Others Overcome Guilt
Psalm 103:10, 12

"He has not dealt with us as our sins deserve or
repaid us according to our offenses . . ."
As far as the east is from the west, so far has He
removed our transgressions from us."

To be *guilty* means we are "responsible for or chargeable with a reprehensible act, having broken a law and committed a crime."[10] Guilt is the condition of being responsible for an offense or wrongdoing and carries with it feelings of pain, anger, remorse, regret, and sometimes the need for repentance. When it comes to our guilt as sinners, and especially believing sinners (i.e., Christians), we must learn what God says and seek to apply His truth to our need. There are many genuine Christians who still feel guilty because they have sinned against God. For some, this guilt haunts them day and night.

> Grace is God providing for us what we don't deserve.

The opposite of guilty is guiltless. We are, in fact, guilty of sinning against God. However, God, knowing this about us and knowing that we deserve a guilty verdict, has intervened and provided a guiltless substitute to take our place. In fact, "God made Him who knew no sin to be sin on our behalf, so that we might become the righteousness of God in Him" (1 Cor. 5:21). When we repent of our sin against God and by faith, receive His eternal forgiveness, we are no longer seen by God as guilty. All of our sin and all the guilt that results from it has been fully, finally, and completely forgiven. In Christ, now, we are *not guilty* even though we may commit an act of sin.

This is really what the grace and mercy of God are all about. Grace is God providing for us what we don't deserve, namely full and final forgiveness and eternal life. Mercy is God withholding from us what we do deserve, namely condemnation, judgment, and eternal separation from Him. When we come to know and follow Christ, He relieves us of the guilt that once condemned us. If we are not guilty any longer, we don't have to live and act as though we are.

> Dear Lord, help me to live in the freedom of Your forgiveness; free of sin's penalty and power over me; free from feelings of guilt and anguish. Thank You! Please show me how to help others, also, in overcoming their feelings of guilt.

A Deacon Ministering to Those Who Mourn
Psalm 6:6-7

"I am weary from my groaning; with my tears I dampen my pillow and drench my bed every night. My eyes are swollen from grief . . ."

If God's heart goes out to those who mourn, and surely it does, then our hearts should go out to them as well (cf. Matt. 5:4). To mourn is "to express or feel grief or sorrow."[11] It is "to mourn for, or lament."[12] It is used in the New Testament of mourning in general (Matt. 5:4; 9:15); of sorrow for the death of a loved one (Mk. 16:10); of mourning for the overthrow of a government (Rev. 18:11,15); of sorrow for sin or for condoning it (Jas. 4:9); and of grief for those in a local church who show no repentance for evil committed (1 Cor. 5:2). In your contemporary ministry, you will, more often than not, work with those who mourn because of a death or a crisis with continuing implications. When mourning persists and is never coped with, it will turn into serious, if not chronic, depression. Depression seems to be more common today, even in the church, than in past generations.

> Encourage those who mourn to turn to the Savior.

Man's immediate solution or quick-fix for this condition is medication. Sometimes drugs may be necessary. But first, we must encourage those who mourn to turn to a compassionate, sympathizing Savior. Jesus said, "Blessed [or happy] are those who mourn for they shall be comforted" (Matt. 5:4). Isaiah the prophet, speaking of Jesus' earthly ministry, said He would "bring good news to the afflicted . . . bind up the broken hearted . . . proclaim liberty to captives and freedom to prisoners . . . to comfort all who mourn" (61:1-2). Before Jesus left to go back to heaven, He gave us the same assignment. He said, "As the Father has sent Me, I also send you" (Jn. 20:21). Look for ways to sympathize with, pray for, and minister to those who are mourning. You could be used to make a remarkable difference for the rest of their lives.

Dear Lord, I do want to be available to You for ministry to those I know are mourning. Help me know how to approach them and what to say and do to give them encouragement and hope.

A Deacon Bringing Hope to the Hopeless
Psalm 146:5

"Happy is the one whose . . . hope is in the Lord his God."

Hope is an overwhelming sense or feeling of favorable and confident expectation. It usually has to do with the unseen or unrealized condition or circumstances of the future. Hope describes the happy anticipation of good (Ti. 1:2), the ground upon which hope is based (Acts 16:19), and the object upon which the "hope" is fixed (1 Tim. 1:1).

People feel hopeless when their thoughts are singly focused on themselves and their immediate circumstances. They find it seemingly impossible to even begin to look up—or out beyond themselves. As their minds become unchallenged, their emotions become raw and their bodies become weak and frail. Their very lives become spiritually dehydrated; they just want to die. They can see or sense no hope for themselves. This is why many people take their own lives. They think they have no hope. The truth is, apart from Christ, none of us has any eternal hope.

You can be used of God to bring hope to the hopeless. It may take some time and energy and maybe some other resources sacrificed to God, but you can make a difference in people without hope. Help them change their minds (cf. Rom. 12:2). Show them who they are or can be in Christ (cf. Eph. 2:4-6; 1 Peter 2:9-10). Speak God's Word of hope into them. Help them to believe in God and in their future (Heb. 11:1,6). Paint word-pictures of a favorable and possible future for them.

> You can be used of God to bring hope to the hopeless.

Help them to imagine what can be with Christ controlling their lives (cf. Eph. 3:20). Let them know that their hope for the future is as bright as the promises of God.

Dear Lord, thank You for the blessed hope You have placed in my heart. I desire to share that hope with others. Please lead me to the hopeless and give me Your words to bring to them.

A Deacon Helping Others to Overcome Failure

1 Corinthians 15:58

"Excel in the Lord's work, knowing that your labor in the Lord is not in vain."

To *fail* is to "prove so deficient as to be totally ineffective; to be unsuccessful; to prove insufficient in quantity or duration."[13] Failures at church, marriage, family, job, or school often make us believe that we are failures in life. Failures usually hurt, and they often hurt a lot. But failure by itself is never the end of the road, and failure in something is surely not the end of you.

We can look at the failures of several men in the Bible and could conclude that they failed in life, but the ends of their stories tell us otherwise. Abraham failed to wait for a child of promise from Sarah and fathered Ishmael by an Egyptian maid named Hagar. But in the end, God gave him Isaac, born of Sarah, the successor to "the father of many nations" (Gen. 24:1). Jacob failed to follow Jewish custom and tricked his brother Esau out of his birthright. But God restored him, re-named him (Israel), and gave him twelve sons constituting the twelve tribes of the Hebrew nation. David's moral failure with Bathsheba and his subsequent sin of murder could have ruined him for life. But through sincere repentance and faith, he remained the king of Israel and provided the human lineage for the Messiah.

> **You may have gone through failures in your life, but that doesn't mean your life is over.**

You may have gone through failures in your life, but that does not mean your life is over. Granted, some failures leave lifelong scars and can forever change the role we fill in the church. But failures in certain areas do not put you on a shelf and render you completely unusable by God. These truths can be shared with those to whom you may be ministering who are trying to get past some big failures. Even if certain of our labors fail, our labor in the Lord is never in vain.

Dear Lord, I acknowledge my failures to You, and I thank You for Your great grace that forgives and reopens doors of ministry for me. I pray that You would increase my faith through my failures and help me to help others overcome their failures.

A Deacon Helping Others Avoid Fruitlessness
Mark 4:19

"The worries of this age, the seduction of wealth, and the desires for other things enter in and choke the word, and it becomes unfruitful."

Jesus uses the parable of the sower to illustrate for His disciples how they can avoid fruitlessness. Clearly, Jesus intends for His children to bear fruit. In John 15 He identifies fruit (v. 2), more fruit (v. 2), and much fruit (v. 5) expected from His followers. And He also makes it clear that we can never produce spiritual fruit unless we abide in Him (vv. 5-7).

So, what holds us back? What prevents us from bearing this spiritual fruit? Jesus pinpoints three "thorns that threaten our fruitfulness." First, the worries of the world pose us with a real problem. Rather than focusing on the spiritual needs of others, we worry about our own needs. In our anxiety, we avoid the clear mandate of Jesus to proclaim the gospel to the ends of the earth.

> Live your daily life with the mind and desire of Christ.

Second, the seduction of wealth or the deceitfulness of riches impresses us more than the call to the harvest. The more money we save for ourselves, the less we give to missions. Instead of using the things to serve and provide for people, we use people to serve and provide for us. Jesus said, "Not even when one has an abundance does his life consist of his possessions" (Lk. 12:15).

Third, the desire for other things will keep us from bearing fruit. If you don't want fruit, you won't have it. And if you don't want it, you don't want what Jesus wants.

Live your daily life with the mind and desire of Christ. Offer yourself and encourage others to offer themselves as laborers in the harvest. Avoid the worries, the wealth, and the things of the world and bear fruit.

Dear Lord, please help me to avoid those obstacles that will prevent me from sowing and reaping the fruit of the gospel.

WEEK 34   **DAY 4**

A Deacon Helping Others Deal With Temptation
1 Corinthians 10:13

"God is faithful and He will not allow you to be tempted beyond what you are able but with the temptation He will also provide a way of escape . . ."

Temptation always comes to us through our senses. We see something, hear something, taste something, or touch something, and instantly we are tempted to sin. Those who are overcoming temptations are hiding God's Word in their hearts (Ps. 119:9,11) and training their senses to discern good and evil (Heb. 5:14). The battle for our thoughts is constantly waged between the world, the flesh, the devil, and God. God does not, and never will, tempt us to sin (cf. Jas. 1:13-15), but Satan can and regularly does.

J. Wilbur Chapman shares an intriguing insight into the matter of temptation:

> Temptation is the tempter looking through the keyhole into the room where you are living; sin is your drawing back the bolt and making it possible for him to enter[14]

So, what can you do to help others deal with temptation? First, follow a good example (Heb. 4:15-16). Second, set a good example (Acts 24:16). Third, teach about good examples (Acts 23:1). Fourth, help hold others accountable through mutual love and transparency. Develop an accountability group with others who are dealing with temptation and sin. Meet or at least touch base weekly and ask the right questions. Be faithful to pray and diligent to resist (Jas. 4:7). You may be pleasantly surprised at your victories.

> **God does not and never will tempt us to sin.**

> Dear Lord, please remind me immediately each time I am tempted to look to You for the way of escape. Help me be a good example of godliness and righteousness to my friends and to others.

A Deacon Meeting the Tangible Needs of Others

Psalm 72:12

"For He will rescue the poor who cry out and the afflicted who have no helper."

This is one of the more specific ways a Deacon can serve the people of God. He can make himself aware of the poor and those in need of tangible, material things and work with others to help meet those needs. This not only fills a very practical need, but it also sets an example of obedience to Scripture. James gives a great illustration of this principle:

> If a brother or sister is without clothing and in need of daily food, and one of you says to them, "Go in peace, be warm and be filled," yet you do not give them what is necessary for their body, what use is that? Even so faith, if it has no works is dead, being by itself (Jas. 2:15-17).

There certainly is more to serving the church than just meeting material needs. However, meeting these needs will very often open the door to other needs that are more spiritual in nature. If you offer to buy and install a set of tires on a widow's car, you may find that she'd really rather have someone pick her up and take her to church. You can still install the tires, but you can also arrange a ride for her to church.

> Meeting needs will very often open the door to other needs that are of a more spiritual nature.

There are also many occasions when a Pastor or ministry staff member has a tangible need. A Deacon can be sensitive to these needs as well and can often meet those needs or indirectly lead others in the church to do so. When you serve in these ways, you will find a great sense of satisfaction in your heart. Never do it for the praise or recognition of man—or even the recipient. Do it as unto the Lord and for His glory.

Dear Lord, please show me ways that I can meet the tangible, practical needs of others with whom I serve. Give me sensitivity to the poor and provide resources for their care.

WEEK 35 **DAY 1**

A Deacon Helping Victims of Broken Promises

1 Samuel 15:29

"The Eternal One of Israel does not lie or change His mind, for He is not man who changes his mind."

Most, if not all of us, in the church have had someone make a promise to us and break it. Pastors have non-attending church members promise them they'll be in worship services on a certain Sunday, and they think nothing of breaking that promise. Husbands break promises to their wives; wives break promises to their husbands; parents break promises to their children and children to their parents. They all have broken their promises. It has become so common we no longer think anything of it. For this reason, mistrust is high in the church.

What is really sad is when a husband and wife break the promises of their wedding vows. Whatever happened to "for better or for worse, for richer or for poorer, through sickness and health, 'till death do us part"? How can we make such promises with such sincerity on our wedding day and so soon break them? Victims of broken promises are all around us—even when we are sitting in church on Sunday morning.

> **Victims of broken promises are all around us—even as we sit in church.**

God has made hundreds of promises in His Word and has always kept every single one. You can buy books and booklets that record these promises. Since God never changes His mind, He will never break His promises. You may not be able to trust some people in your life, but you can always and forever trust God.

God promised a Savior " . . . and we preach to you the good news of the promise made to the fathers, that God has fulfilled this promise to our children in that He raised up Jesus . . ." (Acts 13:32-33). He has promised every believer the gift of eternal life (1 Jn. 2:25). He will never, ever break His promise to you.

Dear Lord, thank You for promising me eternal life.
Help me to live in Your promises and at the same time,
help others to trust Your promises for themselves.

A Deacon Helping the Rejected
Isaiah 53:3

> "He was despised and rejected by men . . .
> and we didn't value Him at all."

We never reject those persons whom we value. If we value our spouses, we will never reject (or leave) them. If we value our parents or our kids or our grandchildren, we will never reject them. It is when they no longer have apparent value to us that we tend to reject them. We usually don't reject certain things when we value them—like our houses, cars, clothes, and toys (big or small). That is, we don't until they are used up and no longer have value to us, at which point we discard them for another.

You may have been a victim of rejection—maybe by a parent, a spouse, or a child. Rejection is almost unbearable. Yet the Bible tells us that Jesus " . . . came to His own, and those who were His own did not receive Him" (John 1:11). That is, His own people rejected Him even as millions do yet today.

> One way to be of service to the body of Christ is to accept those who have been rejected by others.

Basically, the opposite of rejection is acceptance. One of the best things you can do for people who have been rejected is to accept them for who God has created them to be. One big way to be of serious service to the body of Christ is to accept those who have been rejected by others. This is exactly what Jesus did for us. When we were unacceptable to God because of our sin, Christ died on the cross for us. With our acceptance of His sacrifice and His salvation, we are now accepted as the children of God.

Look for someone in your church who seems to be shunned by most everyone else—maybe because of his looks, his clothes, his personality, his poor social skills—and express God's love to him. Accept him even as Christ has, let others see your deed of kindness, and let God receive all the glory.

> Dear Lord, I thank You for receiving me into Your family. I desire to show Your love and acceptance to others. Guide me to those who feel rejected and help me provide acceptance for them.

A Deacon Dealing With Church Conflict

1 Corinthians 3:3

"Since there is envy and strife among you, are you not fleshly and living like ordinary people?"

Conflict can be defined as "a state of open, prolonged fighting, a state of disharmony."[15] Some churches have regular church fights during long business meetings, while others just exist year after year with a climate of disunity and disharmony. In either case, there are many churches, perhaps over half of all the churches in America, that are conflicted over something.

> **Deacons can be a part of the problem or part of the solution. You decide!**

Conflict always results when churches turn inward. It's like corralling a herd of horses and giving them lots of feed and water but never letting them out of the corral. They start kicking and biting each other and kick fences and gates. Confinement results in conflict. Many of our churches have confined themselves—indeed their Christian lives—to a building with the same people Sunday after Sunday and year after year. Inevitably, conflict builds and either some break out or they send the Pastor out in an attempt to solve the problem. All the time the problem is they have lost their vision, forgotten their mission, and become internalized.

Deacons can be a part of the problem or part of the solution. You can help the church get back on track or you die with it. God has not called us to fight among ourselves. He has called us as soldiers in His army to ward off the world, the flesh, and the devil and take the gospel to the ends of the earth. The best way to resolve conflict is to completely change the church's focus—off herself and on a world in need of Christ.

> Dear Lord, I know You hate conflict in the church among Your people. I pray You will help me to be a catalyst to encourage peace but also to help my Pastor bring new vision, mission, and purpose to the church.

A Deacon Confronting Troublemakers

Acts 15:24

"We have heard that some to whom we gave no authorization went out from us and troubled you with their words and unsettled your hearts."

You may or may not have encountered persons in the church who are troublemakers. We do have them from time to time. The early church had them. As an example, Euodia and Syntyche were women who apparently brought some trouble to the Philippian church (Phil. 4:2-3). Hymenaeus, Alexander, Phygellus, Hermogenes, and Philetus were all troublemakers for Paul and Timothy in their ministries (cf. 1 Tim. 1:20; 2 Tim. 1:15; 2:17). These were not all "wolves in sheep's clothing" (Matt. 7:15), but they did have agendas of their own, and they wanted to influence others in favor of that agenda. Often these persons surround themselves with others of like mind and assume authority for themselves that neither God nor the church has given them. They become troublemakers.

> Troublemakers assume unwarranted authority.

So how can you, as a Deacon, confront such persons in your church? Identify, as much as possible, the root of the problem in the person's life. Has he been a perpetual troublemaker who is "always opposed to everything and everyone"? Or is he reacting to personal or family problems that have caused him to take his frustrations out on the church? Enlist another Deacon, or if the troublemaker is a woman, ask your wife to go with you to visit. Pray earnestly for the person and yourself and the encounter. Be prepared to ask a few pointed questions that should reveal the heart of the problem. Be prepared with a few key Scriptures following the admonition of 2 Timothy 4:2: "Be ready to reprove, rebuke, exhort, with great patience and instruction." Ask the person to acknowledge his specific role in troubling the church and ask him to be willing to turn from that and pray for God's forgiveness. Pray with the person and follow up with both encouragement and accountability.

Dear Lord, thank You for entrusting to me this ministry of service to the church. By Your Spirit, through Your Word, enable me to help others who have become troublemakers.

WEEK 35   **DAY 5**

A Deacon Relating to Wayward Church Members

1 John 2:19

> "They went out from us, but they did not belong to us; for if they had belonged to us, they would have remained with us."

Many churches in America face the issue of inactive church members. These are people who, at one time, publicly acknowledged Christ as their personal Lord and Savior, surrendered their lives to Him, and were baptized as believers but now have completely dropped out. Most of these people are merely ignored after a few months and eventually are either placed on an inactive (non-resident) membership roll or dropped from membership altogether. How should the church in general, and the Pastor and Deacons in particular, relate to these wayward members?

Theologians usually, and correctly, use this verse in 1 John 2:19 to refer to the kind of persons we would call wayward or backslidden. Jerry Vines, in his commentary on this epistle refers to these as "deserters." He says they are physical deserters—they just never show up anymore for anything. Then there are moral deserters—they lead their lives apart from the discipline of the church and what their lives stand for becomes a total contradiction to all the church. There are also intellectual deserters; these apostatize from the faith. In almost all of these cases we are observing unbelievers who, in spite of their casual decisions, never were genuinely saved.

> **You have the responsibility to treat them as unbelievers and pray for their salvation.**

Thus, you have the responsibility to treat them as unbelievers and begin to pray for their salvation. Pray that those who might actually be saved will be deeply convicted to return to service. Be prepared to love them and witness to them and bring them under the clear proclamation of the gospel.

Dear Lord, show me those who are detached or have deserted the church, and help me know how to relate to them, pray for them, and appeal to them for new or renewed commitment.

The Deacon's Doctrine

The Deacon's Doctrine: The Bible
2 Timothy 3:16-17

"All Scripture is inspired by God and profitable for teaching, for reproof, for correction, for training in righteousness . . ."

This is one of two premier verses in the New Testament that clearly describe the nature of the Bible (the other is 2 Pet. 1:21). *"All Scripture"* refers to all sixty-six books of the closed canon of the Old and New Testaments in your Bible. The word *inspired* literally means "God-breathed," indicating clearly that the Bible came from God. It really is historically and grammatically God's written and preserved Word for us. As Jesus said in His prayer to the Father, "Your word is truth," we have every reason to believe that the Bible is reliable, authoritative and absolutely true (cf. Ps. 19; 119; Jn. 17:17).

> **The Bible is reliable, authoritative and absolutely true!**

For us, as servants of God and His people, there is no other written authority that even compares with the Bible. The apostle cites four specific benefits for the believer from hearing, reading, studying, meditating on, and memorizing the Bible. It is profitable for teaching or doctrine, showing us the path to walk on; reproof, showing us where we get off the path; correction, showing us how to get back on the path; and training, showing us how to stay on the path. These benefits are invaluable to you as you live your life, love your church, and light the world with the gospel.

John Brown summarizes it well:

> The doctrines of the Bible are all practical and its laws all reasonable. Every doctrine has its practical *therefore* and every law its doctrinal *because*.

D.L. Moody is often quoted as saying, "The Bible was not given to us to merely increase our intellect but to change our lives." You will never be effective in pleasing God, much less serving others, unless your life has been transformed by the Word of God. Each and every day of your life, it must be "a lamp to [your] feet and a light to [your] path" (Ps. 119:105).

> **Dear Lord, help me believe the Bible is Your Word without any mixture of error and let that result in me becoming a more holy servant.**

THE DEACON'S DOCTRINE: GOD

Genesis 1:1

"In the beginning God created the heavens and the earth."

When it comes to the existence of God, there are atheists, who don't believe there is a god at all. There are agnostics, who believe there may be a God but they have no regard for Him and no need of Him. And of course, there are those who believe that God exists based on either natural arguments (creation, cause and effect, etc.) or biblical arguments (all that the Bible says about God is true and accurate). Merely expressing intellectual assent to the existence of God does not, by any means, suggest that a person is saved. "You believe that God is one, you do well; the demons also believe, and shudder" (Jas. 2:19).

As New Testament believers and Deacons in the church, we have come to believe, unequivocally that "there is one God, and one mediator also between God and men, the man Christ Jesus, who gave Himself as a ransom for all, the testimony given at the proper time" (1 Tim. 2:5-6). Though God has chosen to manifest Himself in three persons—Father, Son, and Holy Spirit—He is but one God. "Hear, O Israel! The Lord is our God, the Lord is one!" (Deut. 6:4). "To you it was shown that you might know that the Lord, He is God; there is no other besides Him" (Deut. 4:35).

> **The God of the Bible is not a god of man's own making or thinking or choosing.**

Charles Ryrie, in his *Survey of Bible Doctrine* lists several attributes of God, such as omniscient (all knowing), omnipotent (all powerful), omnipresent (all present), immutable (never-changing). In summary he says, "This is the only God that exists. The God of the Bible is not a god of man's own making or thinking or choosing, but He is the God of His own revelation."[2] This is the God you have come to know in Jesus Christ, His Son (cf. Jn.14:6). He is your total reason for existence and life on earth. You must daily live and serve in the light of this truth.

Dear Lord, I know you are God and God alone.
All things, from mighty to small, were
created by You for Your glory.

The Deacon's Doctrine: Christ
Matthew 16:16

"Simon Peter answered, 'You are the Messiah, the Son of the living God.'"

This short but profound declaration of Simon Peter captures the essence of who Jesus is and provides for us a confessional statement upon which this doctrine is built. There are many attributes and characteristics in the Bible that describe Christ. He is the Messiah or "anointed one" of Israel. But specifically for New Testament believers, He is the Lord Jesus Christ. The apostle Peter states this well: "Therefore, let all the house of Israel know for certain that God has made Him both Lord and Christ—this Jesus whom you crucified" (Acts 2:36). He is Lord, signifying His absolute rule and reign over His followers. He is Jesus, "God with us," indicating His incarnation—God, becoming flesh (Jn. 1:14). He is the Christ, the anointed one of the Father sent to the earth from heaven.

> You are charged to know Him, love Him, serve Him and share Him.

He was born of a virgin, lived a perfectly sinless life, died an atoning death, was raised bodily from the grave, appeared to over five hundred witnesses, commissioned His Church, and ascended back to heaven with a promise to return to the earth as King of kings and Lord of lords.

Jesus Christ is at the center of our faith. "There is salvation in no one else; for there is no other name under heaven that has been given among men by which we must be saved" (Acts 4:12). He is, in fact and function, "The author and perfecter of our faith . . ." (Heb. 12:2). As one of His servants in the church, you are charged to know Him, love Him, serve Him, and share Him. He is your personal Lord and Savior. He has saved you from your sin and assured you of a home in heaven. He has matured you in your faith where the church has recognized you and set you apart for special service. He anticipates your daily obedience and expects you to be a good example of the Christian life.

You have the wonderful privilege of "making known what is the riches of the glory of this mystery among the Gentiles, which is Christ in you, the hope of glory" (Col. 1:27).

Dear Lord, remind me daily to surrender to You as Lord, allowing You to rule and reign in my life.

The Deacon's Doctrine: Holy Spirit
1 Corinthians 6:19-20

"Your body is a sanctuary of the Holy Spirit who is in you, whom you have from God. You are not your own, for you were bought at a price . . ."

Though it is hard for us to fully understand, the Holy Spirit is a person. He is the third person of the triune Godhead (the Father, the Son, and the Holy Spirit). Just because we lack understanding or comprehension does not preclude this biblical truth—the Holy Spirit is a person. All the attributes used to describe one person of the Godhead can be accurately used to describe all three. He is one God who shows Himself to His Creation (namely, us) in three persons.

The Holy Spirit is actively involved in your salvation. He convicted you of your sin and convinced you, in your mind and spirit, that you needed to be saved (Jn. 16:8-11). He regenerated you, or caused you to be born again, through His supernatural intervention (Ti. 3:5; 1 Pet. 1:3). He indwells you, having taken up residence in your mortal body, and living out His own life in and through you (1 Cor. 6:19). He has "baptized you" or submersed you (mind, emotion, and will) into Himself. This occurs only once, at the point of the rebirth, and never needs be repeated. It is something God does by Himself and for Himself in order to unite you with Himself (1 Cor. 12:13). He has sealed you or secured you in your salvation, supernaturally confirming that you are a child of God and will remain so from the point of your rebirth throughout all eternity (Eph. 4:30).

> God has sealed you in your salvation, supernaturally confirming that you are a child of God.

As a child of God, and especially as a Deacon in the church, the Holy Spirit has gifted you to serve Him (cf. Rom. 12:6-8; 1 Cor. 12:8-10). He desires to fill or control you (Eph. 5:18) so that His fruit (Gal. 5:22-23) can be produced through you and you can exercise your spiritual gifts in the church. Make it your priority to discover your gifts, develop your gifts, and devote your gifts to serve God in your church. You'll be glad you did!

Dear Lord, thank You for saving me. Please help me to exercise the gifts You have given me.

The Deacon's Doctrine: Angels
Hebrews 1:14

"Are they not all ministering spirits sent out to serve those who are going to inherit salvation?"

Dr. Ryrie, in his *Survey of Bible Doctrines,* states, "If one admits the biblical evidence, there is no problem in proving the existence of angels. Indeed, the evidence is overwhelming."[3] Of course, we believe the biblical record and approach this doctrine from that perspective. Angels are personal, created beings that possess intellect (1 Pet. 1:12), feelings (Lk. 2:13), and a will (Jude 6). They are spirit beings created by God and thus are different from God. Man is a special order of creation, as are angels. Neither ever becomes the other. When a person dies, he does not become an angel, though angels may take on human appearance at times (e.g., Gen. 16:7-11).

> Angels are very active in your life.

Perhaps the most well-known angel is actually a fallen angel named Lucifer (Isa. 14:12), whom we know as Satan. According to Scripture, one-third of all created angels fell with Lucifer, resulting in a large number of demons scattered throughout the world. This, of course, allows for two-thirds of all created angels still acting under God's direction to minister to the needs of the people of God. Of these active, unfallen angels only two are named in Scripture—Michael, an archangel (Jude 9), and Gabriel, "a man of God" (Lk. 1:19).

Angels are very active in your life even when you are unaware of them. Specifically, they minister to you in answering your prayers (Acts 12:7), giving encouragement in times of danger (Acts 27:23-24), and caring for you at death (Lk. 16:22; Jude 9). Of course, God would not have to use angels to carry out some of His work in and for us, but He has chosen to do so.

As you follow Christ and faithfully carry out your service as a Deacon, remember angels are watching over you, and especially "the Angel of the Lord," Jesus Himself (cf. Ex. 3:2; Acts 7:29)!

Dear Lord, I am so grateful You send Your angels to watch over me.

The Deacon's Doctrine: Satan

1 Peter 5:8

"Your adversary the devil is prowling around like a roaring lion, looking for anyone he can devour."

Satan is a real being. He is not some fictitious figure with horns and a pitchfork. He was originally created as Lucifer, an angel. He rebelled against God and fell (Isa. 14:13-14). He was cast by God from heaven into the earth and since the first century, at least, has been identified as "the god of this world [or age]" (2 Cor. 4:4). The very name Satan means "adversary" (1 Pet. 5:8), while the word devil means "slanderer" (Rev. 12:10). He is viewed in Scripture as the evil one (1 Jn. 5:19), the tempter (1 Thess. 3:5), murderer (Jn. 8:44), liar (Jn. 8:44), and confirmed sinner (1 Jn. 3:8).

Satan works in two specific areas in an attempt to discount or destroy the people of God. He uses the evil world system (1 Jn. 2:15-16) to constantly tempt us to love the world and the things in the world more than we love God. He also uses the flesh—the lower, sinful nature of man—to tempt us to compromise our biblical and moral values (Rom. 6:1-11).

> The biggest defense against the temptations of Satan is the Word of God.

Of course, as a child of God, you have the Holy Spirit of God resident in your life. Scripture makes it clear, "Greater is He who is in you than he who is in the world" (1 Jn. 4:4). Since God, who is in you, is more powerful than Satan, who is in the world, then you have all the power you need to be victorious over temptation (1 Cor. 10:13). The biggest defense you have against the temptations of Satan is the Word of God. This is exactly what Jesus used when He was tempted (cf. Matt. 4).

You need not fear Satan or any of his schemes (Eph. 6:11). In Christ, you have everything you need to overcome Satan and faithfully follow and serve your Savior. May it be said of you, "They overcame him because of the blood of the Lamb [Calvary], and because of the word of their testimony [confession], and they did not love their life even when faced with death [commitment]" (Rev. 12:11).

Dear Lord, I pray that You will be my defense against Satan. Help me resist him and trust You.

The Deacon's Doctrine: Demons

Ephesians 6:12

"Our battle is . . . against the rulers . . . the authorities . . . the world powers of this darkness, against the spiritual forces of evil in the heavens."

Demons are angels who fell with Satan, who is called the prince of demons (Matt. 12:24). Demons, like angels and Satan, display a great deal of intelligence. The Bible gives indication that they know
Jesus (Mk. 1:24), they know their own eventual doom (Matt. 8:29), they are acquainted with the plan of salvation (Jas. 2:19), and they have and promote a well-developed system of their own doctrine
(1 Tim. 4:1-3). It is this doctrinal deception that has become so blatant in our day with the rise of Mormonism, Jehovah's Witnesses, Islam, and several "emergent preachers" who distort a biblical view of grace.

More than anything, demons attempt to counterfeit the Word of God by providing "deceiving alternatives" to biblical truths. They will try to lead us to believe a lie. Likewise, they can inflict diseases (Matt. 9:33, Lk. 13:11, 16), they can possess animals (Mk. 5:13), and they promote false doctrine (1 Tim. 4:1). Demons are often identified as affecting nations— especially nations that have rejected God and His Word and His Son (cf. Dan. 10:13; Isa. 14; Ezek. 28).

> A true believer cannot be possessed by a demon.

It is clear in Scripture that a true believer cannot be possessed by a demon. However, we can be oppressed by evil spirits and influenced by them. A strong safeguard is to maintain a daily devotion to God and allow His Spirit to daily control us—mind, emotions, and will. We must faithfully resist the devil and he will flee from us, as we see in James 4:7.

Be aware of demonic forces as you continue in your service through the church. But don't look for a "demon behind every bush." If you are daily devoted to God and His work and are living under the control of the Holy Spirit, then you will be victorious over any evil spirit that might be dispatched by Satan to try to attack you.

Dear Lord, I pray You will so control my life that the forces of Satan would be guarded from me. Help me to walk in Your Spirit and gain Your victory.

THE DEACON'S DOCTRINE: MAN
Psalm 8:4-5

"What is man that You remember him, the son of man that you look after him? You made him a little less than God and crowned him with glory and honor."

Basically man is material or physical (body) and immaterial (soul or spirit). Both aspects were the direct result of God's creative activity (Gen. 2:7) in which He made man in His own image (Gen. 1:26, 5:1). In both senses, material and immaterial, we are "fearfully and wonderfully made" (Ps. 139:14). And though created by God and for God, man chose to disobey God and subsequently fell from his glorious position in the Garden of Eden to a fallen condition outside the garden. Because the sin of Adam has been transmitted through the generations (Rom. 5:12), we too are fallen in our sin and in need of reconciliation to God. In Christ, this is exactly what God has done. He has provided a way for us to be restored to Him.

> Live your life as a man of God, servant of Christ, and blessing to the church.

When you, as a lost and sinful man (Rom. 3:23), repented of your sin (Acts 2:38), simultaneously placed your faith in Christ alone to save you (Jn. 1:12), and surrendered your life to Him (Acts 26:20), you became a new man (2 Cor. 5:17). As a new man, you've been given a new capacity—a new nature—to live a brand new life (Rom. 6:4)! You have become a permanent child of God, and you will spend an eternity with Christ in heaven (Jn. 14:-16).

But what about now? I hope you will progress toward becoming a man of God. Such a man is described by Paul in 1 Timothy 6:11-16. There, Paul says a man of God is known by what he flees from (v. 11a), what he follows after (v. 11b), what he fights for (v. 12), and what he is faithful to do (v. 14). Through Christ, you have been given "everything pertaining to life and godliness" (2 Pet. 1:3). Live your life now as a man of God, a servant of Christ, and a blessing to the church.

Dear Lord, I desire to become a man totally given over to You. In You, I am not just a man but a man of God. Please empower me to live as Your man.

The Deacon's Doctrine: Sin
Romans 5:12

"Sin entered the world through one man, and death through sin,
in this way death spread to all men, because all sinned."

Man was created by God without sin but with the capacity to sin. Sin entered the human race when Adam and Eve violated the direct command of God by eating the forbidden fruit in the Garden of Eden (Gen. 3:6). Adam's sin affected all future generations because all men thereafter chose to sin (Rom. 5:12-21).

The New Testament word for *sin* (Gk: *hamartia*) literally means, "a missing of the mark."[4] It is essentially man's feeble and failing attempt to live up to the standards of God. Try as we may to hit those high biblical standards of absolute perfection, we cannot. We always have and always will miss that mark. Since we are sinners by nature and by choice, we have no recourse for forgiveness and reconciliation but to receive the finished work of Christ as full payment (atonement) for our sin (Rom. 6:23). Fortunately, by God's grace, we have been saved (Eph. 2:8-9). Technically, we have been saved by grace alone, through faith alone, in Christ alone, and that, solely, for the glory of God. For this we can be eternally grateful.

> **Though we are eternally saved, we need to confess our sins daily.**

Still, there is the matter of daily living and the acts of sin that we commit even as forgiven sinners. Though we have been and remain eternally saved, we have the need to daily, or as often as necessary, "confess our sins" for "He is faithful and righteous to forgive us our sins and to cleanse us from all unrighteousness" (1 Jn. 1:9). Though you have a new nature (of righteousness) in you, you still have an old nature (of sin) in you, as well (cf. Rom. 7:13-15). Therefore, daily remember to "consider yourself to be dead to sin, but alive to God in Christ Jesus" (Rom. 6:11). Though you may never experience a sinless life, you will sin less and less each year that you live if you will apply God's Word with regularity.

> **Dear Lord, I know I am a sinner by nature and by choice. But I pray that You will daily cleanse me of sin and help me live in Your forgiveness.**

THE DEACON'S DOCTRINE: SALVATION
Luke 19:10

"For the Son of Man has come to seek and to save that which was lost."

If we assume the need for salvation, we must also assume that there is something from which we must be saved. We must also assume that there is a means by which we can be saved and a purpose for which we are saved. The Bible gives us clear instruction in these assumptions, which are accurate and require divine intervention.

That from which we need to be saved is God's judgment for our sin. All have sinned and come short of the glory of God (Rom. 3:23), and the wages of sin is eternal separation from God (Rom. 6:23). God always has and always will pass eternal judgment on our sin. He either does this directly toward us, in which case we are condemned to hell forever, or He does this indirectly through Christ and His blood atonement, in which case we are eternally forgiven of our sin and assured of a home in heaven. If we confess with our mouth that Jesus is our Lord and believe in our hearts that God raised Him from the dead, we will be saved (cf. Rom. 10:9-10).

> We must assume there is a purpose for which we are saved.

The doctrine of salvation may best be described in three tenses. There is a past tense aspect that says, "I have been saved from the penalty of sin and am therefore justified by Christ's finished work on the cross." There is a present tense aspect that says, "I am being saved from the power of sin and am therefore being sanctified by the progressive work of the Holy Spirit in my life." There is a future tense aspect that says, "I will be saved from the presence of sin and will be fully glorified by God the Father in heaven." All three tenses are assured and certain for every born-again child of God.

You now live in the present tense. Your life and service are in process. You are being progressively set apart unto God for His use now and His glory forever.

Dear Lord, I yield all that I am and all that I have to You . . . again . . . today! Thank You for seeking me and saving me so I can serve You now and live with You forever.

The Deacon's Doctrine: Church
Matthew 16:18

"On this rock I will build My Church, and the forces of Hades will not overpower it."

Though the New Testament Church did not officially come into existence until Pentecost (Acts 2), Jesus, here, clearly introduces His intention to establish it. In Matthew 18:15-20, He further indicates how the church should be disciplined. Of course, we are recipients of His great blessing called His Church. The term *church* literally means "called-out ones." By virtue of the rebirth (and only by that means), we have been supernaturally placed into the body of Christ—the Church.

Acts 2:41 is a key verse indicating the criteria under which we become members of the church: "So then, those who had received his word were baptized; and that day there were added [to the church] about three thousand souls." Though baptism was not an absolute prerequisite for one to be saved and enter the universal body of Christ, it is an ordinance intended for every member of the local church. The verse gives the correct order. We believe in Christ as we receive His Word (gospel) and are saved. We then are baptized as a public expression (i.e., confession) of our private or personal rebirth experience.

> **The term church means "called-out ones."**

The church can be viewed from both a universal viewpoint, in which case it includes every genuine believer who has been saved since Pentecost, as well as from the standpoint of a local congregation of believers assembling together regularly in a smaller, localized group. Essentially, New Testament believers are seen as a vital part of the church and included in both descriptions. That is, you are a member of both the universal and the local church.

Furthermore, you are a called-out Deacon in the church. You should understand the institution that Jesus created. You should love and serve the church. You should be an integral participant in the life and ministry of the church. Begin today to put your church and your service to the church closer to the top of your priority list.

Dear Lord, I know You have placed me in Your church to serve You and Your people. Please help me do that in a way that brings glory to You.

The Deacon's Doctrine: Future Things
John 14:3

"If I go away and prepare a place for you, I will come back and receive you to Myself, so that where I am you may be also."

The theological term for the doctrine of last things is *eschatology*. In short, it is "the study of what will happen when all things are consummated at the end of history, particularly centered on the event known as the Second Coming of Christ."[5] Many churches, perhaps even the one in which you serve, are known for their commitment to the book (i.e., Bible), the blood (i.e., Christ's atonement), and the blessed hope (i.e., redemption of all believers at Christ's return). These are fundamental beliefs that we hold near to our hearts.

> The future is bright for the believer but dark for the unbeliever.

Someone has well said, "We may not know all that the future holds, but we do know Who holds all of the future." There are many things we do know from God's Word about the future, and especially about heaven. Some of these are drawn directly from John 14. Heaven is a prestigious place (the Father's house), a prepared place (to prepare a place for you), a promised place (I will come again and receive you to Myself), and a prescribed place (believe in God, believe also in Me). The future is bright for the believer but dark for the unbeliever. Just as there is a heaven, there is also a hell. Hell is a real place prepared for "unprepared people" (Rev. 20:14-15).

There are varieties of views as to the timing of future things. But you can be absolutely certain of one thing: Jesus is coming back again to this earth. Each and every one of us who has been "born again to a living hope" (1 Pet. 1:3) will be with Jesus for all eternity. Your responsibility now is two-fold. One, be sure you are prepared to meet the Lord—be sure you are genuinely saved—and two, be faithful to tell others how they too can prepare. This is your reasonable service in the body of Christ. Give yourself to it wholeheartedly!

Dear Lord, as Your child I know I will live with You forever. I know You have prepared a place for me in heaven. I pray that I will be faithful to serve You until I get home.

The Deacon's Doctrine: Baptism
Acts 2:41

"So those who accepted his message were baptized . . ."

Three major positions on the nature of baptism exist among Christian groups. The sacramental view holds that baptism is a means by which God conveys grace. According to this view, the person baptized receives remission of sins and is regenerated. It is a view held mainly by Roman Catholics and Lutherans. The covenantal view holds that baptism is a sign or seal of the covenant—God's pledge to save mankind. The covenant, according to this view, is the means of salvation, and baptism is the rite that brings persons into the covenant. The symbolic view holds that baptism is a sign or symbol of a private and personal experience of salvation. It serves as a public identification of the believer with Jesus Christ and thus also a public testimony of the change that has occurred. Most Baptists and mainline denominations hold to this third view.

Baptism is one of two ordinances (not sacraments) of the church. The other is the Lord's Supper. Both are intended to be observed by the church until Jesus returns. Baptism is to be done in obedience to Christ's Great Commission (Matt. 28:19-20). It is to be by immersion following the true meaning of the word and the example of Jesus Himself (Mk. 1:9). It is, of course, to be observed by genuine believers—thus the term "believer's baptism." It does not save anyone—only God's grace appropriated by faith (Eph. 2:8-9) can save us. Rather, it is a symbolic, public acknowledgment of a supernatural, private salvation that has been experienced by the believer at the point of the rebirth (Jn. 3:3).

> **Baptism does not save anyone.**

Deacons, like Pastors, may be authorized by the church to administer baptism and/or the Lord's Supper. The one administering the ordinances is important but not as important as the meaning of the ordinance and of course, the meaning to the recipients of the ordinances. Be faithful to work with your Pastor and other ministry staff in observing the ordinance of believer's baptism. It will be a blessing to them and to you.

Dear Lord, I thank You for the death, burial, and resurrection of Jesus. I thank You that I have been raised with Him to live a brand new life.

The Deacon's Doctrine: Lord's Supper
1 Corinthians 11:26

"As often as you eat this bread and drink the cup, you proclaim the Lord's death until He comes."

Historically, there have been three primary views regarding the Lord's Supper. All the views have grown out of Jesus' Last Supper with His disciples (Matt. 26:17-30), which took place on the night in which He was arrested and later crucified. The view commonly held by Catholics is called *"transubstantiation,"* meaning the bread and wine literally become the actual body and blood of Christ when sacramental words are spoken by the priest. A second view, *"consubstantiation,"* means Christ's body and blood are truly present "in, with, and under" the bread and wine. This is the view often held by Lutherans. Then, there is the *"symbolic view"* or memorial view where the bread and wine are seen only as symbols of the sacrificed body and blood of Christ. It is a memorial ceremony of Christ's finished work.

> **The Lord's Supper is intended for genuine, born-again believers.**

From 1 Corinthians 11:23-34, we glean several points of significance from the Lord's Supper. First it is a thanksgiving ordinance ("when He had given thanks"). Second, it is a memorial ordinance ("do this in remembrance of Me"). Third, it is an evangelistic ordinance ("you proclaim the Lord's death"). Fourth, it is a prophetic ordinance ("until He comes"). Fifth, it is a disciplinary ordinance ("we are disciplined by the Lord").

The Lord's Supper is an ordinance intended for genuine, born-again believers who share a common faith with fellow recipients. Thus, it calls for us to examine ourselves thoroughly before we actually partake of the elements. We need to look back at the sacrifice of Christ. We need to look ahead at the promise of Christ. We need to look within at our relationship with Christ. We need to look around at our relationship to other believers. Having so examined ourselves, we may then eat the bread and drink of the cup in a worthy manner.

Dear Lord, if I am called upon to administer this ordinance along with my Pastor, please help me take my responsibility seriously! Help me serve You and serve the church by serving the Supper.

The Deacon's Doctrine: The Trinity
Matthew 28:19

"Baptizing them in the name of the Father, and of the Son and of the Holy Spirit."

Nelson's Bible Dictionary describes the Trinity as:

> The coexistence of the Father, the Son, and the Holy Spirit in the unity of the Godhead (divine nature or essence). The doctrine of the trinity means that within the being and activity of the one God there are three distinct persons: Father, Son and Holy Spirit.[6]

It has never been easy for Christians to understand, much less communicate, the Trinity. Nonetheless, the Bible affirms that God is a Trinitarian God. He is one God in three persons. He is not three gods. He is one God. Yet, He has chosen to reveal Himself in three persons. All three persons are co-equal. They all carry the identically same attributes as the other. But in the incarnation (Jesus becoming flesh), God purposed to limit Himself of some of the uses of some of His attributes (i.e., omnipresence).

> **The Bible affirms that God is a Trinitarian God. He is one God in three persons.**

Pastors and Bible teachers occasionally try to illustrate the trinity by referring to H2O or water. They suggest that the Trinity may be compared to H2O, which may manifest itself as liquid, ice, or steam while retaining its essence as H2O. God is One God whose essence remains the same and who chooses to manifest Himself as Father, Son, or Holy Spirit depending on the way in which He relates to His creation at a given time.

Interestingly, the Father is seen predominantly (but not exclusively) in the Old Testament, Jesus in the gospels, and the Holy Spirit in the Acts and the epistles. Nonetheless, all three persons are all present in all the books of the Bible. All three persons are all active in the salvation of souls and the work of the Church.

> **Dear Lord, I want to get to know You (my Father), Jesus (my elder brother), and the Holy Spirit (my Divine Comforter). As I do, my effectiveness in serving You will be enhanced three-fold ... actually, three hundred-fold and more! Thank You!**

The Deacon's Greatest Challenges

A Deacon's Draw From Genesis
Genesis 32:10

*"I am unworthy of all the kindness and faithfulness
You have shown Your servant."*

Though it took him several years to realize it, God had placed a servant's heart in Jacob. He had stolen the birthright of his twin brother, Esau. He had tricked his father, Isaac, into giving him the blessing of the first born. He ran from home to live with his uncle and eventually tricked him in the management of his livestock. But the time came when God spoke to Jacob and told him to return home and humble himself before his family. He was finally obedient and returned. On the way he "wrestled with God" (Gen. 32:24), and that encounter stripped from him everything except a servant's heart. He began to fulfill God's call and promise found in Genesis 32:9-12.

> It is not unlikely you have had some years trying to discover your own servant's heart.

It is not unlikely that you have had some years trying to discover your own servant's heart. They may have been years of running or just waiting to discover God's use of your life. As with Jacob, you may have found yourself far from home—that is far from your family, your church, or God. You may recall a "wrestling match" in your own experience with God. If so, you have had the unique opportunity to be "delivered from yourself" (Gen. 32:30) and replaced in the family of God as a genuine servant.

What an extraordinary work God has done in you! He has once again shown Himself strong on your behalf and put you into service. Never take that for granted! Remember, God has brought you through the molding years of your life so He may set you as an example before future generations.

> **Dear Lord, thank You for teaching me through the experiences of my life what it means to have a servant's heart. Thank You for Your willingness to wrestle with me until I found deliverance from myself and unreserved devotion to You.**

A Deacon's Draw From Exodus
Exodus 14:31

"The people feared the Lord and believed in
Him and in His servant Moses."

No doubt, the Exodus of the Israelites from Egypt across the Red Sea on dry ground was one of the greatest miracles of God. Moses was used as a servant to God's people from the time he appealed to Pharaoh for their release from slavery until he died forty years later on Mount Pisgah, overlooking the promised land (cf. Deut. 34). In his earlier years, Moses had experienced expulsion from Egypt because he misunderstood God's intended purpose for his life. After forty years of service as a shepherd in Midian, God once again spoke to Moses and placed him into His service. God used Moses to deliver His people from bondage under the cruel Pharaoh.

> It is not unlike God to postpone His greatest use of us until our later years.

When God had fulfilled His purpose for Moses, Moses died. Then God said to Joshua "Moses My servant is dead" (Josh. 1:2). Moses was brought through three forty-year periods of his life. He spent forty years in Egypt, forty years in Midian, and forty years in the wilderness of Sinia. Strange as it sounds, his greatest years of service were in the last forty—in the wilderness.

It is not unlike God to postpone His greatest use of us until our later years. You may think, because God has not yet used you as significantly as you had hoped, that your best days of service are past. The truth may be that the best days and years of your service are just ahead of you—even if you're in the last third of your life. "Moses was 120 years old when he died; his eyes were not weak, and his vitality had not left him" (Deut. 34:7). May this be said of you when the time comes for you to die—not that you would have mere physical strength, but that you might be remembered by others as a mighty, influential servant of God.

> Dear Lord, please control my life even as You did Moses's so I may be used as Your servant all the days of my life, including this day. Because of my service, may people "fear You and believe in You."

A Deacon's Draw From Leviticus

Leviticus 10:3

"I will show My holiness to those who are near Me, and
I will reveal My glory before all the people."

Aaron was Moses' brother and as a priest, is seen as a type of Christ, the Great High Priest. Aaron's sons Nadab and Abihu, also considered priests, "presented unauthorized fire before the Lord . . . Then the flames leaped from the Lord's presence and burned them to death before the Lord" (Lev. 10:1-2). The priests were considered to be servants of God. Whereas the prophets brought God's Word to the people, the priests brought the people's needs before the Lord. They served to pray, make intercession, burn incense, and make animal sacrifices to God for the people.

Of course, this access to the heavenly Father has now been brought emphatically and conclusively by our Great High Priest and eternal Intercessor the Lord Jesus Christ. As the Old Testament priests made temporary sacrifice for remission of sin, Jesus the Suffering Servant has made permanent sacrifice for all of our sins.

Aaron's sons made a big mistake in thinking they could exercise their servant duties in their own sinful, selfish ways. It cost them their lives. In the process, God demonstrated His holiness to those who were there.

> How you serve God and the heart with which you serve God are just as important as whether you serve God.

How you serve God and the heart with which you serve God are just as important as whether you serve God. Do your character and conduct reflect that of Christ? Are you interested in serving God with a pure heart? Holiness of life and lifestyle still matter to God. He would much rather receive glory for Himself from your humble, obedient, and faithful service than from the example of immature, selfish service, resulting in premature death. Devote yourself today to serve in holiness.

Dear Lord, I pray that You would enable me to live and serve as a holy man of God. I desire to be Your humble, faithful, and obedient servant.

A Deacon's Draw From Numbers
Numbers 14:24

"My servant Caleb has a different spirit and has followed Me completely."

Caleb was one of twelve spies that Moses sent into the Promised Land. He and Joshua were the only two who came back with a positive report. Caleb saw all the good in God's Promised Land. The others saw all the bad. Caleb focused on God while others focused on the enemy. He had a different spirit. Indeed, he had a servant's heart, desiring to serve God rather than men.

We glean from this text that a servant of God is most clearly identified as having a different spirit and following God completely. That means he thinks differently and has a different attitude about God and His work than most do. It means he has devoted himself without reservation or hesitancy to the service of God. At least in Caleb's case, it meant that he would take an unpopular and even criticized stand in obedience to God and His Word.

> Caleb focused on God while others focused on the enemy.

Like Moses, Caleb saw the best years of his service following the forty years in the wilderness. Unlike Moses, however, Caleb entered the Promised Land with Joshua. He requested the mountain he had surveyed forty years earlier and captured it for his inheritance. As he had served Moses, he also served Joshua. Caleb has gone down in God's history as "My servant, Caleb."

What greater legacy could you leave? Even if it costs you years of sacrifice, disappointment, and uncertainty, will it not be worth it when you are remembered by God as "My servant"? You have been called by God to that end. You are being molded and prepared for that end. You now have only to follow Him completely to that end.

Dear Lord, grant to me a unique anointing of Your Holy Spirit so I might serve You with all my heart. Help me to remain faithful and true to the last day of my life on earth.

A Deacon's Draw From Deuteronomy

Deuteronomy 9:27

"Remember your servants Abraham, Isaac, and Jacob."

The great patriarchs of the Old Testament are some of the best examples of servanthood among all the characters of the Bible. Abraham, in particular, illustrates for us the kind of servant to whom God commits Himself in covenant. In Genesis 12:2-3 we discover the words of the Abrahamic Covenant. In many ways these are promises for the people of God today:

> I will make you into a great nation, I will bless you, I will make your name great, and you will be a blessing. I will bless those who bless you, I will curse those who treat you with contempt, and all the peoples on earth will be blessed through you.

Even though the most accurate fulfillment of this covenant is in the nation of Israel, the New Testament assures us that "as Abraham believed God, and it was credited to him for righteousness, so understand that those who have faith are Abraham's sons . . . So those who have faith are blessed with Abraham, who had faith" (Gal. 3:6-9). Thereby we have the promises made to Abraham.

> As a servant of God in your church, you will do well to remember the faith and character of the patriarchs.

As a servant of God in your church, you will do well to remember the faith and character of the patriarchs, especially Abraham. As you believe God, your faith will also be credited as righteousness. You will also be blessed and be a blessing to others. Because of your faith and obedient service to God through your church and beyond, "all the people on earth will be blessed through you."

Dear Lord, I do place my faith totally and exclusively in You and Your Word. I believe You have made great promises to me and I want to be faithful to serve You from those promises.

A Deacon's Draw From Joshua

Joshua 24:15

*"Choose for yourselves today the one you will worship . . .
As for me and my family, we will worship the Lord."*

Joshua's life and service to the Israelites is well documented in this book by his name, as well as by extrabiblical history. He is primarily known as a military commander who succeeded Moses in leading God's people. He led the people across the Jordan River and into the Promised Land. He conquered large cities and territories, designating the land to the tribes of Israel.

> As a good soldier of Christ Jesus, be well-trained, well-equipped, and ever available.

His service was unique in some ways. Not every servant of God is called upon to command an army. However, many of God's servants are intricately involved in a "spiritual army" some as commanders, some as followers, but all as soldiers. Paul reminded Timothy (both faithful servants) to "share in suffering as a good soldier of Christ Jesus" (2 Tim. 2:3).

From the summation of Joshua's life and service we learn at least four things (Scripture taken from the *New American Standard Bible*):

1. Serving God is a *serious* thing (v. 14a, "serve in sincerity and truth").
2. Serving God is a *decisive* thing (v. 15a, "choose for yourselves").
3. Serving God is an *urgent* thing (v. 15b, "today").
4. Serving God is an *active* thing (v. 24, "we will serve the Lord our God and we will obey His voice").

As you further develop your own service in and through your church, always remember that you have been enlisted by God to do so. As a good soldier of Christ Jesus, be well-trained, well-equipped, and ever available. You are a very valuable person. God will use you to positively affect future generations, even as He did Joshua.

Dear Lord, I choose again today to serve You and You alone. I know I do so by serving others. Help me to remain a faithful soldier of Christ, Your Son.

A Deacon's Draw From Judges
Judges 2:10

"After them another generation rose up who did not know the Lord or the works He had done for Israel."

It is a sad thing when a servant of God gives himself to a large group of people over several years and those people fail to pass God's Word and works on to the next generation. This is exactly what happened in the life of Joshua. Joshua 24:31 says, "Israel worshipped the Lord throughout Joshua's lifetime and during the lifetimes of the elders who outlived Joshua . . ." But in just a few short years "that whole generation was also gathered to their ancestors. After them another generation rose up who did not know the Lord or the works He had done for Israel" (Judges 2:10).

How could so much faith and truth and service be lost in only one generation? Apparently service meant something different to Joshua and the elders of his day than it did to their children and grandchildren. Whether the elders failed to pass them on or the next generation rejected them outright, the word and works of the Lord were forgotten.

> No greater work is yours than to be sure the next generation hears God's glorious gospel.

In his research for *The Bridger Generation*, Thom Rainer discovered some alarming statistics in four generations of Americans. Of the *Builders* born between 1910-1945, 65 percent are professing Christians. Of the *Boomers* born between 1946-1964, 35 percent are Christians. Among the *Busters* born between 1965-1976, 15 percent are Christians. Of those born between 1977-1994, the *Bridgers,* only 4 percent claim to be born-again Christians.[1]

No greater work is yours as a Deacon of God's people than to be sure the next generation hears and receives His glorious gospel.

Dear Lord, please remind me daily of my responsibility to pass Your Word and Your works on to my children and grandchildren. Use me to serve in my generation for the salvation of the next.

A Deacon's Draw From Ruth
Ruth 1:16

"Wherever you go, I will go, and wherever you live, I will live; your people will be my people, and your God will be my God.

These words are those of Ruth to her mother-in-law, Naomi, who encouraged her to leave and return to her original family following the death of her husband. In context they speak volumes of the character, commitment, and genuine servanthood of Ruth. By way of application, these words challenge every servant of God to be faithful wherever, with whomever, and for however long necessary.

> These words challenge us to be faithful wherever, with whomever, and for however long necessary.

Ruth was moved by God to stay in a foreign country, live as a widow with a widowed mother-in-law, and work as a common laborer in the fields. Because of her faithfulness as a servant to God, to Naomi, and to her employer, she was rewarded in exceptional ways, not the least of which was her place in the genealogical lineage of Christ.

Whenever you feel, as a servant of Christ in your church, that you are out of place, out of step, or out of energy, remember the servanthood of Ruth. Be willing to commit yourself even more during trying times. Stay true to your calling and work even when you don't understand it all. As you do, you will find that God can change your heart, illumine your mind, and empower your spirit to serve Him "in spite of the circumstances." And perhaps, as with Ruth, God will dramatically alter your circumstances to make you a powerful example of Christian servanthood.

Dear Lord, as Your servant in and through my church, I want to remain steadfast and true. I want to follow You faithfully regardless of the circumstances in which I serve.

A Deacon's Draw From 1 Samuel
1 Samuel 3:10

> "The Lord came, stood there, and called as before, 'Samuel, Samuel!' Samuel responded, 'Speak, for Your servant is listening.'"

The story of Samuel is a beautiful example of how God speaks and calls servants into His work. Samuel had a godly mother, Hannah, who dedicated him to God's service at a very early age. She declared, "I now give this boy to the Lord. For as long as he lives, he is given to the Lord" (1 Sam. 1:28). Once dedicated, Samuel "served the Lord in the presence of Eli the priest" (1 Sam. 2:11). He was especially attuned to God's voice and was clearly directed by God to serve as he did. He not only listened but listened with a heart of obedience.

You may or may not have had a godly mother who dedicated you to the Lord's service. But however different your call may have come, you are now in a servant role in the church. In light of that, you have assumed responsibilities and ministries you had not planned for or even known about a few years ago. This means you must be as sensitive as you can be to the voice of God in your own life. There is no question but that He will speak to you. The only question is, will you be listening when He does?

> **You must be sensitive to the voice of God in your own life.**

E.W. Blandy captures this thought in a hymn he wrote in 1890:

> I can hear my Savior calling,
> I can hear my Savior calling,
> I can hear my Savior calling,
> Take thy cross and follow, follow Me.[2]

You have the same opportunity that Samuel had to say, "Speak, for Your servant is listening." And as with Samuel, you can serve the Lord through your church for the rest of your life. What an opportunity!

> **Dear Lord, please keep my mind and heart sensitive to Your Holy Spirit's prompting. Remind me daily through Your Word how and where I am to serve. Speak, Lord, Your servant is listening.**

A Deacon's Draw From 2 Samuel
2 Samuel 9:8

"What is your servant that you take an interest in a dead dog like me?

King David wanted to show respect for the family of Saul, his predecessor to the throne of Israel. So he inquired of one of his servants, "Is there anyone left of Saul's family I can show the kindness of God to?" (1 Sam. 9:3).The servant identified Jonathan's son, Mephibosheth, who had been lame in his feet since birth. Mephibosheth yielded himself to King David saying, "I am your servant." Clearly this man was not one "most likely to succeed." He thought he had absolutely nothing to offer and saw himself as useless as a "dead dog.

Obviously, God had different plans for Mephibosheth. David, no doubt under the direction of God, brought the young man into his temple and provided for him all of his life. The king assigned the land owned by his grandfather, Saul, to him and engaged workers to attend it for him. Mephibosheth became a master with servants under him because of the loving-kindness of the Lord.

You may have felt very unworthy when God began to call you into service. You may have seen yourself as having nothing to offer. If so, you soon discovered that a man of God with that heart and attitude is just the one God is looking to place in service. Our service has far more to do with God working in and through us—even our weaknesses—than it does with us working for God in our perceived strengths. God takes great interest and will seriously use a man who will humbly yield to Him for service.

> Dear Lord, I acknowledge that I have nothing of real value to offer You. But I also know You will take my yielded heart and use me in Your service. Here, I give my all to You.

A Deacon's Draw From 1 Kings

1 Kings 3:8

"Your servant is among Your people You have chosen, a
people too numerous to be numbered or counted."

Solomon is another good example of a servant of God. He certainly didn't do everything right. But at a particular point in his life, he makes this special request of the Lord. In his prayer he identified God's placement in his life (v. 7 "You have now made Your servant king . . ."), accentuated God's people in his life (v. 8 "Your servant is among Your people You have chosen"), and appealed to God for wisdom in his life (v. 9 "So give Your servant an obedient heart . . . to discern between good and evil.").

This picture of Solomon helps us, as servants of God and His people, to better prepare for ministry in the local church. It is important that we see ourselves "placed by God" as Deacons. God must be the one who orchestrates our placement. Likewise, we must always remember it is God's people whom we serve. They are His "chosen people, a great people." They need your attention, and they deserve to be served. And of course, you must serve with the wisdom of God (cf. Acts 6:3). You do not do what you do out of mere human ingenuity or personal creativity. You serve the people of God, at the pleasure of God, by the wisdom of God, for the glory of God.

> It is important that we see ourselves "placed by God" as Deacons.

J. I. Packer said, "The kind of wisdom that God waits to give to those who ask him is a wisdom that will bind us to Himself."[3] The closer you are to God, the greater your wisdom to serve God. You are God's servant among God's people to minister the grace of God. Be faithful in your service!

**Dear Lord, I realize that I am but a servant to
Your people. I desire to be obedient in heart and
serve with Your wisdom and discernment.**

A Deacon's Draw From 2 Kings

2 Kings 4:1

"Your servant, my husband, has died. You know that your servant feared the Lord."

Here is a story of the wife of a prophet who was left destitute, even though her husband was a faithful student and servant of God. She was left a widow with two children. Her cupboard was bare, and her heart was broken. But God intervened and met her need through the prophet Elisha, another faithful servant of God.

Serving God does not guarantee an easy or necessarily a long life. Though we may fear the Lord and faithfully serve the church, there is no certainty as to how long we will do so. Death is no respecter of age or stage or even devotion. God knows how long we are to serve. When He is finished using us, He will call us home. If we have been faithful to Him, to our family, and to His people, He will surely take care of those we leave behind. That is precisely what He did with this widow in 2 Kings, and that is exactly what He will do for you.

> Service in this life may only be met with reward in the next.

It is important to remember, however, that God cares for and rewards the survivors of those who "fear the Lord" and serve Him faithfully. We live and serve in the confidence that, given our faithful stewardship of time and resources, God will see to it that our needs and the needs of our loved ones are met. Service in this life may only be met with reward in the next. But it will be rewarded, whether to the servant himself in heaven or to those who survive him on earth (cf. Rev. 2:10).

John Calvin has stated it well, "We shall never be fit for the service of God if we look not beyond this fleeting life."[4] We serve here and now but we also serve for there and then.

Dear Lord, I acknowledge that my service and time of service is in Your hands. I desire to be faithful with whatever time or place You give me. Help me always to revere You and stay close to You as I serve Your people.

A Deacon's Draw From 1 Chronicles
1 Chronicles 17:19

"Lord, You have done all this greatness, making known all these great promises because of Your servant and according to Your will."

King David came to a place in his own life and service where he was literally overwhelmed at the goodness of God. He sat in the Lord's presence (v. 16), acknowledged God's provision (v. 17), was humbled at God's providence (vv. 18-20), and was amazed at God's power (vv. 21-22). He could hardly contain himself as he thought about the miraculous way in which God had blessed him and his people.

The greatest servants of God in the Old Testament and today are those who, with all humility, acknowledge the marvelous, matchless grace of God. David was a humble shepherd boy before he became the king of Israel. One good way to check your effectiveness in service is to honestly assess your attitude of humility. This is not easily done because we are not always honest with ourselves. When we think we are most humble is usually when we are least humble.

> One good way to check your effectiveness in service is to honestly assess your attitude of humility.

Humble service is the best service. It is developed over time and always grows out of us "doing nothing out of rivalry or conceit, but in humility considering others as more important than ourselves" (Phil. 2:3). In his best years of service, King David put the interests of others (especially God's people) ahead of his own. In your best years of service, you will do the same. And as you do, you will experience some overwhelming times in your own life. You too will be humbled at all the great promises of God made evident to you and the great blessings of God poured out upon you. Has God not done for you great and mighty things according to His divine will?

> Dear Lord, as Your servant I pray that my heart will remain true to You. I pray that my mind will focus upon You and that my attitude would exhibit genuine humility as I seek to serve Your people.

A Deacon's Draw From 2 Chronicles
2 Chronicles 6:19

"Listen to Your servant's prayer and his petition, Lord my God, so that You may hear the cry and the prayer that Your servant prays before You."

This is one of the longer prayers in the Old Testament. It is a prayer of Solomon regarding the dedication of the Temple. As phenomenal as the temple was, it paled in comparison to Solomon's perception of God. In verse 18 he says, "Even heaven, the highest heaven, cannot contain You, much less this temple I have built." Yet, Solomon also saw God as a personal God who hears and answers prayer. As a servant of God, Solomon could approach God in prayer with great confidence, just as we can today.

This "servant's prayer of Solomon," as we might call it, places primary emphasis upon who God is, what He had already done, and how Solomon desired God to work in the future. It sets the stage for that most familiar response from God in 2 Chronicles 7:14:

> [If] My people who are called by My name humble themselves, pray and seek My face, and turn from their evil ways, then I will hear from heaven, forgive their sin, and heal their land.

> As a servant of God, Solomon could approach God in prayer with great confidence, just as we can today.

When we pray, as God's servants in the church, we do so believing that God will hear us, forgive us, and heal us. It is quite all right to petition God for your needs. But it is especially important to acknowledge Him for who He is and what He has already done. When you pray in this manner out of a sincere heart of obedience and unreserved allegiance to God, you may be assured that He will listen and answer according to His perfect will.

Dear Lord, I make my prayer before You today with full acknowledgment of Who You are and what You have done in my life. "Hear the cry and the prayer that Your servant prays before You.

A Deacon's Draw From Ezra

Ezra 7:10

"Ezra had determined in his heart to study the law of the Lord, obey it, and teach its statutes and ordinances in Israel."

In several places within the context of Ezra 7 it is said of him "The gracious hand of God was on him" (vv. 6, 9). Ezra was a skilled scribe in the Law of Moses. But he was also seen as a unique servant to God's people at a time of rebuilding the spiritual climate of Jerusalem. One of the ways that he served God's people was by studying the Word of God and communicating it to the people.

Not every servant in the church is gifted to teach, but every servant will be used in some way to bring God's Word to the people. All of us should have a desire to serve with the gracious hand of God on us. Since we know that only God's Word can change and transform lives (cf. Heb. 4:12), we must be certain that our service directs people to the Word of God. Even if your service does not include specific Bible teaching, it should be rendered in such a way that it gets people under the Word. Serve them and invite them to Bible study or worship services where God's Word will be proclaimed.

> All of us should have a desire to serve with the gracious hand of God on us.

On the other hand, you may be a servant who is gifted to teach or preach. You will want to do as Ezra did, determine in your heart to study the Word of God, obey it, and teach it to the people. The greatest service you can render in a person's life is to get them in the Word of God and get the Word of God into them. This calls for both a commitment and sincere determination on your part. It takes time to prepare. You must make time to pray, study, organize your lesson or message, and show up early to teach. As with Ezra, be sure you give them the *"statutes and ordinances"* of God (i.e., His Word from the Bible). You will be providing a very important service to your church.

Dear Lord, as Your servant in the church, I want to be faithful to Your Word. I want to get people into Your Word and help get Your Word into people.

A Deacon's Draw From Nehemiah
Nehemiah 1:6

"Let Your eyes be open and Your ears be attentive to hear Your servant's prayer that I now pray to You day and night for Your servants, the Israelites."

This prayer of Nehemiah was offered at a time when he and God's people were in captivity in Babylon and the city of Jerusalem was in ruins. He had received this report from his brother, Hanani, and it disturbed him greatly. He began to fast and pray, appealing to God for revival of the city and of the remnant that were still there. The prayer was not a quiet, impersonal, perfunctory prayer. It was a prayer offered out of a broken heart and a disturbed spirit. So earnest was his prayer that he prayed "day and night" for God's people.

Have you ever found yourself in a church that was headed for spiritual ruin? As a servant in the church, did your heart break over the situation? How long has it been since you have prayed day and night—even losing sleep—over the dire need of the church? Unfortunately, there are numerous churches in America that are in this very condition. They desperately need servants of God who will pray for them and be willing to act boldly and sometimes sacrificially to bring restoration.

> **Our churches need servants of God who will pray for them and be willing to act boldly to bring restoration.**

In verse 11, Nehemiah further prayed, "Please, Lord, let Your ear be attentive to the prayer of Your servant . . . [and] give Your servant success today, and have compassion on him in the presence of this man [i.e., his king]." Nehemiah appealed to God and then to the human authorities, to allow him to go back and rebuild the walls of Jerusalem. You may find yourself in such circumstances. If so, remember Nehemiah "was graciously strengthened by his God" (2:8). Never underestimate what God will do with you and for you to bring revival to your church.

Dear Lord, please strengthen me and direct me to know how to best serve You and Your people at this particular time in my life.

A Deacon's Draw From Esther

Esther 4:16

"I will go to the king even if it is against the law. If I perish, I perish."

The story of Queen Esther gives us many exceptional lessons about serving God in the midst of a godless government. Godless King Ahasuerus took young Esther, a Jewess, as his queen. Esther became burdened for the Jews' freedom to worship the true God, and the king resisted that. In fact, the king was intent on destroying his Jewish captives. Esther prayed and went before the king with great boldness and courage for the sake of her people. Her guardian father, Mordecai, said to her, "Who knows, perhaps you have come to the kingdom for such a time as this" (4:14). She then determinately made the announcement of verse 16.

You may not find yourself in a similar situation as Esther. But you will likely be called upon to take a stand for Christ and His church in a godless environment. As with Esther, you may be placed by God in a specific town or community "for such a time as this." Your faith and your actions may be tested even to the point of risking your life for the sake of the gospel. What are you doing in your spiritual life to prepare for such a probability? Obviously, you are in your present role as a Deacon because other believers have confidence in you. They believe you will serve them by standing for truth. Some believe you would die for them if necessary.

> You will likely be called upon to take a stand for Christ in a godless environment.

Are you able to say with Esther, I am willing to even appeal to government authorities if necessary to hold out for truth? Do you have such conviction about this that you would do it regardless of the consequences? What if it cost you your life? Your job? Your freedom? Whatever it may cost will be worth it in eternity. Even if you die in your service, "[You] will not perish, but have everlasting life" (Jn. 3:16).

Dear Lord, I desire to follow You and obey Your Word, regardless of what it may cost me. Please embolden me to stand for Your truth even in the midst of godless people.

A Deacon's Draw From Job

Job 2:3

"Have you considered My servant Job? No one else on earth is like him, a man of perfect integrity, who fears God and turns away from evil."

Apparently God considered Job to be one of His faithful servants. He refers to Job as a unique servant ("no one else like him"), an honest servant ("perfect integrity"), a reverent servant ("fears God"), and a righteous servant ("turns away from evil"). It is clear that God could depend on the faithfulness of Job no matter what. Therefore, whenever Satan was looking for someone to devour (1 Pet. 5:8), he heard God say, "Have you considered My servant Job?

Of course, the book of Job clearly pictures the long-suffering and steadfast faithfulness on the part of this servant of God. God knew Job completely, and Job knew God. God trusted Job's faithfulness enough to even allow Satan to "try to destroy" his life. The trial became almost unbearable for Job, but he stayed true to God. At one point he said, "Even if He kills me, I will hope in Him" (13:15). What a servant of God!

None of us ever wishes to be a "Job." We look at all that he suffered and assume that God would never expect that of us when, in fact, the greatest Servant who ever lived gave His own life on a cross for us.

> When being tested, like Job, we should remain faithful and righteous.

Most of us probably have not been tested as Job was. But that does not mean that we should be any less faithful or any less righteous. Can you honestly think of yourself as a unique, honest, reverent, righteous servant of God? If not, maybe this is a good time to develop that spirit.

Make a new, fresh commitment of your life in service to Christ. Discipline yourself in the virtues of the faith. Be as prepared as you can and don't be caught off guard if God says to Satan, "Have you considered my servant (your name)?

**Dear Lord, I know I am Your servant in the church.
I also know that my character and integrity need
Your powerful work of grace. Please make
me a servant with perfect integrity.**

A Deacon's Draw From Psalms

Psalm 31:16

"Show Your favor to Your Servant; save me by Your faithful love."

Nothing can compare to living under the favor of God. This is especially true for those who serve as Deacons in a local church. David was an imperfect man, but he saw himself as a servant of God. He trusted God completely (31:14) to set the course of his life (31:15). He trusted God to take care of those who opposed him. God did all of that in David's behalf out of His divine favor and because of His faithful love.

We often think of grace as the unmerited favor of God. And certainly it is. As God's servant in His church, you are compelled to trust Him with your life. He is trustworthy, and as you faithfully follow Him, He will show His favor to you. God will not only favor your service to His people, He will also save you from the intended effects of your enemies. He does this because He loves you.

Annie Johnson Flint has captured this thought in poetic form:

> He giveth more grace when the burdens grow greater,
> He sendeth more strength when the labours increase;
> To added affliction He addeth His mercy,
> To multiplied trials, His multiplied peace.[5]

This is a direct reference to the teaching of Titus 2:12. God does not favor your life and service merely so you can feel good about what you are doing. He favors you in order to conform you to the image of His Son Jesus Christ. He provides grace for you so you can be saved and serve with a transformed life.

> **God does not favor your life and service merely so you can feel good about what you are doing.**

Perhaps you have found yourself trying to serve God without His Spirit's enablement. That is, you have tried to serve without the favor, grace, and anointing of God. If so, you may need to sincerely join David in his prayer.

Dear God, please show Your favor to Your servant. Deliver me from those who would oppose You. Save me and sustain me by Your faithful love. I desire and commit myself to faithfully serve You and Your people with my life.

A Deacon's Draw From Proverbs
Proverbs 3:5

"Trust in the Lord with all your heart,
and do not rely on your own understanding."

Proverbs 3:5-6 have become favorite verses to many growing believers. Some consider them to be their "life verses." That is, they have quoted and applied these verses in many circumstances of their lives. They have taught others to learn them as well. You would benefit a great deal, as a servant-model in your church, to memorize and regularly apply these verses in your own life.

These verses present us with three very specific mandates before assuring us of a glorious promise. First, we are to *trust* in the Lord. Trust is faith, and faith is trust. We are expected not only to put our trust in Him, but we must simultaneously entrust our lives to Him. It is one thing to trust Him for all He has for you. It is yet another thing to entrust all you are and have to Him. Second, we *depend* on Him and not ourselves. We all rely on something or someone every day we live. You may try to rely solely upon yourself—your own thinking, feeling, judgment, etc. Or you may rely expectantly upon your spouse, your parents, your employer, or some other person. But it does not take long to discover that relying upon your own understanding alone, or even the understanding of a few others, is not sufficient. You must learn to depend upon God's wisdom found clearly in God's Word. Third, we *acknowledge* Him in all we do. Of every move you make or decision you face or service you render, ask yourself, "Am I thinking about Him in this? Is this what He wants? Will this bring glory to Him?" God's desire and will should be at the heart of all you do.

> You must learn to depend upon God's wisdom found clearly in God's Word.

Once these mandates are obeyed, you may then expect God to "guide you on the right paths" (3:6). He will make a clear and straight way for you to fulfill your calling as a Deacon in God's church.

Dear Lord, I do trust You. I desire to trust You with all my life for all my life. I refuse to depend upon my own understanding. I sincerely need Your wisdom and direction. Please clear the way for me to serve You and I will faithfully follow.

A Deacon's Draw From Ecclesiastes

Ecclesiastes 3:1

*"There is an occasion for everything, and a time
for every activity under heaven."*

Solomon lists several examples of *"every* activity under heaven" in Ecclesiastes 3:1-8. I hope you will take time to read and meditate on these:

> A time to give birth and to die; a time to plant and to uproot.
> A time to kill and to heal; a time to tear down and to build.
> A time to weep and to laugh; a time to mourn and to dance.
> A time to throw stones and to gather stones;
> a time to embrace and to avoid embracing.
> A time to search and to count as lost; a time to keep and to throw away.
> A time to tear and to sew; a time to be silent and to speak;
> A time to love and to hate; a time for war and for peace.

Then, in verse 11, the writer says, "He has made everything appropriate in its time.

Have you ever heard, or perhaps spoken the phrase, "God's timing is perfect"? Most of us have. As a Deacon among God's people, you are constantly confronted with the internal question, "Is the timing right for this?" In many cases we miss a blessing from God or an opportunity to minister to others because we fail to answer this question. Frankly, we often postpone or put off a deed of service, convincing ourselves that the timing was not right when, in fact, the time was exactly right.

> We often postpone a deed of service, convincing ourselves the timing was not right.

You will do well to pray without ceasing, listen carefully and consistently to God's still, small voice (His Holy Spirit), and be prepared to act obediently and immediately when God prompts you. That is His timing. He will make His will clear to you in His perfect time.

> Dear Lord, help me develop the kind of relationship with
> You that I will hear Your voice, sense Your prompting,
> and be obedient to You. Help me know Your timing
> when You call upon me to serve in a particular way.

A Deacon's Draw From Song of Solomon
Song of Solomon 8:7

"Mighty waters cannot extinguish love; rivers cannot sweep it away. If a man were to give all his wealth for love, it would be utterly scorned."

With this verse in mind, John Phillips writes:

> Love is what it is all about! It was love that drew our Beloved down from the skies. It was love that took Him to Calvary and on down into the regions of death. His love was invincible, the love that many waters cannot quench, that the floods can never drown . . . Love is what wins out in the end.[6]

Most men who serve as Pastors or Deacons are married with families. This rather unique book in the Bible is essentially the love story of Solomon and the Shulammite. Though Solomon, over all, sets a less than good example to us with multiple wives and concubines, we glean from this book keen insight into marital love. As he brings his book to a close he summarizes, as it were, the marriage of a man and a woman as a union established on and held together by love. He identifies this love as being "as strong as death" (8:6).

Among other things, God has called you out and set you apart in the church as a servant whose marriage and family is as powerful as love and as strong as death (cf. 1 Tim. 3:12). You are setting an example for the next generation. Be so devoted to God and your wife and family that whatever floods of disappointment, discouragement, despair, or even death may come your way, they will not "sweep you away." You have been given wonderful gifts from God—your salvation, your wife, your family, your church, your calling, and your life. Count your many blessings and turn them into a life of service and you will acquire a good standing for yourself, and great boldness in the faith that is in Christ Jesus (1 Tim. 3:13).

> **Count your many blessings and turn them into a life of service.**

Dear Lord, place Your love in me for You, for my family and for my church. Prevent me from ever allowing adversity to extinguish that love.

A Deacon's Draw From Isaiah

Isaiah 44:21

"You are My servant; I formed you, you are My servant,
Israel, you will never be forgotten by Me."

Jacob was one of the patriarchs of the Old Testament, along with his grandfather, Abraham, and his father, Isaac. Jacob had an extraordinary encounter with God, whereby God changed his name to Israel (Gen. 33:28). His twelve sons became the twelve tribes of the nation—the special people of God. Isaiah, the prophet, speaking for God, refers to Jacob as "My servant." Like his father and grandfather, Jacob became a very important servant among God's people. He didn't necessarily plan it that way for himself. In fact, the name *Jacob* means "supplanter or trickster," whereas the name *Israel* means "persists with God." God not only changed his name; He changed his life.

> You too, like Israel, have been formed and preserved by God for service.

You too are a servant of God. You likely did not plan that for yourself. Your former way of life or reputation may have had little to do with God or His church. But now you are at His disposal to serve His people. There is a sense in which you, like Israel, have been formed and preserved by God for service. You have a similar promise from God. To Israel He said, "You will never be forgotten by Me." To you He has said, "I will never leave you or forsake you" (Heb. 13:5).

God has begun a good work in you, and you can be assured that He will complete that work. As a Deacon, you are called upon not to be perfect but to be available and faithful. God has transformed your life and in a sense, given you a new name—Christian. You will be a good servant of Christ Jesus. You will demonstrate to others what servant-leadership is like. Give yourself anew and afresh to Him to that end.

Dear Lord, as You changed and transformed Jacob and made him one of Your servants, please change me however You need to in order to use me as a servant in Your church.

A Deacon's Draw From Jeremiah

Jeremiah 46:27

"But you, My servant . . . do not be afraid, and do not be discouraged . . . for without fail I will save you from far away and your descendants, from the land of their captivity."

Though this was a special and somewhat unique promise made to Israel for their deliverance from captivity, we too are assured of eventual deliverance "from this corrupt generation" (Acts 2:40). This does not mean that you will live your life free of fear or discouragement. It does mean that you can confidently depend upon God to bring you through. He will use you as His servant even amidst great challenge and opposition. He will give you ample opportunity to invest in another generation so your descendants after you will also serve the Lord.

The Abrahamic promise of God passed on through Isaac and Jacob and the nation of Israel carries with it some promise for us. Charles Ryrie, in the footnotes of 1 Peter 2:9-10 of the *Ryrie Study Bible* says, "The church possesses blessings similar to those Israel had, though it has not become the 'new Israel.'"[7] First Peter 2:9-10 says of the church—even us today— "You once were not a people, but now you are God's people . . ."

> He will use you as His servant even amidst great challenge and opposition.

With this wonderful promise of God made to us, you can now serve Him in and through His church with much confidence. Like Israel, you do not need to be afraid or discouraged. You are His servant to His church at this particular time. You can live in the promise of God, and you can show others how to do the same. Your service will be more relaxed and yet more effective as you rest on His promise. You can have confidence in God's "end game." He will come through for you and for all those whom you serve in His name. Make the most of it for His glory!

Dear Lord, I do want to serve You in my church with the full confidence that I am under Your blessing and favor. I know You will provide all that I need to honor my commitment to You. Thank You!

A Deacon's Draw From Lamentations
Lamentations 3:22-23

"Because of the Lord's faithful love we do not perish, for His mercies never end. They are new every morning; great is Your faithfulness."

Faithfulness is one of the greatest virtues in the Christian life, perhaps second only to love. The term in the New Testament means dependability, loyalty, and stability, particularly as it describes God in His relationship to believers. This faithfulness is also expected of us. We must be dependable and loyal to the truth and to the church. God depends on us, and God's people depend on us.

As children, we are expected to be faithful to our parents. In school, we are to be faithful to our teachers. In our marriage, we must be faithful to our spouses. On our jobs, we must be faithful to our employers. Likewise, in the church, we must be faithful. Faithfulness to Christ, to His Word, and to His people is essential for the servant of God. You will be known by your faithfulness.

> **Faithfulness to Christ, to His Word, and to His people is essential for the servant of God.**

One of the greatest hymns ever written speaks of God's faithfulness to us. The words of Thomas Chisholm in 1923 still ring true for us today:

> Great is thy faithfulness, O God my Father, there is no shadow of turning with thee; Thou changest not, thy compassions, they fail not; as thou hast been thou forever wilt be. Great is thy faithfulness! Great is thy Faithfulness! Morning by morning new mercies I see: All I have needed thy hand hath provided; Great is thy faithfulness, Lord unto me![8]

This truth should give you a new sense of motivation and encouragement to be faithful in your service as a Deacon. God will depend on you to do so. The individuals and families in your church will depend on you to do so. Your faithfulness will be rewarded in this life, but especially in the next.

Dear Lord, I want to be a faithful follower and a faithful servant. I pray that You would keep control of my life and order my steps. I wish to give my unrestricted loyalty to You.

A Deacon's Draw From Ezekiel
Ezekiel 3:10

"Son of man, listen carefully to all My words that
I speak to you and take them to heart."

To effectively communicate biblical principles to others, we must first hear and apply His Word ourselves. God really does have much to say to us. When we faithfully hear, read, study, meditate on, and memorize God's Word, then we will be prepared to share it with others. When God spoke these words to Ezekiel sometime prior to 570 BC, He had a very important message to deliver to the nation. He said that Babylonian captivity and slavery were a result of God's people disobeying His Word.

> To take God's Word to heart is to obey it.

Sometimes Deacons and Pastors are called upon by God to bring a message to the church that is not easily heard or well received. Once we have heard from God and taken His Word to heart, we will be able to convey even the most challenging message. When God's Word is faithfully proclaimed to His people it brings "teaching, rebuking, correcting and training in righteousness" (cf. 2 Tim. 3:16). When received and applied, God's Word changes the hearts of people. It may or may not change our immediate circumstance—the Israelites remained in Babylonian captivity for seventy years—but it significantly changes the way we view and adapt to our circumstances.

It calls upon us to listen carefully and consistently to God's Word as He speaks to us through it. It is imperative that we take it to heart—that is, apply it to our personal lives today and each day we live. To take God's Word to heart is to obey it. Ezekiel was a great prophet to the nation for at least twenty-two years (1:2; 29:17-21). Perhaps God will use you to "Go to your people, and speak to them" (3:11). He may give you more than twenty-two years to do it!

Dear Lord, give me ears to hear, a mind to understand, a heart to receive, and a voice to share Your precious Word.

A Deacon's Draw From Daniel
Daniel 6:20

"Daniel, servant of the living God . . . has your God whom you serve continually been able to rescue you from the lions?"

Though King Darius had ordered God's servant to be thrown into the lion's den, he regretted doing so. The king was obligated to punish Daniel because of disobedience to the king's edict. Daniel had continued to pray to the true God rather than give allegiance to godless law and godless authority. Yet, while in the midst of the lion's den, Daniel's life was spared miraculously (6:22), and the king's heart was changed. He made a new decree that Daniel's God was the living God who endures forever (6:26). In verse 28 we read, "Daniel prospered during the reign of Darius and the reign of Cyrus the Persian.

> As a servant of God, you may find yourself being judged for following Christ.

Clearly this story is a graphic example of the faithful servanthood of Daniel and the faithful and miraculous power of God on his behalf. Even the king, in passing a death sentence on Daniel, knew him to be a genuine servant of God. In verse 16 the king says, "May your God, whom you serve continually rescue you!" And God did rescue his servant.

You too are a servant of God. You may find yourself being judged or sentenced by human authority for continually following Christ. God may rescue you, or your obedience could cost you your physical life. But whether you live or die, you are the Lord's servant

(cf. Rom. 14:7-9). You have the same God as Daniel. You have a similar relationship to God as His servant. Whatever He calls upon you to do, wherever He calls upon you to go, and whatever the cost of your obedience, you remain a servant of the most high God.

Dear Lord, I desire to take my servant role as seriously as Daniel. Please empower me by Your Spirit to meet whatever opposition may come. If You should so will it, prepare me for the lion's den.

A Deacon's Draw From Hosea
Hosea 6:6

"I desire loyalty and not sacrifice, the knowledge of God rather than burnt offerings."

The virtue of loyalty is regarded highly by most employers. It is a necessity for a quality military. Likewise, loyalty on the part of God's servants is greatly valued by Him. This has never been truer than in the twenty-first-century church.

Webster defines *loyalty* as "firm allegiance to one's government, homeland, or sovereign; faithful to a person, custom, or ideal."[9] In the text cited above, God says through Hosea, the prophet, "I desire loyalty and not sacrifice." The reference is loyalty to the true God rather than sacrifice to a false god. God was commanding His people to be loyal to Him instead of offering sacrifices to other gods.

It would be easy to assume that we are loyal to our God because we don't make public sacrifices of animals to false gods. But the truth is, we are tempted daily to move our allegiance and faithfulness away from Jesus to other things or other people, or even to a system of religious activity.

> Loyalty on the part of God's servants is greatly valued by Him.

Christ alone is deserving of all our loyalty. He is our Sovereign God (1 Tim. 6:15). As a Deacon and servant-model in your church, you are known for your loyalty to Christ—or your lack of it. The more you grow in your knowledge of God and your relationship to Him, the greater your loyalty to Him. Your faithfulness is to a person—the Lord Jesus Christ. Your service is primarily to Him, even as you faithfully serve His church.

Dear Lord, I pray that You will remind me daily where my loyalties lie. Empower me to not only know You but to follow You faithfully. You are absolutely deserving of all my allegiance and service.

A Deacon's Draw From Joel

Joel 2:13

"Tear your hearts, not just your clothes, and return to the Lord your God. For He is gracious and compassionate, slow to anger, rich in faithful love . . ."

Judgment is not a subject often discussed in today's church because we heavily emphasize the judgment Christ received for us. We should faithfully proclaim the believer's freedom from the penalty of sin. However, in the whole counsel of God (i.e., all of the Bible), we discover several different kinds of judgment. In Joel, we have an example of God's judgment upon His own people for their disobedience. God loves us, but He hates our sin. When we willfully and habitually sin against God, He passes judgment upon us—not to condemn us to hell but to correct us and condition us for heaven.

> Sin has always been a heart problem before it becomes a hand problem.

This text states God's desire for us when we have sinned against Him. Sin has always been a heart problem before it becomes a hand problem. If we are to genuinely repent of sin, we will do so from our hearts and not just from our mouths.

Many servants of God committed acts of sin and were subsequently judged by God. You may find yourself experiencing God's judgment because of sin in your life. You probably know the sin or sins that have broken your fellowship and removed you from God's power and blessing. You have become ineffective and may even feel useless in God's service. There is only one solution: repent of your sin and return to the Lord your God. When you do—sincerely—you will find His gracious, compassionate, loving forgiveness. He will restore the joy of your salvation and the desire to serve Him again through His church.

Dear Lord, please show me the sin(s) of my life even today. Show me how to repent and enable me to do so. Restore to me the joy and fullness of Your salvation and once again, use me in Your service.

WEEK 44 **DAY 5**

A Deacon's Draw From Amos
Amos 5:14

> "Seek good and not evil, so that you may live; and the
> Lord, the God of Hosts, will be with you . . ."

One of the most powerful commands in all of the Old Testament is in Amos 5:4, where God says to His people, "Seek Me and live!" Then in the text above He says, "Seek good . . . so that you may live." Who and what we seek in our lives is of utmost importance if we intend to serve God and His church and spend eternity with Him in heaven.

Seeking God and seeking good follow each other. Because God has made Himself known to us, we need not search very long or far to find Him. Remember His words to His people through Jeremiah (29:13)? "You will seek Me and find Me when you search for Me with all your heart." Every time the Israelites sought and discovered (or re-discovered) their relationship with God, they soon experienced the goodness of God, and with that, the very life of God. They sought God, they sought good, and they lived.

> **Who and what we seek after in our lives is of utmost importance.**

The same is true of you today. As you seek the Lord—His person, His presence, His power (cf. Phil. 3:10)—you will find Him. Because of His great love and mercy and grace, He will do good for you. He will provide life for you . . . His life (cf. Phil. 1:21). Once you establish a genuine, heartfelt, soul-saving relationship with Jesus Christ, you will know His life and you will begin (or continue) to live in Him. You will experience a full and meaningful life (cf. Jn. 10:10) here on earth and an eternal life in heaven (cf. Jn. 3:16; 14:1-3).

This is both a message for the servant of God and a message to be proclaimed by the servant of God. Pause right now. Seek God, seek good, and know the life and mission of God for yourself!

> Dear Lord, help me to seek You with all my heart.
> Please let me see and experience
> Your goodness and Your life.

WEEK 45 — **DAY 1**

A Deacon's Draw From Obadiah
Obadiah 1:15

"For the Day of the Lord is near, against all the nations. As you have done, so it will be done to you; what you deserve will return on your own head."

Most of us are familiar with the phrase, "What goes around, comes around." Essentially, what we mean by that is the way we live and the decisions we make early in our lives will eventually come back to either bless us or curse us later in life. The apostle Paul told the Galatian churches, "Don't be deceived: God is not mocked. For whatever a man sows he will also reap" (Gal. 6:7).

Obadiah, a rather unknown prophet, pronounced pending judgment upon the Edomites, who had rejoiced over the misfortunes that had befallen Jerusalem. He was making it clear to these unbelieving critics of God's people that God would have the last word. The Day of the Lord refers to a final judgment day on which God will render eternal judgment upon all those who reject Him and remedial judgment upon His servants who have neglected Him.

These words say a couple of things clearly to the servant of God in the twenty-first-century church. One, we serve in the present for the sake of the future. What you do in your present service for Christ will count for all eternity. Don't neglect it, and don't take it lightly! The Day of the Lord will also reveal your deeds of service (cf. Rom. 14:12) and all the nations, including yours, will be judged.

> **We serve in the present for the sake of the future.**

Second, we serve in the present the way we would want to be served. What "you have done, so it will be done to you." The Golden Rule, found in Matthew 7:12, applies to all of us: "Whatever you want others to do for you, do also the same for them." As you fulfill your calling to Christian service in the church, remember, you will be held accountable for how you serve and will be judged by God accordingly. Live and serve in such a way that you can look forward to what you'll receive.

> **Dear Lord, I desire to serve You faithfully so that I may, one day, stand before You with a clear conscience knowing I've done what You expected me to do.**

A Deacon's Draw From Jonah

Jonah 3:1

"Then the word of the Lord came to Jonah a second time."

As with most of us, the clear revelation of God did not come easily or quickly to Jonah. Jonah 1:1 says, "The word of the Lord came to Jonah." Now, in 3:1 "The word of the Lord came to Jonah a second time." What happened to Jonah between these two verses gives us great insight into the seriousness and intention of God—for us.

When God speaks to us through His Word, the Bible, and confirms His command or intention for us, through life opportunities, we can either obey or disobey. The cost of disobedience can be very high. For many in the Bible, disobedience cost them their lives. For others it cost them a life of pain and suffering and grief. Jonah is an example of this. Because of his disobedience to God's Word, he went down to Joppa, down into a ship, down into the sea, and down into the belly of a great fish. His descent came from his disobedience. Once he came to a place of repentance and obedience, he began to see God literally save a city.

> Jonah's descent came from his disobedience.

How are you doing when it comes to obeying the word of the Lord? Perhaps God has spoken to you about a matter and you have simply ignored Him. Or maybe you have heard Him but have justified your disobedience by trying to reinterpret what He meant. In your heart of hearts, you know what He has said, but in your mind you have convinced yourself, "He surely didn't mean that!"

Would you be willing today to acknowledge any disobedience in your life and make a fresh commitment to obey God when He speaks to you? Take to heart the words of John H. Sammis, which he wrote in 1887: "Trust and obey, for there's no other way to be happy in Jesus, but to trust and obey."[10]

Dear Lord, please help me to hear You when You speak! Help me to obey the first time and avoid the pain of disobedience. I desire to willingly and deliberately renew my commitment to obey You and do what You say when You say it.

A Deacon's Draw From Micah
Micah 6:8

"He has told you men what is good and what it is the Lord requires of you: only to act justly, to love faithfulness, and to walk humbly with your God."

Through the prophet, God explains to His people that He is not all that impressed with their human, fleshly attempts to please Him. He was not asking them to surrender more burnt offerings or blood sacrifices or even their children (as some heathen gods would call for) but simply to act in spiritual obedience to a personal, loving God. All God expected of His people then, and all He expects of us now, is that we act justly, love faithfulness, and live humbly with Him.

This seems simple enough. But most of us, even as dedicated servants of God in the church, don't get this. To act justly means we are willing to stand for the truth and support those who are unfairly accused or socially disadvantaged. We must do what we can to help deliver the weaker or wronged party by passing godly judgment upon the oppressor. To love faithfulness or mercy means that anyone who is in a weaker position, due to some misfortune or another, should be delivered. This should be done out of a spirit of generosity, grace, and loyalty. To live humbly with God is merely the intentional commitment to bring one's life into conformity with God's will.

> God requires we know Him, love Him, follow Him, and serve Him by serving others.

God does not reject our offerings outright. But He receives them when given out of a sincere heart of justice, faithfulness to others, and humility and obedience to God. This is akin to the great commandment that we love God with all our hearts and our neighbor as ourselves.

As a servant of God in the church, you will do well to know what God requires of you—first and foremost. He desires that we know Him, love Him, follow Him, and serve Him by serving others in His name. That is what is good and what the Lord requires of you.

> **Dear Lord, I have heard and understand what You expect of me. Please empower me to live my life and serve my church according to Your Word.**

A Deacon's Draw From Nahum

Nahum 1:3

"The Lord is slow to anger but great in power;
the Lord will never leave the guilty unpunished."

Nahum was the only prophet whose message focused extensively upon Nineveh's coming condemnation. In this way it complements the book of Jonah, in which God's judgment against Nineveh was averted. Ultimately, God will judge all His enemies, and His kingdom will triumph. As God's people, and as His servants, we should never doubt the seriousness of His wrath against sin, despite apparent delays in carrying out His justice.

> Ultimately God will pass judgment upon the unbelieving, unrepentant sinner.

When it comes to judging sin, and especially the sin of unbelievers, God shows great patience and longsuffering. However, His patience does not nullify His inevitable justice. God "does not delay His promise, as some understand delay, but is patient with you, not wanting any to perish, but all to come to repentance" (2 Pet. 3:9). Ultimately God will pass judgment upon the unbelieving, unrepentant sinner. For the believing sinner, judgment has already been passed in and through the atoning death of Christ on the cross (cf. Rom. 8:1), but the Lord will never leave the guilty unpunished.

Knowing the reality of sin and God's judgment upon it, and knowing the reality of the cross and God's forgiveness in Christ, we are compelled to proclaim the gospel. Your family members, friends, and those with whom you work who do not yet know Christ are subject to the judgment of God. We are compelled, as God's Deacons in the church, to tell the good news. God is patient with sinners, giving them ample time and opportunity to hear and respond to the gospel. He is also just and will bring sure and certain judgment to those who reject His gospel.

You will want to be faithful and consistent in your witness for Christ. Don't wait for a better time or place. Just be faithful now!

Dear Lord, I want to faithfully share Your gospel with others. Please empower me with Your Holy Spirit and present divine opportunities for me to do this. I recommit myself to that end.

A Deacon's Draw From Habakkuk
Habakkuk 3:2

"Revive Your work in these years; make it known in these years."
In Your wrath remember mercy."

Those of us who have served in the church for many years have experienced some amazing works of God. With even a passive reading of the Bible, we discover greater and more phenomenal works of God. It is easy for us to look at ourselves and our churches today, especially in America, and see significantly fewer works of God—at least works that we would consider phenomenal or miraculous.

> It is easy to look at the churches in America and see fewer miraculous or phenomenal works of God.

Apparently the prophet Habakkuk had come to such a time in his own life. In this book he actually offers three prayers to God. He prays first with a question, "How long, Lord, must I call for help and You do not listen?" (1:1). Then he prays, with an exclamation, "Are You not from eternity Yahweh my God?" And finally he prays with an appeal, "Revive Your work in these years!"

Perhaps it would do us well to pray the first two prayers ourselves before we so quickly appeal for revival in our church or community. We may need to acknowledge before God how long it has been that we have lived without revival (How long, Lord . . .). Maybe we should, once again, acknowledge privately and publicly who our God is (Yahweh or Jehovah, my God.). Then we might have a better perspective to pray, "Revive Your work!"

How long has it been since you have seen a prolonged, powerful movement of God in your church or community? How often do you hear others speak more of the things God has given them rather than of God Himself? How many times have you or your church prayed for revival and revival has not come?

> Dear Lord, I acknowledge that real revival has not come to me or my church and You alone are the only eternal God who can bring it. Please, show Yourself strong and work Your mighty works of renewal and salvation in me and my church.

A Deacon's Draw From Zephaniah
Zephaniah 3:9

"For I will then restore pure speech to the peoples so that all of them may call on the name of Yahweh and serve Him with a single purpose."

In their context, these words refer to the final restoration of all believers to God for all of eternity. But by way of application, they also speak of believers' understanding of God, based on His name, and the need for us to serve shoulder to shoulder in fulfilling His kingdom purpose.

We all look forward with great anticipation to God's full restoration of the nations—the time when the gospel will have been preached to those who lived on the earth, and to every nation and tribe and tongue and people; the time when "at the name of Jesus every knee should bow . . . and every tongue should confess that Jesus Christ is Lord, to the glory of God the Father" (Phil. 2:10-11). But until then, what shall we do?

> As we await God's final restoration, we will serve Him with a single purpose.

As we await God's final restoration, we will "serve Him with a single purpose" or shoulder to shoulder. This is an especially meaningful verse for Pastors and Deacons who desire to serve together in the church. The words shoulder to shoulder or a "single purpose" carry with them the idea of unity and mutual appreciation for God's mission in the world. This principle is well stated by Paul in Philippians 2:2: "fulfill my joy by thinking the same way, having the same love, sharing the same feeling, focusing on one goal.

You have the wonderful privilege of serving your church and your Pastor with your focus on one goal. That goal, of course, is to "make disciples of all nations" (Matt. 28:19). Until Jesus returns and God's full and final restoration comes, you will serve Him now, where you are, with what you have, for the sake of His Great Commission.

Dear Lord, show me how to serve side by side and shoulder to shoulder with my Pastor and fellow Deacons for the purpose of fulfilling Your Great Commission.

A Deacon's Draw From Haggai
Haggai 2:8

"The silver and gold belong to Me—the declaration of the Lord of Hosts."

The pronouncement of Haggai 2:1-9 was a word of great encouragement and promise for the people of God. However, the entire book calls for God's people to "consider your ways!" (1:5, 7; 2:15, 18-19). God's temple had been horribly neglected while the people built their own houses and barns (or businesses). God, through the prophet, calls upon His people to consider and correct their ways, realizing that their problem was not a lack of resources but a lack of priority.

> Once you are satisfied that your priorities are perfectly in line with God's, then you can count on God to provide for what He orders.

Many churches today evaluate their present or future ministries based on what they can afford. Unfortunately, these churches usually assume that God is blessing their feeble efforts and their conservative spending when, in fact, just the opposite may be true. We must always be good stewards of God's resources, but this is not to say that we arbitrarily decide how much we give or how much we spend on certain ministries. Often, it is our priorities that prevent us from fulfilling our mission. It was this same problem which God said could only be solved by "Considering your ways!

You may be one of those servant-leaders in your church who is responsible for the use of finances. You must consider your priorities and along with your Pastor, consider the priorities of the church. Once you are satisfied that your priorities are perfectly in line with God's, then you can count on God to provide for what He orders—no matter how impossible it may seem to be to you or to others.

> Dear Lord, show me the difference between my ways and the ways of my church and Your ways. Help me to realign with Your ways so Your work may be done with Your provision and blessing.

A Deacon's Draw From Zechariah

Zechariah 4:6

"This is the word of the Lord . . . not by strength or by might, but by My Spirit, says the Lord of Hosts."

Zechariah described his prophetic call as simply, "the word of the Lord." For more than fifteen years, the Jews had been back in Jerusalem from Babylonian captivity. However, the city was still in ruins and the people were doubting the future. God raised up Zechariah to encourage these Jews with a vision of Jerusalem's glorious future. It became very obvious to the people that if the city would be rebuilt it would take a miracle of God. Rather than continuing to depend upon their own strength or human might, the prophet gave them these powerful words from God, "but by My Spirit.

> Transformation is a work accomplished exclusively by the Holy Spirit.

It was the breath of the Lord that worked in creation (Gen. 1:2) and opened the Red Sea and closed it again (Ex. 15:8, 10). In the vision given to Ezekiel, the wind brought dead people to life (37:1-14). A similar divine intervention was needed in order to complete the building of the Temple and the restoration of Jerusalem.

So it is in many churches today. A miraculous work of God's holy and powerful Spirit is necessary for church revival and national awakening. Perhaps you serve in a church that is in need of revitalization and renewal. There likely are many people in your church and community who need to be brought to new life. You can participate with God in that miracle. You cannot do it in the flesh, no matter how many dollars, buildings, vehicles, or other resources you may have available to you.

The work of transformation is not a work accomplished by military strength, human ingenuity, or mere persuasion of man. It is a work accomplished exclusively by the Holy Spirit of God. We must pray as never before and proclaim the gospel as never before in order to see a glorious revival of the church and a transformational awakening in the nation. Will you participate?

> Dear Lord, I desire to see Your powerful Spirit bring revival in my life, my church, and my community. Guide me to do Your work and serve as I should.

WEEK 46 — **DAY 4**

A Deacon's Draw From Malachi
Malachi 3:10

> "Bring the full ten percent into the storehouse so
> that there may be food in my house."

For most Pastors and Deacons, this text is well known. In fact, in an ordination service, pastoral or deacon candidates are almost always asked, "Do you believe in and practice tithing?" Malachi's total message was not about tithing. It was more about God's people neglecting their proper and intended worship of God. He accused the people of doubting God by quoting their own words, sometimes prefaced by "you ask." For example, "But you ask: 'How have You loved us?'" (1:2); "Yet you ask: 'How have we despised Your name?'" (1:6); "Yet you ask: 'How have we wearied (Him)?'" (2:17); and "You ask: 'How do we rob You?'" (3:8).

Malachi 3:10 is God's word to the church member who would quickly and easily neglect his responsibility to tithe. It was a command under the law and is a starting place for New Testament grace-giving. It is intended for the local church (i.e., storehouse). It is an acknowledgment of God's bountiful supply in our lives. In no other discipline does God say to us, "Test Me in this way." When you give at least 10 percent of your income to the Lord through your church, you are proving to others that God is truly who He says He is—"One who opens the floodgates of heaven and pours out a blessing for you without measure" (3:10b).

> **You should see your tithe as a starting place.**

You may be a faithful giver in your church. It is the conviction of most church leaders today that those who serve as Pastors and Deacons should set an example for the rest of the church. That includes tithing—giving 10 percent of your income to the Lord through your church. If you tithe, don't ever stop! If you don't, start this Sunday and don't stop!

Of course, all that you have belongs to God. You should see your tithe as a starting place from which you increase your giving. Giving above and beyond will only add to the "floodgates of blessing" being poured out on your life.

Dear Lord, I commit to return unto You, through my church, at least 10 percent of my income. Please help me discipline my life and exercise good stewardship of all You have entrusted to me.

A Deacon's Draw From Matthew
Matthew 6:24

"No one can be a slave of two masters, since either he will hate one and love the other . . . You cannot be slaves of God and of money."

As the Old Testament concludes with teaching on tithing (Mal. 3:10), so the New Testament begins with Jesus's teaching on giving and the effects of money on our lives. In this text
(Matt. 6:24), Jesus was saying that no one can be a slave to two owners. We cannot serve both material possessions and, at the same time, serve Jesus Christ as our Master. No compromise is possible, no matter how hard we try to reconcile the two.

This principle is amplified by Jesus when He poses the question, "What will it benefit a man if he gains the whole world yet loses his life? Or what will a man give in exchange for his life?" (Matt. 16:26). He also said, "One's life is not in the abundance of his possessions." These are probably not new ideas to you. You may understand them well and perhaps have even taught them to others.

> As a true follower of Christ, you no longer own anything, not even yourself.

Yet, for many church members, this is a confusing idea. Many have not yet come to surrender all their possessions to the Lordship of Christ. Mistakenly, they think they can faithfully follow Christ and at the same time, keep their material possessions for themselves. This is a clear violation of Jesus's teachings.

When we sing and pray the words "I surrender all!" we must understand that to mean *all*. Yes, *all* of your sin and guilt . . . *all* of your broken relationships and feelings of bitterness, resentment, and unforgiveness. It also means *all* your money and material possessions. As a true follower of Christ, you no longer own anything, not even yourself. "You are not your own, you were bought at a price . . ." (1 Cor. 6:19-20). Does God own you? All that you have? All that you are? All that you will ever be?

Dear Lord, as one of Your servants, I want to again surrender all of my life and all that You have entrusted to me back to You, my rightful owner.

A Deacon's Draw From Mark

Mark 10:45

"For even the Son of Man did not come to be served, but to serve, and to give His life—a ransom for many."

The central division of the book of Mark and the central theme of the book is Mark 10:45. Chapters 1 through 10 speak of the service of the Savior while chapters 11 through 16 speak of the sacrifice of the Savior. He is, in fact, the Suffering Servant. Indeed, much of His service included suffering, while all of His suffering was in service to the Father and in our behalf. Jesus—the Son of God and Son of Man—came to this earth not to be served by men as a reigning king but to serve man as our redeeming Savior. He did not come to find His life or save His life; He came to give His life.

> We cannot give our lives as a savior, but we can give our lives as servants.

We cannot give our lives as a savior, but we can give our lives as servants. Jesus said, "As the Father has sent Me, I also send you" (Jn. 20:21). You have a Savior. You are a servant. As a servant of Christ, you have been placed in a church for His purpose and His glory. Just as Jesus came not to be served, neither should we expect others to always serve us. Even if you own your own business or supervise many other people, you will only succeed to the level you are willing to serve them. In the church, you are not in a position of authority or supervision. You are in a place of service, whereby you give your life, time, talent, money, influence, and giftedness—in the interest of others.

In light of all the ways in which Christ has served you, would you not give yourself anew and afresh to His service? Is this the sincere desire of your heart? Are you faithfully following the example of your serving Savior? Perhaps this is a good time in your life to renew your commitment to serve Him with all that you are and all that you have.

> Dear Lord, I wish to recommit my life in service to You through my church. I pray You will take my life and let it be consecrated, Lord, to Thee.

A Deacon's Draw From Luke
Luke 4:8

"It is written: Worship the Lord your God, and serve Him only."

When Jesus first spoke these words, He spoke them to Satan, who had been tempting Christ to worship him instead of His Heavenly Father. Satan was trying to convince Jesus that all of the kingdoms of the world belonged to him; that all the authority over those kingdoms was his; and that he would be willing to give some of that to Jesus if only He would bow down and worship him. Jesus's response was brief but profound. Jesus placed worship and service side by side. He was saying, in essence, to worship Satan would be to serve Satan. Jesus knew, as we must come to know, that there is one, and only One, true and living God whom we must worship and serve.

Unfortunately, God's people are still tempted to worship other gods. Satan will be sure that the temptations come at his most opportune times. Jesus was tempted after spending 40 days in the wilderness without food or water. We will be tempted in our weakest hours or days as well. You may be in a wilderness of your own, not particularly fasting or praying but very much subject to the temptations of Satan. Satan may be tempting you directly to worship him, or he may be tempting you through your fleshly desires to worship yourself. He may be tempting you to worship the world or the things in the world (cf. 1 Jn. 2:15-16).

> God's people are still tempted to worship other gods.

In any case, when you are tempted you can know that God will provide the power and capacity to resist and overcome the temptation (cf. 1 Cor. 10:13; Jas. 4:7). You, too, can say to yourself, to others and, if necessary, to Satan himself, "I am committed to worship the Lord my God and serve Him only." Do whatever you need to do to make that kind of commitment. The temptations are coming . . . again!

Dear Lord, I acknowledge that You alone are God and You alone are deserving of all my praise and worship. Please empower me daily to resist temptation and yield myself only to You.

A Deacon's Draw From John

John 12:26

"If anyone serves Me, he must follow Me. Where I am, there My servant also will be. If anyone serves Me, the Father will honor him."

Jesus made this statement in response to Philip and Andrew reporting to Him that there were some unbelievers attending a festival who wanted to meet Jesus. At that point in the Passion Week, Jesus was focused on His impending crucifixion. However, He took the time to explain to Philip and Andrew what it really means to be a follower of Christ. He said, "The one who loves his life will lose it, and the one who hates his life in this world will keep it for eternal life" (v. 25). He then explained that serving Him called for genuine followship ("follow Me"), fellowship ("there My servant also will be"), and receivership ("the Father will honor him").

On October 28, 1949, at age twenty-two, soon-to-be missionary Jim Elliot entered into his journal these words: "He is no fool who gives what he cannot keep to gain what he cannot lose." Six years later, on January 8, 1956, Elliot was killed on the Curary River, Ecuador, by the Wasdani Indians to whom he was bringing the gospel.[11] At age twenty-eight, Jim Elliot gave up what he could not keep to gain what he will never lose.

> He is no fool who gives what he cannot keep to gain what he cannot lose.

As with Jim Elliot, each one of us must come to a level of commitment for which we are willing to give our lives. Serving Jesus means following Him wherever He goes even if it is to a hostile, unbelieving, heathen people group. With such a commitment comes the absolute certainty that Jesus will be with us. He has promised in Matthew 28:20, "I am with you always, to the end of the age," and in Hebrews 13:6, "I will never leave you or forsake you.

While you serve Him with your life, follow closely. You need never fear what man may do or say to criticize your Savior. You must serve Him with absolute abandon.

Dear Lord, please keep me close to You wherever that may take me. Show me daily the adjustments I must make to follow You. Give me a willingness to forsake all and follow You.

A Deacon's Draw From Acts

Acts 13:36

"For David, after serving his own generation in God's plan, fell asleep, was buried with his fathers, and decayed.

A great many Pastors and Deacons would love for that to be said of them after spending their lives in the service of Jesus Christ. Pastor Rick Warren refers to this verse as his life verse, quoting it from the New American Standard, "David . . . served the purpose of God in his own generation . . ." From this verse he was inspired to write The Purpose Driven Life, which has been read by millions of people around the world.

> God does not call upon you to hide out and passively live with little or no direction.

God does not call upon you to hide out and passively live with little or no direction. He has not saved you, called you, and placed you in ministry merely so you can coast to retirement and then heaven. You have a purpose. God has a master plan for you. He has sovereignly allowed you to live in your generation for a reason. He wants you to reach your generation with the gospel. To what extent have you discovered God's purpose or plan for your life? Though His full and complete will comes to us gradually and progressively, He gives us enough insight for us to follow Him today. One step of faith and obedience always leads to more steps. All of the time, God desires that we serve Him by serving our generation.

Take advantage of every opportunity God gives you in your church and through your church to serve Him. Don't be afraid or hesitant to do what He leads you to do. Remember, it is His responsibility to place you. It is your responsibility to obey and go and be placed. Then it can be said of you one day, "He served the purpose of God in his own generation; fell asleep, and was laid among his fathers . . .

Dear Lord, prepare me, even from this point on in my life, to serve Your purpose and carry out Your plan in and for my generation.

A Deacon's Draw From Romans
Romans 14:18

"Whoever serves the Messiah in this way is acceptable to God and approved by men."

The context of this verse is Paul's teaching on the doctrine of the weaker brother. Paul admits that certain foods not permitted by the Levitical law could be eaten by Christians. However, just because they could be eaten did not mean they should be. For the sake of those less mature believers whose faith was hindered by the eating of certain foods or drinking wine, it was perfectly fine for the more mature to abstain from eating and drinking. Paul concluded, "It is a noble thing not to eat meat, or drink wine, or do anything that makes your brother stumble" (14:21).

> God is never pleased when our actions cause another believer to stumble in his or her faith.

We often hear someone in the church argue in favor of social drinking or recreational gambling or some other activity, suggesting that they are not at all uncomfortable or offended by it. The argument is often made without any regard whatsoever for the potential impact their actions may have on a younger believer. There seem to be plenty of scriptural principles condemning such activity. But even if there aren't, that does not mean that we have the right to do as we please. One of the rights you surrender when you give your life to Christ is the right to do as you please. You now have the obligation to please Him. He is never pleased when our actions cause other believers to stumble in their faith.

If you know an action or an attitude in your life that is offending another believer, you should immediately discontinue that action or adjust that attitude in order that you not cause other believers to be weakened in their faith. Jesus said, "Whoever causes the downfall of one of these little ones who believe in Me—it would be better for him if a heavy millstone were hung around his neck and he were drowned in the depths of the sea" (Matt. 18:6).

Dear Lord, please show me any action or attitude in my life that is hurting a younger believer and empower me by Your Spirit to rid myself of it.

A Deacon's Draw From 1 Corinthians

1 Corinthians 13:13

*"Now these three remain: faith, hope and love.
But the greatest of these is love."*

Without question, the thirteenth chapter of 1 Corinthians is the most well-known "love chapter" of the New Testament. In these thirteen verses, Paul identifies several qualities needed in a servant of the church—speaking, preaching, believing, giving, sacrifice. However, he always qualifies the qualities by adding "but do not have love" (vv. 1-3). This is still one of the greatest admonitions ever given to the twenty-first-century church. It is also a great personal admonition for those who serve as a Pastor or Deacon of a local church, because without His love, we are *"nothing"* (vv. 2-3).

You may have many gifts, talents, and qualities with which to serve the Lord, but if your heart is not right and your motivation is impure, then your effectiveness will be limited. You must deliberately embrace the love of God. Learn of His love, accept His love, and by faith, apply His love in your own life. Only then will you be able to speak, preach, believe, give, or sacrifice with the blessing of God.

> **If your motivation is impure, then your effectiveness will be limited.**

For the love of God to be borne out in your life requires you to clear your mind and heart of every other motivation. Paul later says to this same church, "Christ's love compels us" (2 Cor. 5:14). That means we cannot be compelled or motivated by reward, money, acceptance, friendship, personal gratification, or any other selfish reason. We are motivated to do what we do in service to Christ and His Church exclusively by "God's love poured out in our hearts through the Holy Spirit who was given to us" (Rom. 5:5). Love really does "bear all things, believe all things, hope all things, endure all things and . . . never fails" (vv. 7-8).

Dear Lord, I do desire to serve You with a sincere, heartfelt motivation of love. Please help me learn how to both experience Your love and live out Your love in my ministry to others.

A Deacon's Draw From 2 Corinthians
2 Corinthians 9:12

"The ministry of this service is not only supplying the needs of the saints, but is also overflowing in many acts of thanksgiving to God."

These words, and indeed all of chapter 9 in 2 Corinthians, provide us with a beautiful picture of generosity. As stated in verse one, it "concerns the ministry to the saints." This means that the financial generosity of God's people toward the "ministry of this service" is of utmost importance.

The money or other resources given by faithful church members to support the work of ministry is essential and provides a way to glorify God in His church. It really does overflow in many acts of thanksgiving to God. The term "ministry of this service" may also be translated the "administration of this service." It is not only our service rendered to the church that matters to God; it is also the way we render service—the administration of the service—that matters. When administered correctly, many persons who become the recipients of the service will primarily give thanks to God.

> The financial generosity of God's people toward the "ministry of this service" is of utmost importance.

This chapter calls upon all of us to participate in the ministry. We are to experience "giving living," which means we give generously (v. 6), voluntarily (v. 7), cheerfully (v. 7), and optimistically (v. 8) to the work of God through His people. We are to be willing to sacrificially invest in the lives and ministry of Pastors, Christian educators, missionaries, and other servants of God.

Perhaps you, as a servant in your church, already understand and faithfully follow this teaching. It is reasonable to say, however, that the vast majority of your fellow church members do not. All Christians in the American church, on average, give less than 2.5 percent of their income to the church. You will do well to practice "giving living" and to strongly encourage it in others.

Dear Lord, please show me how to practice faithful giving and empower me to faithfully encourage others to do the same.

A Deacon's Draw From Galatians
Galatians 2:20

"I no longer live, but Christ lives in me. The life I now live in the flesh, I live by faith in the Son of God, who loved me and gave Himself for me."

This is perhaps one of the most profound, and yet absolutely essential, characteristics of the believer's life in Christ. It is a principle that most believers—even Pastors and Deacons—do not understand and therefore, neither live it nor teach it. It is not a big, mysterious secret that only the "super-spiritual" can grasp. It is not a kind of life reserved only for "those other church members." This life of identification with Christ (v. 20a) and indwelling by Christ (v. 20b) is intended for every single born-again believer. Possibly the reason so many American churches are in decline, spiritually anemic, and internally focused is because they have lost this glorious truth of Scripture.

There is a big difference between you trying your best to live for Jesus and daily surrendering your mind, emotions, and will to the absolute Lordship of Christ. It's the difference between living for Jesus and allowing Him to live through you. Since you did not die for Him (actually He died for you), neither can you, technically, live for Him (actually He lives in and through you).

So when it comes to serving Christ in His church, how we do it is the big difference. You want to allow Christ to so operate in you that, even though you live in a body, it is Christ who lives in you. Even though you work with your hands, they are, as it were, the hands of Christ. Though your voice speaks, it is actually Christ speaking through you. This is all to be done by faith in and full dependence upon the Son of God, who loves you and gave Himself for you.

> This life of identification with Christ is intended for every born-again believer.

Dear Lord, I confess that I have tried to serve You merely through my human limitations. I desire to serve with You in complete control of my life. Please control my body, soul, and spirit so that I live solely by faith in You.

A Deacon's Draw From Ephesians

Ephesians 4:11-12

"He personally gave some to be . . . Pastors and teachers, for the training of the saints in the work of ministry, to build up the body of Christ."

Since Jesus is the founder of the Church and has established it on earth, He certainly has total authority to organize it as He desires. He has determined what the churches should look like in the world, who should be members, who should be leaders, what would be its purpose, how it would be structured, and ultimately how it would be taken to heaven and presented to Himself.

In this chapter of Ephesians, Paul sets forth both the unity and diversity of the Body of Christ (the Church). We are to live and serve in a "one another" relationship "accepting one another in love, diligently keeping the unity of the Spirit with the peace that binds us" (vv. 2-3). Though unified in Spirit and purpose, we are diverse in terms of giftedness and application. Thus, we see the uniqueness of the leadership team of the church.

God has given to the church apostles (i.e., missionaries), preachers, evangelists, Pastors, and teachers. You may actually serve your church in one of these areas. If not, you certainly support these leaders and do all you can to align with them in ministry and mission. You would especially want to understand and support the Pastor. He has a special calling and responsibility to "train the church in the work of ministry." In many cases, He can train you. In most cases, you can help him train others. The unity and effectiveness of the church depends upon your willingness to pray for and support your Pastor.

> **Though unified in Spirit and purpose, we are diverse in terms of giftedness and application.**

Dear Lord, I acknowledge You as the supreme Head of the Church. I also acknowledge that You have placed my Pastor in my church so I can support him. I pray You will lead me by Your Spirit to faithfully fulfill my role.

A Deacon's Draw From Philippians
Philippians 1:1

"Paul and Timothy, slaves of Christ Jesus: To all the saints in Christ Jesus who are in Philippi, including the overseers and deacons.

This epistle is the only one in the New Testament that includes the title of *Deacon* in its salutation. From a close reading, it can be concluded that much, if not most, of the letter applies directly to the men serving as Deacons in the Philippian church. Therefore, the principles of Philippians are worth review for you and every other servant in your church. Just in this salutation, we can identify several persons who make up the ministry team of the church: missionaries (both Paul and Timothy), members (saints), Pastors (overseers), and Deacons (servants). The mission and ministry of a local church involve everyone—everyone who is a genuine child of God and identified with that congregation.

> The mission and ministry of a local church involve everyone.

The mission of the church is carried out by all the members through God's grace and in a spirit of peace. These are realized only in the person and work of Jesus Christ (v. 2). Paul quickly identifies these members' participation and partnership in the gospel from the time the church was started (v. 5).

Your role as a Deacon, a servant of God to the church, is vital in the fulfillment of Christ's Great Commission to us. You are a crucial player on the ministry team of your church. You align with your Pastor and other Deacons in service to the members. You also seek out opportunities to give testimony of your faith to those outside the church. You set a good example in character and conduct. You assist other believers to follow God's will for their lives.

These are among many other admonitions clearly given in this epistle. They present God's challenge to you to faithfully participate in the gospel from this day forward. Be bold enough to take the challenge!

> Dear Lord, I pray You will remind me daily of my role and function in the church. Help me to fulfill my responsibility from this day forward.

A Deacon's Draw From Colossians

Colossians 3:24

"You will receive the reward of an inheritance from
the Lord— you serve the Lord Christ."

Some very clear instruction for the Christian family is found in Colossians 3:18-25—wives submitting to their husbands, husbands loving their wives, children obeying their parents, and parents training their children. We also find instruction for employee/employer relationships. Central to all of this instruction is an admonition and a promise.

We are admonished, "Whatever you do, do it enthusiastically, as something done for the Lord and not for men" (v. 23). This means no matter what role or roles you fill in the family, in the church, or on your job, you are to faithfully fill that role as if you were doing it directly for the Lord. Of course, there is a sense in which you are doing it for the Lord. After all, it is God who has given you life, a partner, a family, a church, a job, and a calling. He has entrusted these people and responsibilities to you with the intention of you reporting back to Him on your progress. So, serve enthusiastically, knowing to whom you will ultimately give account.

We are promised, "You will receive the reward of an inheritance from the Lord" (v. 24). You are not to serve with your constant thoughts on the reward you'll receive. But you can serve faithfully knowing that God is watching and taking notes. The day will come when your deeds of service will be evaluated by God (cf. Rom. 14:10-12; 1 Cor. 13:13-15). You do have something extremely special to look forward to simply because you have placed your faith in Christ (cf. Acts 20:32). But you must always remember, no matter what your current roles are in life, "You serve the Lord Christ."

> **You are not to serve with the constant thought on the reward you will receive.**

Dear Lord, I thank You for saving my soul and giving me a life to live for You. I am grateful to You for both Your admonition and promise to me. I desire to serve You with all my heart for all my life. Please accept my commitment to do so.

A Deacon's Draw From 1 Thessalonians
1 Thessalonians 1:9

"You turned to God from idols to serve the living and true God."

The apostle Paul wrote these words to a congregation of believers that had exhibited a work of faith, labors of love, and endurance of hope in Christ. It was a church, not unlike many today, that had been recently begun with converts from heathenism and idolatry. So, as Paul begins his letter he commends them for their faith and growth. In fact, he says, "you became an example to all the believers" in the larger region of Macedonia and beyond. This sharp reminder in verse 9 is intended to encourage them all the more in their service.

> What have you turned from to serve the true and living God?

Serving God goes beyond doing additional activity intended to help others live more securely. It is an intentional and deliberate turning away from serving a false god or gods and focusing exclusively on serving the true and living God. That sounds noble and certainly sounds scriptural. However, not every believer is willing to do that. For some, it seems possible to hold on to the hidden idols of their lives while at the same time serve the true God. Of course, that attempt is always doomed to failure. God is a jealous God. In the very first of the Ten Commandments He stated emphatically, "Do not have other gods besides Me," as we read in Exodus 20:2. God properly defends His own sovereignty and glory. "For the Lord your God is a consuming fire, a jealous God" (Deut. 4:24).

What is it that you have turned from to serve the true and living God? Perhaps you've turned from some, but not all, of the "idols" in your life. Idols can be anything that attracts your attention and call for your allegiance or affection more than God. That which is truly god in our lives is that which consumes our time, our talents, our money, and our promotion. Does that describe your servant-relationship to God or is there another?

> Dear Lord, I pray You will reveal to me any hidden gods in my life so that I may turn away from them and serve You alone. And enable me, by Your own power, to not return to gods of my past.

WEEK 49 **DAY 3**

A Deacon's Draw From 2 Thessalonians

2 Thessalonians 2:16

"May our Lord Jesus Christ Himself and God our Father . . . encourage your hearts and strengthen you in every good work and word."

Encouragement is a wonderful thing. *Webster* defines it, "to inspire with hope, courage, or confidence: *hearten*."[12] The Greek word in this text and verse 17 literally means "to call by the side" or "a calling of one person to aid another by verbal counsel, consolation or comfort."[13] The apostle Paul used this word to let the servants of Christ in Thessalonica know that they may be encouraged in heart and spirit to passionately pursue every good work and speak every good word. We notice it is not merely Paul encouraging them. It is Paul praying that the "Lord Jesus Christ Himself" would encourage them. This is a reference to the exceptional love of God demonstrated through His daily encouragement of His people.

> **God has provided a Divine Comforter for you.**

You may be in great need of God's encouragement today. Perhaps the circumstances of your life, the limitations of your current ministry, or the frustrations of the world and the flesh have greatly discouraged you. You may even be feeling a sense of hopelessness. There is good news for you. God has provided a Divine Comforter for you. He is the Holy Spirit who lives in you. He is ready and able to give you His encouragement. Pray and acknowledge your need. Ask God to encourage you. He loves you and wants to come alongside you, put His arm around you as it were, and speak great love and encouragement to your heart.

If you are living in the encouragement of God, you must thank Him for that and daily seek to encourage others (cf. 2 Cor. 1:4). Encouragement really is a wonderful thing, and God Himself offers it to you.

Dear Lord, I acknowledge my need for Your daily encouragement. I thank You that by Your indwelling Spirit, You have given me great comfort.

A Deacon's Draw From 1 Timothy

1 Timothy 3:10

"And they must also be tested first; if they prove blameless, then they can serve as deacons."

This verse is found in the middle of a paragraph in 1 Timothy 3 that speaks specifically to the qualifications of a Deacon in a local church. There are no less than twelve qualities listed in verses 8 through 13. The two that are identified in verse 10 are proven service record and character that is blameless. Both Pastors and Deacons are usually evaluated and scrutinized by other Pastors and Deacons before they are ordained or placed into service. This does not mean that they have only begun to serve. They should already have a good track record of service in the church before they are ordained. Likewise, they should have a character that is beyond reproach. They are not perfect, but they are consistently committed to living a godly life that reflects the fruit of the Holy Spirit and holding to high moral standards (cf. Gal. 5:22-23).

Essentially, the man who would serve in a local church in the office of Deacon should be characterized by holiness. Again, this is not absolute perfection—it is simply living a morally transparent life. He has no hidden sins and is completely unpretentious in his conduct. Morally, a Deacon is called to holiness; dynamically, he is called to service.

> Morally, a Deacon is called to holiness; dynamically, he is called to service.

Now would be a good time for you to evaluate your own life and service. Have you had a good track record over an extended period of time of service in your church? Do you honestly and consistently live a morally and ethically pure life? Are you still just as willing and eager to serve God as when you were first set aside by the church as a Deacon? Rather than think you don't measure up, why not recommit yourself to "grow into a mature man with a stature measured by Christ's fullness" (Eph. 4:13)?

Dear Lord, I submit myself to You again today for service in Your church.

A Deacon's Draw From 2 Timothy

2 Timothy 1:3

*"I thank God, whom I serve with a clear
conscience as my forefathers did . . ."*

One of the best preventions of stomach ulcers is living with a clear conscience before God and men. That is what is meant by living "above reproach." The *conscience*, according to *Webster's Dictionary*, is "The faculty of recognizing the difference between right and wrong with regard to one's conduct."[14] *Vines Dictionary of New Testament Words* defines the biblical meaning of conscience as "that faculty by which we apprehend the will of God, as that which is designed to govern our lives; the process of thought which distinguishes what it considers morally good or bad, commending the good, condemning the bad, and so prompting to do the former and avoid the latter."[15]

> The state of your conscience will have a big effect on the state of your service.

A noble objective for a servant of God is to train his senses to distinguish between good and evil (cf. Heb. 5:14). The best way to know the difference between right and wrong or good and evil is to hide God's Word in your heart. If conscience is a "process of thought," then we must think correctly—the way God thinks—in order to have a clear or clean conscience. To think like God thinks is to embed in our mind, even in our subconscious minds, those biblical commands that describe right and wrong. The psalmist put it this way: "I have treasured Your word in my heart so that I may not sin against You" (Ps. 119:11).

What about your conscience? Is it clear, clean, or callous? The state of your conscience will have a big effect on the state of your service. Always remember, "The blood of the Messiah, will cleanse our consciences from dead works to serve the living God" (Heb. 9:14). Let Jesus and His Word be your conscience.

**Dear Lord, please show me how to live with a good
conscience before You and before my church and
before others with whom I live and work.**

WEEK 50 — **DAY 1**

A Deacon's Draw From Titus
Titus 3:14

> "Our people must also learn to devote themselves to good works for cases of urgent need, so that they will not be unfruitful."

Paul wrote to Titus particularly to offer instructions about church organization, identifying congregational officers and various age groups. This book especially shows the necessary relationship between sound doctrine and sound behavior. In chapter 3, Paul places a big emphasis on good works (vv. 1, 5, 8, 14). In this verse 14, he summarizes the chapter by challenging Pastor Titus to teach the church to be devoted to good works, especially in cases of emergencies or urgent need. As the church practiced this, they became very fruitful in the gospel.

This is a valuable point of instruction for all Pastors and Deacons in the contemporary church in America. We must learn to devote ourselves to good works and as a result, bear spiritual fruit. Many church leaders, especially evangelistic leaders, de-emphasize works in favor of grace, proclaiming salvation by grace through faith. They often quote Ephesians 2:8-9 to teach that truth—and it certainly is truth that we are saved by faith and not by works. However, Ephesians 2:10 says, "We are created in Christ Jesus for good works, which God prepared ahead of time so that we should walk in them." This is what Paul is saying to Titus, and through him, to the churches in Crete, where Titus served.

> **We must learn to devote ourselves to good works and as a result, bear spiritual fruit.**

Some of the good deeds in which we should engage are implied in Romans 12:9-21: Bless and do not curse, weep with those who weep, associate with the lowly, respect what is right, be at peace with all men, never take your own vengeance, feed and serve your enemies, and overcome evil with good. These good deeds are not done by us naturally. We must live under the control of God's Spirit, allowing Him to produce His own fruit through us (cf. Gal. 5:22-23). Do this and you too will bear fruit.

> Dear Lord, teach me how to devote my life to good works, serving the church and the community and pleasing You in the process. I want to be faithful and fruitful. Please direct my life in this way.

A Deacon's Draw From Philemon
Philemon 17

"So if you consider me a partner, accept him as you would me."

Paul wrote his friend, Philemon, to urge gentle treatment and forgiveness of a runaway slave, Onesimus. This brief letter addresses slavery, an ethical problem that has vexed human life—and Christianity—for centuries. The book teaches that in Christ both masters and slaves are to consider each other as brothers. When the concept of the basic equality of all who are in Christ prevails, slavery will not endure as an institution. This truth has demonstrated its power in many cultures throughout history.

> You may need to serve your Pastor by affirming him to the church.

This is a good example of spiritual equality, along with unique functionality. In Paul's day, slavery was a reality. Onesimus was a slave, and Philemon was his master. Paul likely led Onesimus to Christ while they were both in a Roman prison (v. 10). From that prison, Paul enlisted Tychicus, a companion, to travel from Rome to Colossae with this and two other epistles (Ephesians and Colossians)—oh, and Onesimus—to be delivered to Philemon. Onesimus may have actually hand-delivered this letter to his master, Philemon, as he turned himself in as a runaway slave.

The letter makes a strong defense for Onesimus. Paul appeals to Philemon as his partner and encourages him strongly to "accept him as you would me." What a reference! What a context!

We learn many lessons from Philemon about interpersonal relationships: accountability (vv. 22-25), accommodation (vv. 8-11), affirmation (vv. 4-7), acceptance (vv. 12-16), and allegiance (vv. 17-21). You may need to recommend someone who, without Christ, may have been unusable but now is useful (cf. v. 1). You may need to serve your Pastor by affirming him to the church. You may need to accept and work with someone you've not even known before. Adjust however you must, and serve the need that is before you.

> **Dear Lord, please give me Your sensitivity to the needs of others so I may lead them to You, and if necessary, lead them to the church.**

A Deacon's Draw From Hebrews
Hebrews 9:14

> "For though by this time you ought to be teachers, you need someone to teach you again the basic principles of God's revelation. You need milk, not solid food."

God's intention for all believers is that they advance to a certain level of maturity in their Christian lives. With the re-birth, we begin as spiritual babies, no matter our earthly age. Like newborn babies, we should have a strong desire for the "milk of the Word" (cf. 1 Peter 2:2). It is by taking in these elementary principles that we grow in respect to our salvation.

But the time comes when every Christian should move beyond the milk (elementary principles) and begin to take in the "meat of the Word" or more solid food (deeper, more theological principles). Then, instead of merely being taught God's Word, we begin to teach ourselves (i.e., feed ourselves). Finally, we are capable of teaching others. This is the challenge from Hebrews 9:14. We must grow in such maturity that we are no longer being spoon-fed by others but are now feeding other new babies ourselves.

> **Every Christian should move beyond the milk and begin to take in the "meat of the Word."**

At what point in this process of maturity would you place yourself? Are you still taking in only the basic principles of Scripture? Are you still merely feeding yourself but only with the very basics of Scripture? Or, have you matured to the point where you are simultaneously being taught and teaching others? This is the level of growth that God desires of all believers, and especially of Pastors and Deacons. In 2 Timothy 2:2 Paul said, "And what you heard from me in the presence of many witnesses, commit to faithful men who will be able to teach others also." Whether or not you are uniquely gifted to teach, you still have the responsibility to mature in your faith so that you might faithfully pass it on to the next generation.

Dear Lord, please help me discipline my time and focus on growing in Your Word. I do desire to mature enough that I might more faithfully share Your Word with others.

A Deacon's Draw From James
James 4:7

"Draw near to God, and He will draw near to you. Cleanse your hands . . . and purify your hearts . . ."

God has not saved us from our sin merely to take us to heaven when we die. He has saved us in order to have a relationship with us while we live on this earth. He has not merely saved us and then turned us loose to fend for ourselves in the world. Nor has He saved us without a purpose.

In your relationship with Christ, it is necessary to daily "draw near to Him." You must make this time intentional and deliberate. It will never just automatically happen. A disciple is a disciplined follower of Christ. That is what you are.

> **God saved us in order to have a relationship with us.**

We have, just in this brief verse, a command and a promise. The command is to draw near to God and the promise is He will draw near to you. Drawing near to Him requires that we confess any sin to Him immediately. We never can come near to God with known, harbored, habitual sin in our lives. The Bible says, "If we confess our sins, He is faithful and righteous to forgive us our sins and to cleanse us from all unrighteousness" (1 Jn. 1:9). We will never be able to claim the promise of His nearness until we have obeyed the command to draw near to Him. We can only draw near to him with clean hands and purified hearts, having confessed all our sins to Him.

Now would be a good time for you to draw near to God. Will you do that . . . honestly and sincerely? It will require some discipline on your part, but that is who you are—a disciple of Christ. You'll never serve as you could, or as you should, unless and until you do.

Dear Lord, I now ask You to remind me of any sin in my life. I confess my sin and accept by faith Your forgiveness and cleansing. I desire to have a close, ongoing relationship with You.

A Deacon's Draw From 1 Peter

1 Peter 3:15

"Always be ready to give a defense to anyone who asks you for a reason for the hope that is in you."

Have you ever had someone ask you why you go to church or why you are a Christian and you've been at a loss for words? Or maybe you did respond with a rather generic answer like, "It helps me live a better life!" or "My family needs a good example!" or "We've gone to church all my life!" Perhaps you are seldom asked those questions because others with whom you work or rub shoulders in the community have no reason to even know if you are a Christian. That would be very sad indeed. But assuming some know and occasionally some ask, what will you say?

> When we deliberately surrender our whole life to the Lordship of Christ, we will be much better prepared to defend our faith.

This verse directs us in our response to these questions. We should always be ready with an answer. The verse actually begins with the essential quality necessary for us to be prepared to give this answer: "Set apart the Messiah as Lord in your heart." When we have deliberately, through faith, surrendered our whole lives to the Lordship of Christ and He is ruling and reigning in our hearts, then we will be much better prepared to defend our faith. If He is not freely given that place, we will always be at a loss for words or have a very shallow and meaningless answer.

Setting Christ as Lord in your heart simply means you abandon all else and all others in terms of your allegiance. It means you daily draw near to Him and invite Him to take complete control of your mind (so you will think like Him), your emotions (so you will feel like Him), and your will (so you will choose like Him). He then becomes the sole object of your day as He leads you to work and relate to others. Would you be willing to begin this day, and each day hereafter, like that?

Dear Lord, I want to be able to tell others why I go to church and why I am a Christian. I pray that You will take control of all areas of my life and give me a clear reason for the hope that is in me.

A Deacon's Draw From 2 Peter
2 Peter 1:3

"His divine power has granted to us everything required for life and godliness, through the knowledge of Him who called us by His own glory and goodness."

One of the big questions a non-believer has about Christianity is, "How can anyone live that way?" They make the false assumption that being a Christian is merely living a moral and holy life and that you have to stop cussing, drinking, smoking, lying, cheating, and numerous other vices. They rightfully acknowledge that they could never live that way. However, that is a false assumption of what it means to be a Christian.

A person can never live like a Christian apart from a personal, powerful relationship with Christ. That relationship is not established by our own attempt at goodness or moral living. Goodness, godliness, and moral living are all by-products of a relationship. The relationship is with Christ. It comes about when a person is convicted of his sin by God's Holy Spirit, hears and understands God's plan of salvation, repents of his sin, and places his faith in Christ alone. This involves a spiritual birth, whereby we are given not just a new start in life but also a new life with which to start. That new life is the life of Christ, resulting in old things passing away and new things coming (cf. 1 Cor. 5:17).

With our new life in Christ comes His divine power, which He grants to us so we can then begin to live a more godly life. To know Christ is to love Him. To love Him is to follow Him. To follow Him is to serve Him. He has given us everything we need to do just that.

> **A person can never live like a Christian apart from a personal, powerful relationship with Christ.**

Dear Lord, I thank You for providing the power I need to live a good, godly life. Please enable me to know You better and do Your will at this time in my life.

A Deacon's Draw From 1 John
1 John 3:14

"We know that we have passed from death to
life, because we love our brothers."

This verse is not to be misunderstood. It is not saying that our salvation comes to us as a result of our love for others. Clearly, it is saying that our love for other believers is a result of our salvation. Love is a byproduct of a genuine love relationship with God. It is impossible to love others—believers or unbelievers—with a God-like love when we have never received His love. That is, when we have not yet received Him.

It is true that one of the evidences that we are genuinely children of God is that we love one another. This is one of the primary threads that run through this entire epistle. The end of verse 14 actually says, "The one who does not love remains in death." In other words, if a person shows no love for the Lord, the church, or a lost person, he is probably not a true believer. He is still spiritually dead.

> One of the evidences that we are genuinely children of God is that we love one another.

Love is a big deal with God. It was His love that caused Jesus to die on the cross for our sin (cf. Jn. 3:16). It was His love that was demonstrated even before we knew Him (cf. Rom. 5:8). It is His love given to us (through His Holy Spirit) for each other that proves to a lost world that we are truly Christians (cf. Jn. 13:34-35). In our own hearts we know that we have "passed from death to life, because we love our brothers."

It is the love of God poured into your life that motivates you to serve as you do. First John 4:11 tells us God's Spirit in us exhibits His own love to others. It is because of God's great love for you, your family, your church, and your community that you serve the Lord. Continue to serve Him with love.

*Dear Lord, thank You for loving me as You do.
I pray that You will show Your love through my
life as I seek to serve You in my church.*

A Deacon's Draw From 2 John

2 John 9

> "Anyone who does not remain in the teaching about Christ, but goes beyond it, does not have God. The one who remains in that teaching, this one has both the Father and the Son."

There are those today who have ignored this verse altogether when it comes to organized religion, and even some denominations of Christianity. For example, the Mormons hold to a *Second Testament of Jesus Christ,* which goes beyond the inspired New Testament of the Bible. Likewise, Roman Catholics hold to the Apocrypha (additional inter-testamental books) as being authoritative Scripture. There are many others that either go beyond the clear teaching about Christ or come up short of it. In either case, those who sincerely adopt those falsehoods do not have God (i.e., they are not true Christians at all according to this text).

> There is great assurance for those who believe the Bible is divinely inspired, totally accurate, and the fully sufficient Word of God.

This is what makes the authority of Scripture so very important to us. For those of us who believe the Bible to be the divinely inspired, totally accurate, and fully sufficient Word of God, there is great assurance. The closed canon of the sixty-six books of the Old and New Testament are altogether truth, without any mixture of error. As we remain in that teaching, we have an abiding and growing relationship with God the Father and Jesus Christ, His Son.

What is your personal conviction about the teaching of Christ (i.e., the New Testament)? Do you believe it to be the Word of God? Do you remain convinced by God's Holy Spirit that the Bible is true without error? If so, then 2 John 9 affirms you as having a genuine relationship with God. It is only with this kind of conviction that you will be effective in serving others in your church or your community.

> **Dear Lord, I affirm the Bible as Your holy and inspired Word. I believe it, trust it, and desire to live by it. I pray You'll help me share it with others.**

A Deacon's Draw From 3 John

3 John 2

> "Dear friend, I pray that you may prosper in every way and be in good health, just as your soul prospers."

Third John was written to advise Gaius, a fellow minister with John, about his responsibility to receive warmly a group of traveling ministers. Gaius was also warned to beware of a troublemaker, Diotrephes, and to welcome a newcomer, Demetrius. In verse two, John offers a prayer for Gaius, asking God to prosper him in every way and grant him physical health. He acknowledges Gaius's spiritual health ("as your soul prospers") as being intact.

You may often find yourself in a position of providing hospitality to traveling evangelists, furloughing missionaries, or other Pastors ministering to your church. These are great opportunities for you to render some very important service to the Lord. You will likely work with your Pastor or other Deacons in the church to accomplish this. Usually, guests need travel, lodging, meals, and sometimes office space to fulfill their assignment. You can either personally supply these needs, arrange for others to do so, or give money enough for these expenses. It is always good to involve other servants in your church to work with you. They'll need the opportunity, and you'll need the help.

> Pray faithfully and earnestly for your Pastor and staff, that they may have all the resources they need and that God would grant them physical health for their ministry.

In addition, pray faithfully and earnestly for your Pastor and staff, that they may have all the resources they need and that God would grant them physical health for their ministry. This seems to be at the heart of John's third epistle, and certainly it is at the heart of God for you.

Dear Lord, I pray that You would bless and prosper my Pastor. I pray You will keep him strong and healthy in mind and body. Please use me to serve the needs of others in ministry.

A Deacon's Draw From Jude

Jude 3

"Contend for the faith that was delivered to the saints once for all."

This brief letter was written to condemn false teachers who were trying to persuade Christians that they were free to sin since they had been forgiven and under God's grace. Jude wanted us to oppose this teaching with truth about God's grace. The word *contend* is a word used to describe hand-to-hand combat in military warfare. It implies a need for us to be willing to fight in spiritual warfare for the sake of the true gospel of grace.

It is always correct to contend for the faith, even when you are in the minority. This has never been truer than the age in which we live. There are more and more groups of so-called Christians that are being organized around false teaching. There are Pastors and churches today preaching and teaching the very thing Jude warns against. For example, when it is taught that we are actually sinless because all of our sins were placed on Christ and "we bear them no more," that is only half true. We do not bear God's eternal judgment for our sin (cf. Rom. 8:1), but we do "die daily" to the sins that so easily entangle us (cf. Heb. 12:1). "What shall we say then? Should we continue in sin in order that grace may multiply? Absolutely not!" (Rom. 6:1-2). We are never given a license to sin, even though we are saved by grace.

> We are never given a license to sin even though we are saved by grace.

We are declared righteous by Christ (cf. 2 Cor. 5:21), but that does not mean that we live righteously every day of our life. It is our goal. We still possess a sin nature that can compel us to sin unless we access Christ's power to resist the temptation (cf. Rom. 7:15-25).

Be encouraged today that you are living in the grace of God, having been forgiven of all your sins—past, present, and future. Contend earnestly for that marvelous grace that "was once for all delivered to the saints" (Jude 3).

Dear Lord, thank You for Your great grace. Thank You for Your Word—the Bible—which I accept as Your written truth once for all given to me.

A Deacon's Draw from Revelation

Revelation 22:3

"The throne of God and of the Lamb will be in the city, and His servants will serve Him."

You just thought your service would be over when you die! This text makes it quite clear that service, communion, and reigning will be believers' privileges for eternity. Some people view heaven as a place where we will be assigned to an isolated cabin that has a rocking chair on a front porch and we'll spend all eternity relaxing. Nothing could be further from the truth. We have neither a cabin nor a rocking chair. Laziness will be a foreign idea for a glorified body indwelt with an eternal Holy Spirit.

> All that you now do in service through your church, you do in preparation for your service in heaven.

Revelation 7:15 describes believers in heaven before God's throne, serving Him day and night in His temple. Apparently, our service to God only begins here on earth. It seems to have no end. The nature of our service will change, because here we serve God by serving people. There, we'll serve God with the people in His temple . . . around His throne.

All that you now do in service through your church, you do in preparation for your service in heaven. Here you have many limitations. There you'll have none. Here you become tired and weary. There you will never grow tired. Here you serve until you die. There you'll serve and never die. Here you serve Christ in His Church. There you'll serve the enthroned Christ surrounded by His Church. Here you serve for a heavenly reward. There you will serve, and that will be your heavenly reward.

So, don't ever stop serving Christ. Keep your focus on Him and your heart pure before Him. One day, fairly soon, you'll be glad you did.

Dear Lord, I praise You and thank You for the privilege I have to serve You while I live on earth. And I look forward to serving You in heaven throughout all eternity.

A Deacon and the Great Conversion

John 17:3

"This is eternal life: that they may know You the only true God, and the One You have sent—Jesus Christ."

What is the one very most important and valuable thing in the human experience of life? Some would say health! Some education! Some marriage or family! Some career or money! Still others power or prestige! Or maybe comfort or peace! Should the most important thing be the same for all people in all generations for all time? Jesus taught clearly that the most important thing was to have a genuine, personal, intimate, and eternal relationship with the One true and living God.

This relationship is wrapped up in knowing, following, loving, and serving God. Knowing God is what we often refer to as conversion. When you consider Jesus's words in John 17:3, you must conclude that knowing Him involves a Great Conversion.

Since you serve as a Deacon in your church, you are seen by the congregation as having experienced this Great Conversion in your own life. This means you were deeply convicted by God's Holy Spirit of your sinful and lost condition (cf. Jn. 16:8). You heard and understood the gospel message of salvation by grace through faith in Christ alone (cf. Rom. 10:13-17; Eph. 2:8-10). You then expressed to God in prayer your sincere sorrow for your sin, acknowledged your sin to Him, turned away from your sin, and by faith, surrendered your life to Jesus Christ as your personal Lord and Savior (cf. Rom. 10:9-10, 13). At that point, you were born again from above by the Spirit of God and placed in God's family as a living child of His (cf. Jn. 3:3,7). You have truly experienced a Great Conversion. You can now live and serve by telling others of the very most important thing in the human experience.

> **Develop a genuine, personal, intimate, eternal relationship with God alone!**

Dear Lord, thank You for saving my soul, making me whole, and giving to me Your great salvation, full and free.

A Deacon and the Great Confession
Matthew 16:16

"You are the Messiah, the Son of the living God."

The vast majority of the people alive today have no earthly idea who Jesus Christ really is. Today, that would mean billions of people are without an understanding of who Jesus is, much less what He has done and what difference He could make in their lives. In the context of this verse, Jesus posed the question to His disciples, "Who do people say that the Son of Man is?" (v. 13). Not really understanding all that He was asking, the disciples replied, "Some say John the Baptist, others, Elijah; still others, Jeremiah, or one of the prophets" (v. 14). Then He posed a second and most important question of all, "But you, who do you say that I am?" (v. 15). Peter, speaking more or less for the group, said, "You are the Messiah, the Son of the living God" (v. 16).

Essentially, Jesus was helping His followers know the difference between public consensus (who the world says He is) and personal conviction (who the believer says He is). This same distinction must still be made today. Who Jesus really is, the Son of the living God, has everything to do with how you serve in your local church and how you share the gospel with others. You do not serve other people merely out of a sense of social concern. You serve out of a deep conviction that Jesus can and will change their lives.

> You serve out of a deep conviction that Jesus can and will change their lives.

This Great Confession of Simon Peter establishes the basic need of every person. When you experienced a spiritual rebirth, you came to this same point. You believed and said, in so many words, Jesus is the Christ, the Son of God who loved me and gave Himself for me. You confessed with your mouth that Jesus is your Lord. You believed in your heart that God raised Him from the dead. You surrendered to Him as your only Lord and Savior, and you were gloriously saved. Now you keep making this confession so others will know Him too!

> Dear Lord, I have confessed You alone as my Lord and Savior. Please empower me to continue telling the story to many others as I serve You.

A Deacon and the Great Commandment
Matthew 22:37, 39

"Love the Lord your God with all your heart, with all your soul, and with all your mind . . . Love your neighbor as yourself."

This is God's command to every believer. He expects us to love Him and to love others. This command is actually Jesus's quotation of Deuteronomy 6:4, known to Jews as the *Shema,* which literally means, "hear." It is a command that all true believers need to hear regularly. God expects us to love!

We love Him for who He is to us—our Creator, Sustainer, Mediator, and Savior. We love Him for what He has done for us—sent His Son and saved our souls. It is not merely our obligation to love Him; it is our mandate. God is love (cf. 1 Jn. 4:16). God does what He does, for and with us, out of a heart of sincere, sacrificial love. It is this love that motivates us to serve as we do.

> **Loving God is absolutely essential if we ever hope to love others.**

Loving God is only half of Jesus's command, but it is the first half. Loving God is absolutely essential if we ever hope to love others. Without His love, you will be unable to love your spouse, your children, your grandchildren, or your church family as you need to. You certainly will not love unbelievers around you. This is true because of the kind of love God has. His love is limitless and sacrificial. He loves the unbeliever and the unlovable. He loves personally and intimately. He loves us as He intends to be loved.

Do you love God with all your heart (the innermost recesses of your emotions), with all your soul (the very "life breath" of God in you), with all your mind (the realm of extraordinary perception), and with all your strength (a God-given capacity or enablement)? This is the Great Commandment! Do you love others as you love yourself? Only as you obey these commands will you be an effective Deacon or servant in your church.

Dear Lord, I pray that You will expand my understanding and increase my desire to love You as You intend. Help me to love others, especially unbelievers, as You love them.

A Deacon and the Great Commission
Matthew 28:19

"Go . . . make disciples of all nations . . ."

We know Christ, follow Christ, and love Him in order to serve Him. When you really know Him, you want to follow Him. When you really follow Him, you grow to love Him. When you really love Him, you will really want to serve Him. The big reason for which we serve is that God may be glorified in the salvation of all the people groups of the world. Thus, before Jesus left the earth for heaven, He left us our marching orders. In essence, He said, "This is how you will serve Me." We have those orders preserved in several places in the New Testament.

The Great Commission, as we often call it, is Jesus's final assignment given to us as His Church in the world. As with the Great Commandment (Matt. 22:37-39), this is a command, not merely a suggestion. God expects us to make disciples of (from among) all the people groups of the world so that one day "every tribe and tongue and people and nation" (Rev. 5:9) will be represented at the throne of God in heaven. "The Lord does not delay His promise [i.e., to return], as some understand delay, but is patient with you, not wanting any to perish, but all to come to repentance" (2 Pet. 3:9).

> The Great Commission is a command, not merely a suggestion.

Here you have your reason to live. Your family, church, community, and world await your service. You have been saved and are now surrendered to Christ so you may serve Him by serving others. You are here to make disciples and teach them to observe all of the same commands of Christ that you are seeking to obey. You have no other assignment from God. Therefore, you need not give yourself any other assignment.

Go now into all the world and proclaim the gospel. Be faithful until death, and He will give you a crown of life (Rev. 2:10). Resume your service today, and don't look back.

Dear Lord, I renew my commitment to Your call and pray You will go before me, prepare the way, and be with me always, even unto the end of my life.

End Notes

Introduction

1. Henry Webb, *Deacons: Servant Models in the Church* (Broadman & Holman, Nashville, 2001), Preface, paragraph 3.

The Deacon's Qualifications

1. *Webster's II New College Dictionary* (Houghton Mifflin, Boston~New York, 1995), p. 1009.
2. W.E. Vine, *Vine's Complete Expository Dictionary of Old and New Testament Words* (Thomas Nelson, Nashville, 1985), p. 562.
3. Kelly Willard, *Make Me a Servant,* as quoted by **hymnlyrics.org**: http://www.hymnlyrics.org/lyricsm/make_me_a_servant.html (accessed October 2011).
4. *Webster's*, op. cit., p. 942.
5. *Vine's*, op. cit., p.527.
6. *Baptist Hymnal* (Convention Press, Nashville, 1975), Hymn No. 294, Used by Permission.
7. *Gathered Gold, A Treasury of Quotations for Christians,* compiled by John Blanchard (Evangelical Press, Hertfordshire, England, 1984), p. 151.
8. *Nelson's New Illustrated Bible Dictionary*, ed. Ronald F. Youngblood (Thomas Nelson, Nashville, 1995), p. 1316.
9. *Gathered Gold*, op. cit., p. 334.
10. John Phillips, *Exploring the Pastoral Epistles* (Kregal, Grand Rapids, 2004), p.86.
11. Ibid., p. 89.
12. *Nelson's New Illustrated Bible Dictionary*, op. cit., p. 295.
13. John Phillips, op. cit., p. 93.
14. *Gathered Gold*, op. cit., p. 26.
15. John Phillips, op. cit., p. 96.
16. *Baptist Hymnal*, op cit., Hymn No. 397, Used by Permission.
17. *Gathered Gold*, op. cit., p. 101.

18. Theodore Roosevelt, as quoted by **Theodore Roosevelt Association** from a speech entitled "Citizens of a Republic," given at Sorbonne, Paris, April 23, 1910: *http://www.theodoreroosevelt.org/life/quotes.htm* (accessed October 2011).

The Deacon's Spiritual Fruit

1. *Gathered Gold*, op. cit., p. 189.
2. Ibid., pp. 189-90.
3. *Baptist Hymnal*, op. cit., Hymn No. 208, Used by Permission.
4. *Webster's II New College Dictionary*, op. cit., p. 805.
5. Jon Mohr, *Find Us Faithful*, as quoted by Steve Green on: *http://www.stevegreenministries.org/lyrics/index.php?song=161* (accessed October 2011).
6. *Gathered Gold*, op. cit., p. 101.
7. Ibid., p. 201.
8. *Nelson's New Illustrated Bible Dictionary*, op. cit., p. 1230.

The Deacon's Personal Life

1. *Webster's II New College Dictionary*, op. cit., pp. 696-97.
2. *Nelson's New Illustrated Bible Dictionary*, op. cit., p. 838.
3. *Webster's II New College Dictionary*, op. cit., p. 386.
4. Heard in a sermon. Quote attributed to Vance Havner, who expanded a quote from Rudyard Kipling. Source unknown.
5. *Gathered Gold*, op. cit., pp. 196-97.
6. *Vine's Complete Expository Dictionary of Old and New Testament Words*, op. cit., p. 540.
7. *Baptist Hymnal*, op. cit., Hymn No. 281, Public Domain.
8. *Webster's II New College Dictionary*, op. cit., p. 689.
9. *Broadman Hymnal* (Broadman, Nashville, 1940), Hymn No. 64, Public Domain.
10. *Gathered Gold*, op. cit., p. 341.
11. Ibid., p. 60.
12. Ibid., p. 61-62.

The Deacon's Commandments

1. *Gathered Gold*, op. cit., p. 118.
2. *Webster's II New College Dictionary*, op. cit., p. 549.
3. *Gathered Gold*, op. cit., p. 159

4. *Baptist Hymnal*, op. cit., Hymn No. 454, Public Domain.
5. *Nelson's New Illustrated Bible Dictionary*, op. cit., p. 771.
6. *Gathered Gold*, op. cit., p. 187.
7. Ibid., p. 103.
8. *Nelson's New Illustrated Bible Dictionary*, op. cit., p. 866
9. *Baptist Hymnal*, op. cit., Hymn No. 323, Public Domain.
10. *Richards Complete Bible Dictionary*, ed. Lawrence O. Richards (Word Bible Publishers, Iowa Falls, 2002), p. 37.
11. Ibid., p. 260.
12. *Baptist Hymnal*, op. cit., Hymn No. 294, Public Domain.

The Deacon's Common Ministry

1. *Nelson's New Illustrated Bible Dictionary*, op. cit., p. 522.
2. *Baptist Hymnal*, op. cit., Hymn No. 164, Public Domain.
3. *Gathered Gold*, op. cit., pp. 128-29.
4. Ibid., p. 105.
5. Ibid., p. 127.
6. *Baptist Hymnal*, op. cit., Hymn No. 403, Public Domain.
7. *Gathered Gold*, op. cit., p. 88.
8. Ibid., p. 215.
9. *Baptist Hymnal*, op. cit., Hymn No. 189, Public Domain.
10. Ibid., Hymn No. 294, Used by Permission.
11. *Gathered Gold*, op. cit., p. 306.
12. Ibid., p. 154
13. *Nelson's New Illustrated Bible Dictionary*, op. cit., p. 586.
14. John Phillips, *Exploring Philippians* (Loizeaux Brothers, Neptune, NJ, 1995), p. 79.
15. *Ryrie Study Bible, New American Standard Version* (updated 1995), ed. Charles Ryrie (Moody Press, Chicago, 1995), p. 1890.
16. *Vine's Complete Expository Dictionary of Old and New Testament Words*, op. cit., p. 197.
17. *Gathered Gold*, op. cit., p. 157.
18. Ibid., p. 154.
19. John Phillips, *Exploring Philippians*, op. cit., p. 94.
20. *Baptist Hymnal*, op. cit., Hymn No. 281, Public Domain.
21. Ibid., p. 189, Used by Permission.
22. Source unknown.
23. John Phillips, *Exploring Philippians*, op. cit., p. 107.
24. Ibid., p. 113.

25. *Vine's Complete Expository Dictionary of Old and New Testament Words*, op. cit., p. 346.
26. John Phillips, *Exploring Philippians*, op. cit., p. 105.
27. Ibid., p. 142.
28. Ibid., p. 143.
29. *Gathered Gold*, op. cit., p. 90.
30. Ibid., p. 90.
31. *Webster's II New College Dictionary*, op. cit., p. 1170.
32. John Phillips, *Exploring Philippians*, op. cit., pp. 152-53.
33. *Gathered Gold*, op. cit., p. 286.
34. *Baptist Hymnal*, op. cit., Hymn No. 389, Public Domain.
35. *Webster's II New College Dictionary*, op. cit., p. 598.
36. John Phillips, *Exploring Philippians*, op. cit., p. 160.
37. *Gathered Gold*, op. cit., p. 339.
38. John Phillips, *Exploring Philippians*, op. cit., p. 162.
39. *Baptist Hymnal*, op. cit., Hymn No. 403, Public Domain.
40. *Gathered Gold*, op. cit., p. 212.
41. *Richards Complete Bible Dictionary*, op. cit., p. 996.
42. *Webster's II New College Dictionary*, op. cit., p. 674.
43. *Richards Complete Bible Dictionary*, op. cit., p. 493.
44. *Vine's Complete Expository Dictionary of Old and New Testament Words*, op. cit., p. 338.
45. Ibid., p. 498.
46. *Richards Complete Bible Dictionary*, op. cit., p. 838.
47. *Webster's II New College Dictionary*, op. cit., p. 648.
48. Ibid., p. 225.
49. John Phillips, *Exploring Philippians*, op. cit., p. 169.
50. *Gathered Gold*, op. cit., p. 90.
51. *Vine's Complete Expository Dictionary of Old and New Testament Words*, op. cit., p. 125.
52. *Webster's II New College Dictionary*, op. cit., p. 307.
53. Reinhold Niebhur, "Serenity Prayer." **WIKIPEDIA**: http://en.wikipedia.org/wiki/Serenity_Prayer (accessed October 2011).
54. *Gathered Gold*, op. cit., p. 80.
55. John Phillips, *Exploring Philippians*, op. cit., p. 178.
56. Steven Curtis Chapman, *"His Strength Is Perfect."* **Lyrics Depot**: http://www.lyricsdepot.com/steven-curtis-chapman/his-strength-is-perfect.html (accessed October 2011).
57. John Phillips, *Exploring Philippians*, op. cit., p. 178.
58. *Baptist Hymnal*, op. cit., Hymn No. 304, Public Domain.
59. *Vine's Complete Expository Dictionary of Old and New Testament Words*, op. cit., p. 10.
60. *Nelson's New Illustrated Bible Dictionary*, op. cit., p. 499.

61. *Baptist Hymnal*, op. cit., Hymn No. 33, Used by permission.
62. *Webster's II New College Dictionary*, op. cit., p. 489.
63. *Baptist Hymnal*, op. cit., Hymn No. 164, Public Domain.

The Deacon's Relational Characteristics

1. *Gathered Gold*, op. cit., p. 213.
2. *Ryrie Study Bible, New American Standard Version* (updated 1995), op. cit., p. 1811.
3. *Gathered Gold*, op. cit., p. 212.
4. Ibid., pp. 189-90.
5. *Nelson's New Illustrated Bible Dictionary*, op. cit., p. 728.
6. *Gathered Gold*, op. cit., p. 108.
7. *Broadman Hymnal*, op. cit., Hymn No. 122, Public Domain.
8. *Ryrie Study Bible, New American Standard Version* (updated 1995), op. cit., p. 1883.
9. *Webster's II New College Dictionary*, op. cit., p. 633.
10. *Nelson's New Illustrated Bible Dictionary*, op. cit., p. 1316.
11. *Webster's II New College Dictionary*, op. cit., p. 371.
12. *Vine's Complete Expository Dictionary of Old and New Testament Words*, op. cit., p. 198.
13. *Webster's II New College Dictionary*, op. cit., p. 229.
14. Ibid., p. 534.
15. *Richards Complete Bible Dictionary*, op. cit., p. 499.
16. Paraphrased from *Standing on the Promises, the Autobiography of W.A. Criswell* (Thomas Nelson, Nashville, 1990).
17. *Nelson's New Illustrated Bible Dictionary*, op. cit., p. 586.
18. *Gathered Gold*, op. cit., p. 155.
19. Ibid., p. 110.
20. *Baptist Hymnal*, op. cit., Hymn No. 256, Public Domain.

The Deacon's Giftedness

1. *Gathered Gold*, op. cit., p. 235.
2. Ibid., p. 79.
3. Bear Bryant. **Thinkexist.com**: http://thinkexist.com/quotation/if-anything-goes-bad-i-did-it-if-anything-goes/532705.html (accessed October 2011).
4. *Gathered Gold*, op. cit., p. 315.

The Deacon's Caregiving Ministries

1. *Gathered Gold*, op. cit., p. 191.
2. Ibid., p. 105.
3. *Webster's II New College Dictionary*, op. cit., p. 325.
4. *Gathered Gold*, op. cit., p. 68.
5. *Nelson's New Illustrated Bible Dictionary*, op. cit., p. 950.
6. *Webster's II New College Dictionary*, op. cit., p. 645.
7. *Broadman Hymnal*, op. cit., Hymn No. 400, Used by permission.
8. *Vine's Complete Expository Dictionary of Old and New Testament Words*, op. cit., p. 110.
9. *Gathered Gold*, op. cit., p. 67.
10. *Webster's II New College Dictionary*, op. cit., p. 494.
11. Ibid., p. 716.
12. *Vine's Complete Expository Dictionary of Old and New Testament Words*, op. cit., p. 418.
13. *Webster's II New College Dictionary*, op. cit., p. 402.
14. *Gathered Gold*, op. cit., p. 310.
15. *Webster's II New College Dictionary*, op. cit., p. 236.

The Deacon's Doctrine

1. *Gathered Gold*, op. cit., p. 19.
2. Charles Ryrie, *A Survey of Bible Doctrine* (Moody Press, Chicago, 1972), pp. 36-50.
3. Ibid, p. 89.
4. *Vine's Complete Expository Dictionary of Old and New Testament Words*, op. cit., p. 576.
5. *Nelson's New Illustrated Bible Dictionary*, op. cit., p. 413.
6. Ibid., p. 1277.

The Deacon's Greatest Challenges

1. Thom S. Rainer, *The Bridger Generation* (Broadman & Holman, Nashville, 2006), pp. pp. 163-175, esp. p. 169.
2. *Baptist Hymnal*, op. cit., Hymn No. 371, Public Domain.
3. *Gathered Gold*, op. cit., p. 334.
4. Ibid., p. 283.
5. Ibid., p. 130.

6. John Phillips, *Exploring the Love Song of Solomon* (Kregal, Grand Rapids, 2003), p. 222.
7. *Ryrie Study Bible, New American Standard Version* (updated 1995), op. cit., p. 1979.
8. *Baptist Hymnal*, op. cit., Hymn No. 216, Used by Permission.
9. *Webster's II New College Dictionary*, op. cit., p. 649.
10. *Baptist Hymnal*, op. cit., Hymn No. 409, Used by Permission.
11. Elisabeth Elliot, *Through Gates of Splendor* (Christian Herald, New York, 1957), paraphrased.
12. *Webster's II New College Dictionary*, op. cit., p. 371.
13. *Vine's Complete Expository Dictionary of Old and New Testament Words*, op. cit., p. 198.
14. *Webster's II New College Dictionary*, op. cit., p. 239.
15. *Vine's Complete Expository Dictionary of Old and New Testament Words*, op. cit., p. 198.

About the Author

Russell R. Cook was the third and youngest son born to Leonard and Venetta Cook and reared on a hog farm near Hannibal, Missouri. He graduated in 1967 from Hannibal Senior High School. In 1969, he graduated from Bailey Technical School in St. Louis, Missouri, as a diesel mechanic. Later he served with the Twentieth Engineering Brigade in the US Army as a heavy equipment operator. When he returned from a tour of duty in Vietnam in 1971, he was honorably discharged with the rank of SP/5. Soon he answered God's call to the gospel ministry.

He enrolled as a ministerial student in 1971 at Hannibal-LaGrange College and began a ten-year educational career. He completed his BA degree at Dallas Baptist University in Dallas, Texas, his MDiv from Southwestern Baptist Theological Seminary in Ft. Worth, Texas, and his DMin from Luther Rice Seminary in Lithonia, Georgia.

In 1971 he married Marsha Ragsdell, from Prairie Grove, Arkansas, who was teaching school near Hannibal when he returned home from Vietnam. They have three married children, Bryan, Phillip, and Joy, and have been blessed with five grandchildren.

Russell Cook has pastored four Baptist churches in Missouri, Texas, and Oklahoma since 1971. He has been active in local, associational, state, and national ministries. He became the Director of Missions for Pottawatomie-Lincoln Baptist Association, a network of sixty-four churches and missions in two counties of central Oklahoma, in 1996. He and Marsha make their home in Shawnee, Oklahoma. Together they have devoted many of their ministry years training Pastors, staff members, Deacons, and their wives for effective service to the local church.

CPSIA information can be obtained at www.ICGtesting.com
Printed in the USA
LVOW06s1325260713

344825LV00001B/60/P